PRAIRIE BACHELOR

Prairie Bachelor

The Story of A Kansas Homesteader & The Populist Movement

Lynda Beck Fenwick

University Press of Kansas

Published by the University Press of Kansas (Lawrence, Kansas 66045), which was organized by the Kansas Board of Regents and is operated and funded by Emporia State University, Fort Hays State University, Kansas State University, Pittsburg State University, the University of Kansas, and Wichita State University.

Library of Congress Cataloging-in-Publication Data
Names: Fenwick, Lynda Beck, 1944– author.
Title: Prairie bachelor : the story of a Kansas homesteader and the populist movement / Lynda Beck Fenwick.
Other titles: Story of a Kansas homesteader and the populist movement
Description: Lawrence, KS : University Press of Kansas, [2020] | Includes index.
Identifiers: LCCN 2020016291
ISBN 9780700630271 (cloth)
ISBN 9780700630288 (paperback)
ISBN 9780700630295 (epub)
Subjects: LCSH: Werner, Isaac Beckley, approximately 1844–1895—Diaries. | Kansas—Politics and government—1865–1950. | Pioneers—Kansas—Biography | Populism—Kansas—History—19th century. | Populism—Kansas—Biography. | Farmers—Kansas—Stafford County—Biography. | Farm life—Kansas—Stafford County. | Stafford County (Kan.)—Biography.
Classification: LCC F686 .F46 2020 | DDC 978.1/02092 [B]—dc23
LC record available at https://lccn.loc.gov/2020016291.

British Library Cataloguing-in-Publication Data is available.

Printed in the United States of America

10 9 8 7 6 5 4 3 2 1

The paper used in this publication is acid free and meets the minimum requirements of the American National Standard for Permanence of Paper for Printed Library Materials Z39.48-1992.

Contents

Illustrations

Introduction

Writing for the local newspaper in 1888, Isaac Beckley Werner said, "After ten years settlement of Stafford County, the fact begins to dawn on our progressive farmers, that many of the difficulties [we face] . . . can only be overcome by a united effort on the part of the farmers themselves."[1] For a decade, homesteaders like Isaac Werner had broken the tough prairie sod and adapted to the undependable rainfall, soils that varied from sandy loam to sticky clay, swarms of insects, and other challenges from Mother Nature, and gradually had made the land productive. However, the challenges of declining markets, increasing interest rates, and higher railroad shipping costs remained. The Populist movement was driven more by their struggles with the business of farming than by their skills as farmers.

Many of the issues with which Isaac and other laborers struggled seemed beyond their control as individuals, but by joining together to confront the power of the wealthy with their greater numbers, they believed reforms were possible.

America had begun as a nation of farmers, small businessmen, and craftsmen, but the Civil War that nearly split the nation had instead transformed it. Industry created cities, and railroads opened markets. Wealth, created by common men's labor, passed power to those men who controlled the railroads, industry, and investments, and that wealth gave those men influence in Washington, DC, and in state capitals. The political power of working people came from their greater numbers at the ballot box. That voting power was recognized, particularly by farmers, in the Populist movement, during which ordinary people came together in the late nineteenth century to create a political party powerful enough for a brief time to challenge Republicans and Democrats alike. Kansas played a key political role during the history of the People's Party, and Isaac and his community played an active role in the movement, which he documented in his daily journal entries.

Following the advice of Henry Ward Beecher, the influential minister and brother of author Harriet Beecher Stowe, Isaac recorded events happening around him rather than focusing entirely on himself. His journal became a record of the Populist movement and the conditions that brought it about, from the perspective of his specific region in Kansas. When trains brought Populist leaders to nearby county seats to speak, Isaac attended and recorded in his journal what they had to say. He regarded his personal library as his most essential possession, and he regularly expanded it with books on history, art, logic, travel, and many other topics. During the Populist movement he added books on government and economics, as well as Populist literature. His formal education had extended into his late teens, and his self-education never ended. His community regarded him as one of the most learned among them.

Working people of that era were hungry for education, not only for their children but also for themselves. Despite limited cash, they bought books and subscribed to Populist newspapers. Local editors and community reporters provided a social network comparable to today's internet connections, and large newspapers sold small-town editors newssheets with national and international news, providing information from beyond their communities, probably not significantly more or less biased than our modern news sources. There was also "yellow journalism" that focused on scandal and sensationalism, largely unencumbered by facts, similar to current tabloids. Today's significance of having an education is apparent in the current cost and competition for school admissions; yet the personal passion for learning seems to have waned, as publishers, small-town newspapers, and even city-wide periodicals have lowered or ceased their operations.

Perhaps surprisingly, many of the issues of that era remain important to us today. Women played an active role, serving as officers and lecturers in the Farmers' Alliance, as well as working alongside their husbands on the farms. In the towns and cities, middle-class women were marching for votes and against liquor. These social movements among women were not unlike the activism of women today.

The problems of post–Civil War growth of cities have similar echoes in the present day. Then, freed slaves crowded into cities in search of work and shelter, overwhelming resources available to assist them. Newly arrived European immigrants and Chinese workers, brought by railroad contractors, were given jobs that displaced existing laborers because the new arrivals were willing to work for less pay and in less safe conditions. The former laborers were angry with the factory bosses and the contractors, but they also resented the workers who replaced them. They were left to search for new employment, often at lower wages, which frequently led to social problems, such as overcrowded tenements and substance abuse. Poverty may wear a different face today, but urban crime and poor living conditions have not disappeared. Nor have prejudice and alienation. Lack of employment then was often linked to public drunkenness, with resulting problems not dissimilar to present-day addictions to alcohol, drugs, and other vices.

Beyond the cities, the Homestead Act had drawn many former Union soldiers west to claim their 180-acre homesteads, whereas those who fought for the South returned to a broken economy and a radically altered way of life. Although these farmers had much in common, their regional differences made it difficult for them to unite politically to reach common goals.

The first entry each day in Isaac's journal recounted the local weather. For most farmers on the prairie, the weather was unlike what they had known back East, and temperatures, rainfall, wind, and other natural conditions were faithfully recorded by Isaac and others to learn when and what to plant. Almanacs predicting eclipses, full moons, and planting dates were of some help but were certainly less dependable than on-the-ground data, as they usually relied on guesswork or on "secret charts." Nothing was available like the current ability to project long-term meteorological changes to the earth. Instead, inaccurate theories and tactics to influence weather, like the belief that "rain followed the plow," or that cannons shot into clouds would cause rain, were employed in attempts to predict and control weather. Near term weather cycles were familiar to farmers, such as dry spells without rain, but in the late 1800s, accurate long-term weather and climate projections did not exist.

The belief that it would take several generations to populate the United States from the east coast to the west coast had been greatly overestimated, and with that settlement achieved, the idea of Manifest Destiny that had fueled the mid-century continental surge west had led many to argue conquest beyond America's shores. Although most Americans may have seen the Spanish-American War as an intervention to aid Cubans seeking independence from Spain, many influential Americans believed Manifest Destiny justified using such wars for American expansion.

As you read about the events that began with Isaac's arrival in Kansas in the final years of the 1870s and continued until 1898 when his estate was finally settled following his death three years before, you will see the changes that occurred, the influences that have been carried forward to the present time, and the similarities between the past and the present. You will also learn about the birth of two terms commonly heard today—Populism and Progressivism. You may have seen many definitions intended to distinguish separate meanings for these two terms, but in fact, their meanings overlap, and the two terms are often used interchangeably. Those attempting to distinguish between Populism and Progressivism often separate the two early movements, describing Populists as representing agrarian and other laboring interests, with Progressives described as more forward-looking and less self-interested. Their goals are often segregated into categories, with Populists more interested in free coinage of silver, government ownership of public services, and government control over monopolies, whereas Progressives are described as more accepting of industrialization and urbanization, and more empathetic toward the less fortunate. The fault with such definitions is not in identification of goals but rather in the assignment of certain goals only to one group or the other. Both terms endure into the present time, but early Populism had more farmers and laborers active in the late 1800s and had declined by the turn of that century, whereas Progressivism was more urban, arising later in the 1890s and growing in the early 1900s. In both movements, people actively sought ways to confront the changing culture and economy during the decades after the Civil War.

The discovery of Isaac's journal roused my curiosity about a too-little-known era in American history. Although the journal provided a front row seat to history, no movement can be understood without an awareness of the social, political, economic, environmental, and cultural conditions that surround it. The Populist movement of the late 1800s is no exception, and to tell its story I began with the people who were there—Isaac, his friends, and the Populist leaders he knew or heard speak. Because the movement evolved, I start at the beginning, not with the creation of the People's Party but rather with the people themselves. From the knowledge of what they experienced and the efforts they made before choosing political activism comes the full understanding of what these people wanted and why they acted as they did.

During those same years, other movements, such as Prohibition and suffrage, were changing America. Those events and their leaders are included in this narrative, sometimes overlapping the activities of rural Populists.

For that reason, the book is organized into chapters year by year. You can see why farmers took out loans they expected to repay quickly with what they raised and were trapped instead when crop prices fell and interest rates soared. You can feel the hopelessness as crops were devoured in prairie fires and when babies died before their first birthdays. You can picture the organizations they joined and the meetings they attended year by year before they turned to the formation of a political party of their own. And, you can learn of the activities happening in cities and different regions during the same time.

With the focus on Populism, you can share the excitement of the political rallies, understand the platforms that parties drafted, and almost believe the promises their candidates made during the successful years of the Populist movement. When you reach the concluding chapters, you will understand the divisions that developed in the party and empathize with the disappointments and regrets. You will also recognize that many of the goals of the movement did not die with the party. Rather, they were absorbed into the old parties and are taken for granted today.

Having met Isaac and those of his generation, you may discover that many of their problems and pleasures were much like our own, despite the inventions and conveniences we enjoy today. Many issues we care about remain the same, and problems they sought to correct remain unresolved, although perhaps in a slightly different guise. Yet, there are lessons to be learned from history, and respect to be gained from recognizing the heritage of those who came before us.

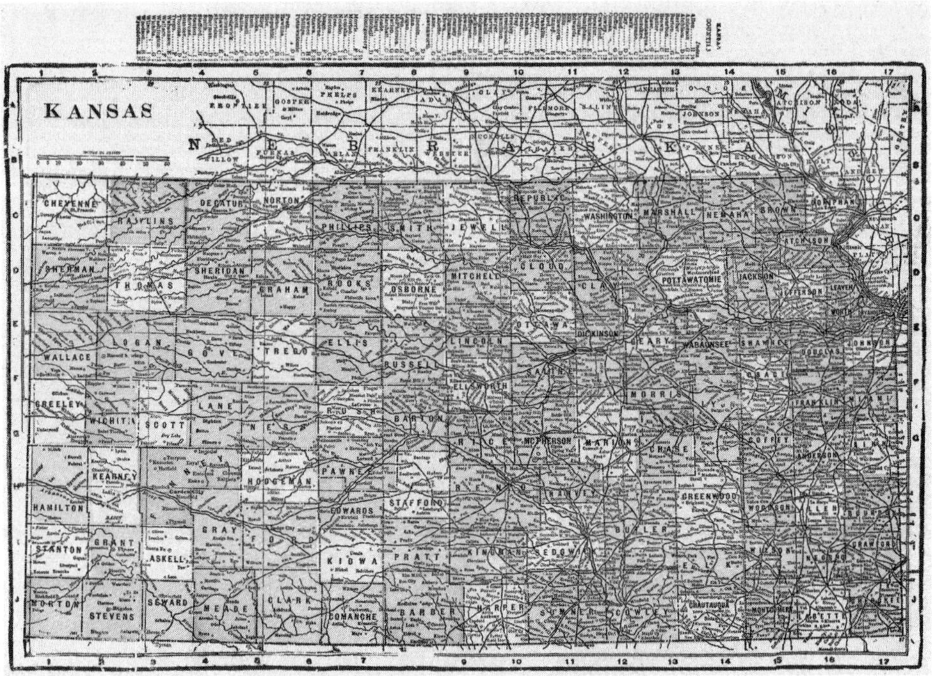

Courtesy of University of Texas Libraries, The University of Texas at Austin.

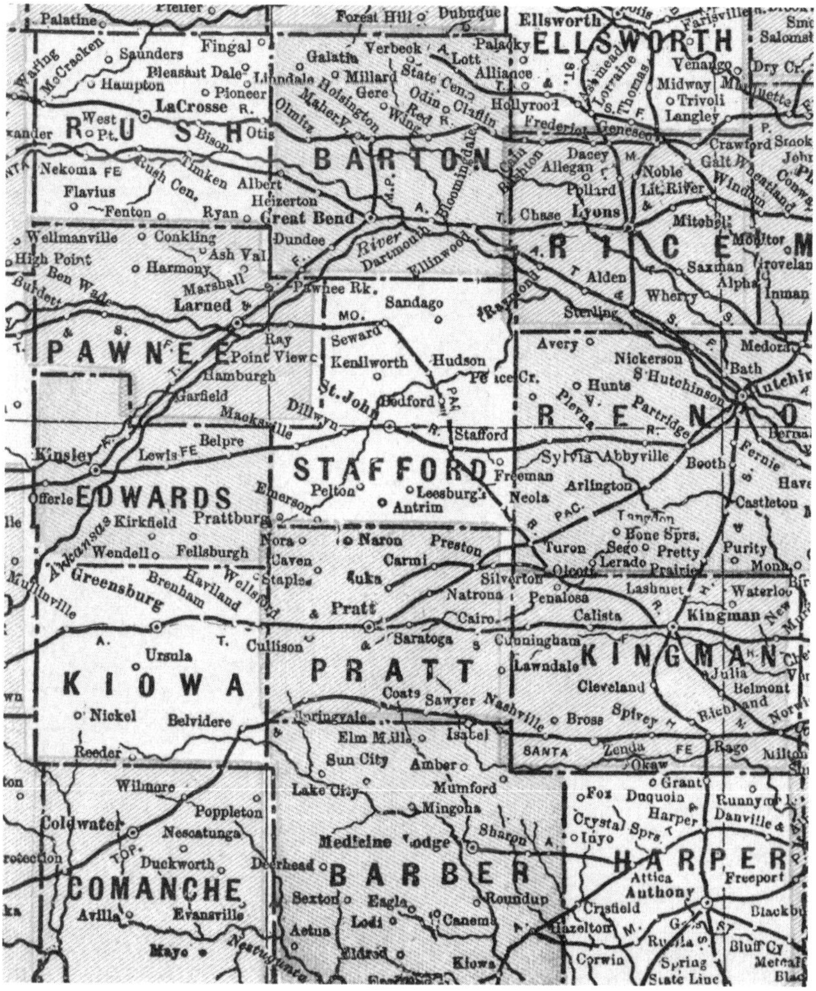

ELLSWORTH
Ellsworth
RUSH
LaCrosse
BARTON
Great Bend
RICE
Lyons
Sterling
PAWNEE
Larned
STAFFORD
St. John
Stafford
RENO
Hutchinson
EDWARDS
Kinsley
PRATT
Pratt
KINGMAN
Kingman
KIOWA
Greensburg
COMANCHE
Coldwater
BARBER
Medicine Lodge
HARPER
Anthony

When I read the book, the biography famous
And is this then (said I) what the author calls a man's life?
And so will someone when I am dead and gone write my life?
(As if any man really knew aught of my life,
Why even I myself I often think know little or nothing
of my real life,
Only a few hints, a few diffused faint clews and indirections
I seek for my own use to trace out here.)

—Walt Whitman (1819–1892)
From *Leaves of Grass*

The Funeral

March 1895

This is a story that begins at the end of the life of Isaac Beckley Werner in 1895, with the details of his amazing life and his involvement in the Populist movement yet to come in the following chapters. For now, it is enough to share a glimpse of Isaac and his neighbors by imagining ourselves as a bystander at his funeral. We know a great deal about him from the 480-page journal he wrote in every day, and although no direct account of Isaac's funeral has been found, what we might have seen had we stood among the other mourners at Isaac's graveside in Neelands Cemetery on that March day can be recreated from many other records. His probate records provide many details, including funeral expenses for specific items. In addition, journal entries during his life identify his closest friends most likely to have attended his funeral, describing their talents and relationships with him. His journal describes funerals he attended at Neelands Cemetery, and the Populist newspaper to which Isaac subscribed also contained accounts of services.[1] Even the country cemetery itself, with Isaac's own gravestone and the inscribed headstones of many of his friends and acquaintances alongside him, add more detail to the story of Isaac and his community.

Much like finding an old jigsaw puzzle whose missing pieces are only revealed when the rest of the puzzle is assembled, researching the past sometimes forces historians to fill in those missing spaces with informed ideas of what the gaps would have contained. Isaac's journal contained much about his life, but many other sources exist to inform the content of the missing puzzle pieces and complete a picture of his life.

The chapters of this book are written in a narrative style, but years of painstaking research underlie the story. Isaac's daily journal entries provide the major evidence of his life, but they are supported by an abundance of primary source texts: his published articles; local newspapers; documents and images in local history museums; information from tombstones; courthouse records; genealogy research for the people mentioned in his journal and the Werner family; interviews of descendants; biographies of Populist leaders; old letters; books that influenced the movement; books enumerated in Isaac's probate inventory and described in his journal; maps of the period; legal opinions and trial transcripts; and books published by historical societies, centennial committees, and local historians. So too have visits to the places Isaac lived, walking the fields and pastures Isaac walked, inspecting farming equipment from the period, and consulting scholarly books and papers devoted to the history of the period enriched our understanding of this Kansas Populist and farmer. With all of these historic puzzle pieces put together, the images of Isaac's life offer a clear picture of the man and the events in which he participated. Isaac's burial service is no longer left entirely to imagination.

LATE MARCH WAS A BUSY TIME of year for farmers in 1895, yet the group of prairie homesteaders, the men dressed in canvas trousers and denim overalls and the women in calico, would surely have left their work long enough to gather around an open grave in Neelands Cemetery to pay their final respects to Isaac.[2] In earlier years the group of mourners would have been larger, but Isaac had been ill for so long that when death finally came for him, he must have been a forgotten man to many people in the community.

Once, he had been a familiar figure at the Farmers' Alliance meetings, stepping to the podium to condemn the greed of Wall Street and monopolies and to urge farmers to recognize that their best hope depended on joining together politically and economically. Some members of the Farmers' Alliance may have noticed his absence and assumed Isaac had finally left to join the farming cooperative in Mexico that he so often described in his lectures at Alliance meetings.

At the District 33 schoolhouse, the privies needed painting, and repairs to the roof had been neglected for months, but only the parents of older students would have remembered the bachelor who believed so strongly in educating both children and adults that he regularly took it upon himself to keep the schoolhouse "thrifty," as he called it. When Isaac became too ill to pick up a paintbrush or a hammer, the little tasks of keeping the building in good repair had often been ignored until they became big jobs. His solitary caretaking was missed, even when the man himself was not.[3]

The cluster of old friends and close neighbors would have been only the remnants of the many acquaintances from his past, those special friends and neighbors who believed Isaac was deserving of half a day's loss of plowing and planting their fields and gardens. News of the time for the funeral would have been passed by word of mouth, but all of his friends knew where to gather.

Isaac had told those who cared for him in the miserable final months of his life—when he was humiliated by the need for help with even those personal matters a man should never be so helpless he cannot manage for himself—that he wanted to be laid to rest in Neelands,[4] where so many other homesteaders in his Kansas prairie community had already been buried. His gravestone was simple, suitable for a man who served his community without expectation of reward and who celebrated achievements and birthdays privately. The inscription read: "I. B. Werner, Died March 21, 1895, Aged 51 Years."

A worker on the Neelands Ranch had been buried in a pasture, and the family had donated the surrounding three acres to be used as a cemetery. It was first called the Livingston Cemetery, after the nearby community, but most people referred to the piece of pasture set aside for burials by using the name of the family who had given the land.[5] Funerals in the country, without embalming, made the delays of traveling to town cemeteries problematic, so there were many country cemeteries scattered around the prairie. Isaac could have chosen the Naron Cemetery down in Pratt County, since his homestead was right on the county line, in fact, closer to Naron than Neelands. But he had always thought of himself as a Stafford County man, and more of his friends were buried in Neelands. That was where he had wanted to be.

George and Theresa Hall were the first ones to take him into their home when he became too ill to live alone, but their four children were still young, and after only twelve days they realized that round-the-clock care was too demanding for them to manage. Then, his nearest neighbors, George and Nancy Henn, had taken him in, perhaps because Nancy remembered how Isaac's advice and attention may have saved her son's life, after the doctor had declared nothing further could be done. If Nancy's motives were gratitude, her husband George had seemed more interested in the financial compensation.[6]

During the last five months Isaac remained in his own home, neighbor G. G. John had checked on him about every day. Isaac loved his claims, with the pastures, fields, gardens, and tree groves he had nurtured so carefully, and he was a proud man who liked his solitude. G. G. John had built Isaac an invalid chair that served for a while, but at last Isaac had to accept that he would live his final days in other people's houses.[7]

In addition to the Henns, the Halls, and G. G. John, most of the others gathered around the grave would have been neighbors with whom Isaac had shared work, and political friends he had come to know as they organized the Farmers' Alliance during those droughty years in the late 1880s when crops teased with promise in the spring but withered and dried up long before harvest. Even when farmers managed to raise something worth selling, the prices were not enough to cover the costs of growing. The settlers and their children who lived near Isaac were as gaunt and dry looking as their withered crops, but at least some of them had managed to survive on their homesteads, hoping for better years to come. Families to the west of Albano Township, only a few miles away, had come about as near to starving as living creatures could, many existing barefooted in winter, surviving on a gruel made of ground wheat mixed with water, neighbors having so little for their own families that they dared not share much with neighbors having even less. It was a time when sickness stalked everyone.

William Campbell, with whom Isaac had spent many evenings discussing politics and attending meetings of the Albano Township Farmers' Alliance and the Stafford County Agricultural Society, would have made a special effort to attend, although his wife, Eliza, was not feeling well in the final weeks of her pregnancy. Another political friend, John Hilmes, was likely to have traveled to the cemetery from St. John. Isaac's friendship with Hilmes had developed when Hilmes was the owner-editor of the Populist newspaper, the *County Capital,* and Isaac had been a frequent contributor of articles promoting the political efforts of farmers, and offering advice about raising potatoes and corn. Both Campbell and Hilmes credited Isaac with helpful strategizing during their Populist political campaigns. Campbell had been returned to the Kansas House of Representatives three times, and Hilmes had been elected probate judge. They would have wanted to show their respect for their old friend.

Isabel Ross would certainly have come with her grown children. After her divorce, she would have found it nearly impossible to survive on the homestead she claimed as a single woman without the countless kind gestures Isaac had made, paying her and her children for picking potato bugs off the vines when Paris Green was not available to poison the bugs, and helping sort potatoes by size and quality for marketing in town. Despite his shy formality with her, he was the most dependable neighbor to help tie down a haystack in a wind storm or bring her a load of his own supply of corn husks to burn, simply out of his concern for keeping her family warm during heavy snows. Her marriage to a man who was physically abusive had made her wary of men, but her bachelor neighbor's awkward kindnesses had restored her confidence in herself and had slowly healed her spirit so that she could move on with less bitterness after the divorce. As Isaac's health had gradually worsened, she must have realized the significance of the jobs he had done for her, for it was unlikely that she would have lasted long enough to prove up her claim without his neighborliness.

Schoolteacher Susan Beck would have attended with her children, Royal and Anna Marie. Although her husband Aaron and Isaac had disagreed politically, Susan had always enjoyed conversations with Isaac, discussions that often centered on books. There had been less time for visits after Aaron's stroke, with the busy teaching schedule she had assumed to help support the family, but she and her children would surely have made a point to be at Isaac's service to pay the family's respects.

The other mourners would have been farmers who lived near Isaac's farm or who were members of the Albano Township Farmers' Alliance. Some of the farmers from Naron Township, Isaac's neighbors to the south down in Pratt County, would have also wanted to be there.

Isaac hadn't cared much for preaching, and neighbors knew what would suit him best was music and perhaps quotes from Shakespeare. Although Isaac disapproved of William Wilson's love of horse racing, and the gambling and drinking that often accompanied the sport, Isaac had visited the Wilson brothers to admire their horses and seek their advice when he was looking for a horse to breed with his gray mare, Dolly. When it came to music, any differences between Isaac and William Wilson evaporated, and had he been asked, Wilson would have been honored to sing at Isaac's service. Wilson was highly regarded for his beautiful voice, so much so that he offered singing classes two nights a week during winter months when there was no field work to be done. For his solo, he might have chosen "Mid pleasures and palaces though I may roam, / Be it ever so humble, there's no place like home." Whether it was his father's farm with its stone house back in Pennsylvania where he was born or the farm he had carved out of the prairie sod, Isaac had devoted most of his life to the soil, and the song's references to home would have suited Isaac's devotion to the land. To satisfy the ladies more concerned for the bachelor's soul, Wilson might have led the group in singing "Softly and Tenderly," the woman singing "Come home," to be answered by the echo of the male voices, making a lovely chorus rising into the early spring sky, with its closing admonition, "Calling, O sinner, come home."[8]

As the sound of their singing drifted away on the prairie breeze, William Campbell would have been an appropriate friend to step forward, with Isaac's *Collected Works of William Shakespeare* resting in his arms. Years of campaign speeches delivered at open-air political rallies had taught Campbell how to project his voice over crowds far larger than any small congregation of neighbors. Perhaps he began with one of Isaac's favorite passages, Ariel's song in *The Tempest*: "Full fathom five thy father lies. Of his bones are coral made; / Those are pearls that were his eyes," his rich politician's voice phrasing the rhymed lines as beautifully as any trained actor could have delivered them. Having finished that passage, Campbell might have turned a few pages aside to another ribbon-marked passage, Prospero's Epilogue, to read, "Now my charms are all o'erthrown, And what strength I have's mine own, Which is most faint."[9]

Perhaps Dr. Isaac "Doc" Dix, Isaac's old friend and neighbor who had moved to Pratt Center a few years before, would have stepped forward to lead the group in The Lord's Prayer, the entire service having been conducted by his friends without the benefit of a minister, and no family present.[10]

Tradition suggests that after the casket was lowered into the grave, the farmers who had met with Isaac so many times at Alliance meetings might have formed a line that moved slowly forward as each one dropped a shovel of soil onto the casket. Isaac would have been well satisfied with such a service.

As attendees walked back toward their wagons, perhaps Isabel Ross pulled Theresa Hall aside to share her disappointment with Isaac's death notice in the *County Capital*. Only eight lines long, the notice made more mention of the Henn's care for Isaac than of his achievements. It was a particular disappointment, given Isaac's close relationship with the *Capital's* previous editor, Hilmes, and the number of articles Isaac had written for that newspaper, especially those organizing the County Agricultural Society and supporting the Farmers' Alliance. Neighbors knew that he not only supported the local Albano Alliance but also frequently lectured at Alliance meetings in Pratt and Edwards Counties, helping fellow farmers with advice and encouraging opportunities for farmers to come together and learn from each other's mistakes and successes.

Others who were almost certainly in attendance at Isaac's funeral were those mentioned frequently in his journal, like young Fay Vosburgh, with whom he had once discussed a joint farming venture, or Charles Waters, who willingly loaned equipment to Isaac because he knew Isaac was likely to clean it up and return it in better condition than it had been when it was borrowed. G. G. John would almost certainly have been among the mourners, perhaps with his wife and their small children, for his kind attendance as Isaac's health declined had allowed the postponement of leaving his home for full-time care.

Many farm families would have made the effort to attend, remembering those lean years, when almost everyone was too far in debt to imagine ever paying more than the interest on their mortgages, and financial successes were few. The encouragement of farmers like Isaac, who were facing the same struggles, was often the only opportunity to regain enough courage not to slip away from creditors in the middle of the night. Many farmers did just that if their wives had family back East who would take them in, or if they were unmarried men who could outrun the creditors by heading west to try making a fresh start. Times had begun to improve, but without the advice of men like Isaac, they might have given up their claims. Because Isaac had no family living nearby, gossip about who might purchase his farm and timber claim would have naturally circulated, especially as Isaac's farm was regarded as one of the finest in the community.

News of funerals was transmitted by word of mouth, country burials done quickly without embalmment. Often those living in other townships did not receive news of the death in time to attend, but perhaps Joseph Cooper might have traveled to Isaac's service. There was great respect between the two men, for although Isaac had been responsible for initiating the County Agricultural Society, General Cooper had been elected president of the organization, and Isaac had been entrusted with the office of treasurer, a change from the secretary's office that he held in almost all of the organizations of which he was a member, perhaps because of his reputation as a learned man.[11]

Not only were burial services held quickly, but initiating the administration of estates was promptly begun. After news of Isaac's death reached the county seat of St. John, Judge Hockensmith, recently elected to replace John Hilmes, had appointed Dr. W. R. Willcox to administer Isaac's estate. Because Willcox had visited Isaac in the final days of his life, he would likely have attended the funeral, especially since his own farm was not far away. He might have heard the gossip and speculation regarding the settling of Isaac's estate, typical when a man without a wife and children dies. The estates of farmers like Isaac were often complicated, with loans among friends that weren't always documented as they should have been, and bank loans that farmers had carried on their backs for years keeping the bankers at bay by paying the interest month by month. Many of them paid more interest than the principal amount of the original loan, but continuing to pay the high interest rates was the only way to avoid foreclosure on their farms. Years before, Willcox and his family had gone to Isaac's farm when a local photographer was using it as a background for posing neighbors whose own farms were less successful. Willcox would have known that the house and its furnishings were far above average, but what must have truly amazed him were all the books. Anyone seeing Isaac's literary collection would have thought him to be a lawyer, or at least a teacher. It was a library of which any learned man would be proud, and Willcox must have known what a responsibility he had assumed.[12]

Given the popularity of famed American poet Walt Whitman during Isaac's life, it is quite possible that Isaac would have read the words of Whitman's poem, asking "Will someone when I am dead and gone write my life?" Whether Isaac expected anyone to read his journal and the articles he published, he has certainly left behind more than "a few diffused faint clews and indirections" as guides to the telling of his life and the story of the Populist movement in his early Kansas community.

This book is written for readers not terribly different from Isaac and his neighbors, ordinary Americans who care about our history. Through Isaac and his community, readers can discover the history of a time and place nearly forgotten but worth remembering by those of us today experiencing many of the same challenges. As David McCullough has said, "No harm's done to history by making it something someone would want to read."[13] For those who wish to read beyond Isaac and his community, the footnotes and the bibliography at the back of the book can guide the way to explore the Populist movement and the other issues of the late 1800s from which we have so much to learn.

PRAIRIE BACHELOR

CHAPTER 1

1884

Isaac Werner arrived on the open plains sometime in the latter half of the 1870s, bringing with him his 480-page journal, the fifth in a series he had kept throughout his life. The whereabouts of the four previous journals are lost to time, but what he labeled as "Vol. 5th" was begun in 1870 and continued into 1871, during the time he was a druggist in Rossville, Illinois. The oversized journal pages were filled from margin to binding in his neat but cramped penmanship, dense with observations about his community, his drugstore business, his book collecting, and news, his tight script filling 128 pages.

Without explanation, his writing ceased for thirteen years, but on August 24, 1884, he resumed keeping his journal, and from that day until the final 480th page was filled, he wrote every day. Pasted inside the cover of his journal was a clipped newspaper column written by the famous pastor and brother of Harriett Beecher Stowe, Rev. Henry Ward Beecher. Isaac copied from Beecher's clipping at length:

> It used to be the fashion, about the time I was a boy, for young persons religiously inclined to keep a journal, and to enter in it, from day to day, the exercises and experiences which befell them.
>
> . . .

> But there is quite another sort of journal. One may trace, from day to day, the mere facts of personal history, the proceedings of the farm, or the books read, visiting made or received, the events of society, the conversations with men of mark, the facts of the weather, the seasons, the aspects of nature, and, in short, a journal for knowledge, in distinction from feeling, might be kept with great profit. It will be likely to cultivate a habit of accurate observation or reading.[1]

Isaac's entries had never been entirely self-centered, but when he resumed writing in his journal in 1884, he seemed determined to follow Reverend Beecher's advice. It made him an excellent recorder of his times.

Once he resumed writing, he sometimes made references to events during the early years in Kansas before he had resumed keeping his daily journal, as well as references to his family and his years in Wernersville, Pennsylvania, providing details from periods in his life outside the dates of his current journaling. In addition, the prominence of the Werner family, especially Isaac's father, had resulted in many published records, and in particular a book published by the family's church. Like the children in the fairy tale who dropped crumbs to be able to find their way home, William Werner and his family also left a literary trail to follow various records back to their beginnings.

WHEN ISAAC WERNER ARRIVED on the treeless prairie about 1878, his initial homes were dugouts, cave-like shelters dug into the prairie sod. Eventually he built a house, with its own basement room, but on days like this he envied his neighbors who still benefitted from the insulation of their earthen homes. One early poet praised the snugness of dugouts, as well as the ability of such a humble dwelling to meet the requirements for establishing a claim: "The dugout homes of Kansas! The lowliest of all; They hold the homestead title as firm as marble hall."[2]

There were some benefits from living in dugouts, such as insulation from winter cold and summer heat, but Isaac did not miss the snakes and bugs that regularly dropped from dugout ceilings. Now it was the fleas and bedbugs Isaac battled for a good night's rest. He controlled the bedbugs by coating oil or kerosene on the legs of the bed frame to keep the bugs from crawling up, but the fleas were harder to control.[3]

With no livestock to tend, Isaac stayed indoors when winds roared across the prairie, driving the cold through the walls. The dried buffalo chips once called *prairie coal* had been picked clean,[4] but in those early years every

"Mr. Beecher's Unprinted Words," an advertisement for Rev. Henry Ward Beecher's secular publication. *County Capital,* January 27, 1893.

dugout or shanty had a pyramid of the dried dung stacked as high as the family fuel gatherer could reach, tall cones near the door of every dugout.[5] The buffalo were gone,[6] and with them, the prairie coal.[7]

Trees planted when nothing taller than prairie grasses decorated the horizons were still too precious to chop for fuel. Most homesteaders made do with corn husks they twisted and tied to slow their burning or used chopped lengths of cornstalks and cobs, once the corn had been stripped. The dried

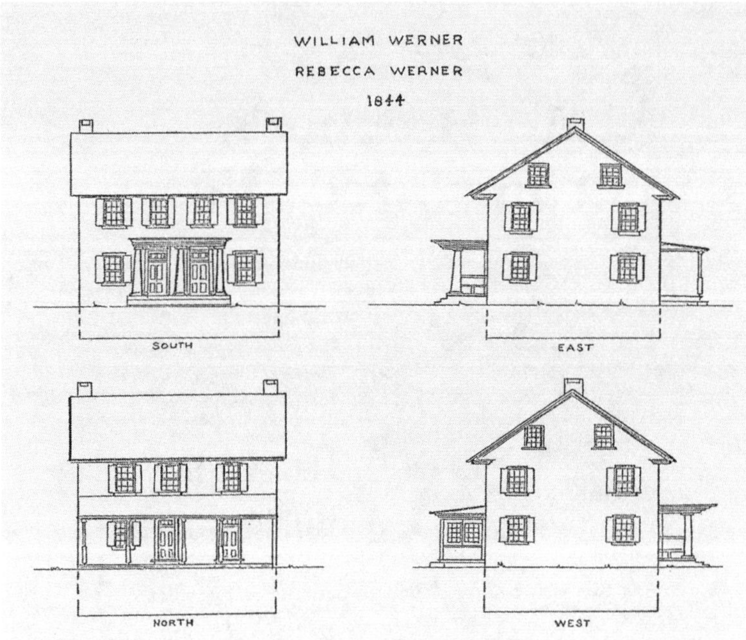

William Werner's stone home in Wernersville, Pennsylvania, where Isaac Werner was raised. From the collection of Jim Werner, by permission.

dung had burned more slowly, with hardly a noticeably odor, and as Isaac sparingly fed the faster-burning corn husks into his stove, he may have wished for prairie coal instead.

The life he had chosen on the Kansas prairie was very different from his childhood in Wernersville, Pennsylvania, the town founded in 1855 by his father William. Isaac's grandfather had come to Lower Heidelberg Township as a boy of ten, settling with his family in the fertile Lebanon Valley a few miles west of Reading, Pennsylvania. His descendants remained in the area, surrounding Isaac with uncles, aunts, and cousins as he and his twin brother grew to manhood. The family center was Hain's Church, which stood on the highest point of land in Lebanon Valley, and the Werner name was carved into many of the gravestones in the Hain's churchyard. Most of the time it must have been fun to exist in the confusion of Werner cousins and uncles—many with the same given names, but occasionally he surely felt lost, just another Werner male among so many others.

Isaac and his twin brother were the firstborn of their parents' children, followed by three girls. Their father had waited to marry until he was forty

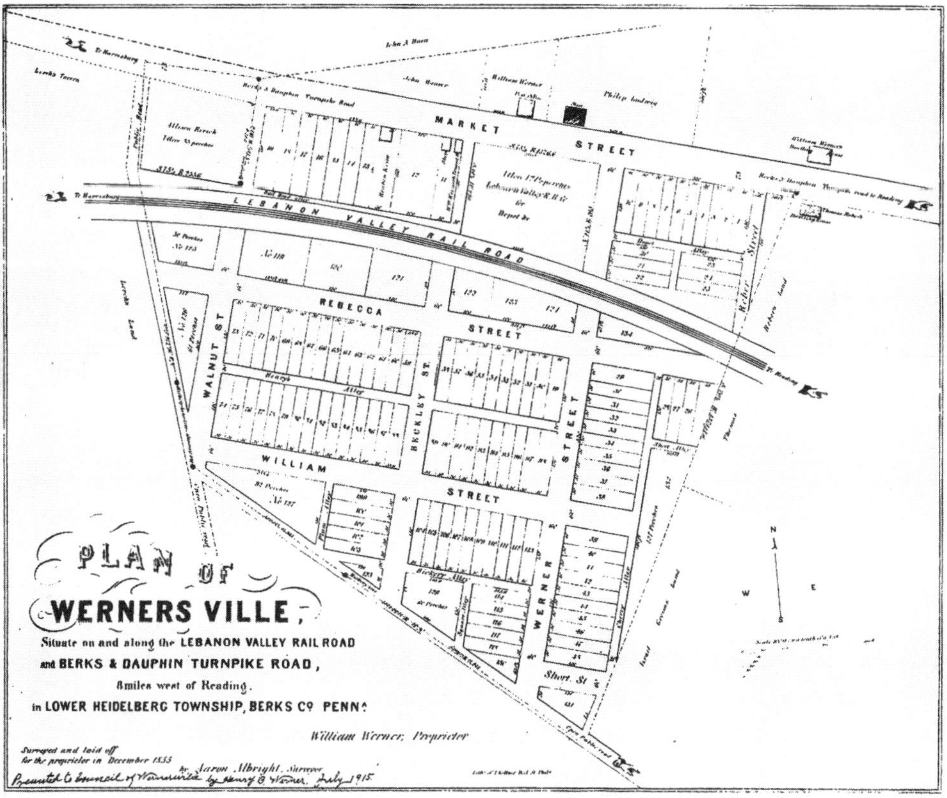

Town plat that William Werner had drawn and titled *Werners Ville*. The plat was given to the city of Wernersville by William Werner's son Henry, July 1915. Courtesy of the Wernersville Public Library, Wernersville, PA.

years old and successful enough to have a fifty-two-acre farm with which to support his new bride. When twin sons were born, the family moved into a new, two-story stone house, and William continued to build rental properties on his land. In 1855, he had a surveyor plat a town on twenty-two acres of his land, with streets of this new town named after himself and his family. Five years later, William and his wife Rebecca allowed the Philadelphia & Reading Railroad Company to lay its tracks across their land, and the railway station bore the name Wernersville, the name William had instructed the surveyor to designate the plat he had drawn. At his death, William owned twelve different tracts of land, comprising 550 acres. He left behind a forty-two-year-old widow, twenty-year-old sons, and two daughters, Emma, nineteen, and Henrietta, fourteen, a third daughter, Elmira, having died in infancy.[8] Isaac had been proud of his successful father, but in his nearly legendary life, William had cast quite a shadow, and Isaac may have been motivated to step outside that shadow to see if he could make his own success where the Werner name meant nothing except what he made of it. Had he stayed in Wernersville, he might never have been known as much more than his father's son and his twin's brother.

When the Civil War ended, and a cousin who had fought for the Union returned home, the two young men headed west. This cousin, named Henry after his own father, was an example of the confusion of names within the Werner family, and in this case, confusion also with Isaac's twin, who shared the given name of Henry. Cousin Henry's journey west with Isaac ended when he took a milling job along the way, but Isaac continued on to Rossville, Illinois, where he became the proprietor of a drugstore. Isaac proudly copied into his journal the complimentary assessment of his store by a drug salesman for Tinney & Moore of Lafayette, Indiana: "You keep the neatest Drugstore I met in a good while . . . indeed you have everything well arranged and keep it in good order."[9]

It was in Rossville that Isaac started his library, ordering books from dealers in New York, Boston, and Chicago, gradually acquiring an extensive library that he brought to Kansas, considering it "his rustic reference fortification." As a homesteader, Isaac could never have afforded all of the expensive books he acquired with income from his drugstore. A single shipment from Putman & Sons in 1871 totaled $54.01 for nine books, a small fortune in those times. Isaac never doubted such large expenditures for books, writing in his journal on January 10, 1871:

> As I been thinking now and then during last 6 months—not liking much anymore the ideas of loaning money out @ 10% and very uncertain when and old devil I will ever get it in or not, how to better, at least more satisfactory, if not even better paying, invest future cash I may be able to spare, and looking around me at the various openings to my judgment, I invariable mostly concluded that in a good Library for few more years to come—excepting risk of burning out . . . I would invest every spare dollar for next two or three years to come.[10]

He added elsewhere, "Whether I really increased the value of my real estate & chattels during this past year or not, I confidently feel that I enriched my mind . . . and in my eye that looks a fortune worth possessing. 'O learn thou young man, God hath provided wisdom the reward of study.'"[11]

As a man in his twenties, Isaac naturally noticed the young ladies in Rossville. It may have been the fact that he had two sisters that made him sensitive to the unequal treatment of women, but the seed of his support for expanding women's rights had grown stronger in Rossville. In January of 1871, a series of entries in his journal evidenced what he obviously considered an unfair thwarting of romance. On the ninth Isaac wrote, "Today Miss Milky commencing as bookkeeper for Henderson & Lee Company, a little novelty for Rossvillions—Female Clerks." Eight days later, his entry showed serious interest in the young lady: "For the first time fairly seen—as she called in for trifle—the late arrived bookkeeper of Henderson & Lee, appearing in quite fashionable 'Harness,' partly approaching the Grecian Bent, eyes pure and bright as crystals, not quite so bad." On Sunday, January 22, Isaac's dreams were dashed, as he wrote, "Soon after breakfast J. R. Lee called in and we indulged in a leisure conversation concerning their late feminine clerk, he telling me how of late some of the young country Romeos tried to coax his bookkeeper into their society attending country dances, but he kindly advising the said clerk concerning her best course of associating to retain credibly said clerkship, which she is filling at present."[12] Isaac took the hint from his fellow businessman. There were no more entries in his journal about Miss Milky.

He had also observed the condescending treatment his landlord showed toward his wife, and one particular example was so offensive that he recorded it in his journal on Wednesday, January 18, 1871. Isaac's landlord had previously acknowledged that his wife had

> bought the furniture and such needly articles of her own saved up money, while she was single. But during my presence at table eating he boldly throwed up to her into her face that she had brought nothing to him but two cannary birds. Elizabeth sat there at the end of table, looking on her plate, said nought, for I guess she had nothing to say, or if she had, she may have thought this had already too much been said. . . . [I] thought—considerable if she deserved such treatment I must been awfully deceived in my judgement, and if she was not, then William should have had his lean stearn booted better than he seen any booting yet executed. But then, I guess she knows about tolerable Blowing . . . and takes his spells accordingly.[13]

Having personally observed the unfair treatment of both Miss Milky and his landlord's wife, Elizabeth—one an unmarried woman and the other a wife—made Isaac better understand why suffragist activists were trying to change the rights of women for the better. Throughout his life he supported their efforts.

After several years, Isaac sold his successful drugstore to enter into a new business venture with his cousin Henry, who had arrived in Rossville on April 1, 1871, after several years of employment at a mill in a neighboring state.[14] With the knowledge Henry had gained and Isaac's business experience, the two cousins joined a third partner to operate a milling business. When cousin Henry decided to return to Wernersville, the milling venture ended and Isaac headed west, drawn by the promise of free land in Kansas.

The lives of his siblings and his mother had also changed after Isaac's father's death. His brother Henry stayed in Pennsylvania[15] and married Eve Hain, who was descended from the family that had donated the land for Hain's Church. They named their only child Charles Hain Werner, cementing his lineage from two of Wernersville's oldest families.

Isaac's mother and sisters had moved from Wernersville to Reading, where his sisters had married and established their own homes. Emma's husband, William E. Good, had a nice job with the railroad and remained in Pennsylvania. However, Ettie's husband, Rev. Samuel Palmer, was called to pastor a church in Abilene, Kansas, and Isaac's mother left Pennsylvania to live with her youngest daughter's family.[16] Although his sister and mother now lived in Kansas, Isaac felt unable to visit any of his family, prohibited by the responsibilities of his farm and his limited financial means.

Would Isaac's father have been disappointed to know how scattered his family had become, only Isaac's twin brother Henry continuing to manage the family land and legacy in Pennsylvania that William had spent a lifetime accumulating for them?

What might his father have thought of Isaac's 160-acre homestead in far south Stafford County, with an adjacent 160-acre timber claim to the north? The founding of St. John, the county seat about sixteen miles from Isaac's claims, occurred in 1878 when an early community of Mormons, who had arrived four years earlier to settle in a colony named Zion Valley, joined with other settlers to petition for the secular town of St. John. Isaac's journal makes no mention of the Mormon's or their leader, William Bickerton, although many of those early Mormon settlers remained in the community.[17] Isaac had arrived around 1878, the same year many of his neighbors had come,[18] and six years later he still lacked a horse, so he swapped his carpentry skills and manual labor in exchange for having neighbors break sod for him, an exchange that limited the number of acres broken. He also focused on his timber claim, which he worked by hand. His diligence was repaid by the healthy growth of his cottonwood trees, but attacking the sunflowers and sand burrs around the tender young trees was a backbreaking battle.

With most of the land having now been claimed by earlier homesteaders, only the poorest land remained unclaimed. Nearly every square mile of land in his community contained three or four families, primarily quarter-section homesteads, with a few timber claims scattered among them. Just to the north of Isaac's timber claim William and Nancy Henn lived with Nancy's seventeen-year-old son from an earlier marriage.[19] The boy, whose name was Frank Curtis, was seriously ill, and a doctor from St. John had diagnosed his case as hopeless.

Over a period of twelve days in September, Isaac recorded his efforts to assist the boy and his mother amidst the rest of his journaling:

> September 6th . . . Frank Curtis another back set in his sickness & sending after the St. John doctor . . .
>
> 7th . . . Eve up to the Henns & sat up most the night. Frank in his relapse and fading . . .
>
> 8th . . . I felt considerable worried about Frank Curtis; proper dieting for his recovery & seen Mrs. Dix & Persis about trying better regimen . . . Evening by Henns & urged better dieting for Frank, he failing fast, his physician expressing it hopeless . . .
>
> 9th . . . A.M. via Henns, Frank improving under Persis's nursing . . . Eve to Henns till midnight . . .
>
> 10th . . . I repaired Frank's bedstead . . .
>
> 11th . . . Morning up to Henn's, fixed windows & door to close tight . . .
>
> 14th . . . Eve up to Henn's, fixed Frank's chair & sat till midnight and [with] Cambell's wife.[20]

During the days these entries were made, Isaac continued describing in his journal the work he was doing on his farm, keeping up with those responsibilities while also assisting in the neighbor boy's care.

Isaac's thoughtful attention to the Henn family was not particularly unusual, for neighbors helped one another on the prairie. Isaac was especially close to the Dix family, who lived a mile to the west of his timber claim, and he took care of Doc Dix's chores when Doc was away. He liked to observe his neighbors' farming methods to see what succeeded and what failed, carefully recording his observations in his journal. The prairie soil was unlike what most homesteaders had farmed elsewhere, and each decision they made about their crops was a sort of experiment.

While Isaac was working there, Susan Dix invited him to join her and little Mabel for their noon meal.[21] Mabel was a pretty five-year-old girl, the pride of her parents. She was an only child, but before she was born there had been three other children. The Dix's firstborn was a boy who had died a few months after his first birthday, all of Doc's skills as a doctor unable to save him. As their grief lessened, they had a son and a daughter, and when both of those toddlers died within days of each other, it must have taken courage to risk having a fourth child. They had decided to make a fresh start in Kansas, where Mable was born, and it was only natural that they doted on her. So often it was the children who paid with their lives for the harsh conditions on the prairie.

Although Isaac sometimes wished for a family of his own, he still felt unable to provide for a family's needs. His tree-growing venture was in its infancy, and although he had cleared enough land for raising what he ate, without a horse to break more sod he could not raise much more to sell. There would have been nothing to sell with a family to feed, and probably not even enough to feed a wife, let alone children.

Musing about a nonexistent family served no purpose, so as the temperatures dropped in September, he focused on harvesting and storing the produce he would need for himself when winter arrived, one afternoon digging sweet potatoes and bagging black-eyed peas. Winter's approach was also a good time to reconcile his accounts of work shared with neighbors, wanting to avoid getting too far behind or ahead with anyone.

The approach of cold weather was not a good time for new settlers to be starting life on the prairie; yet, for several days he had noticed "sand hunters" around, looking at the last pieces of land still available to homestead. What land was left in Stafford, Pratt, and Edwards counties was only the least desirable, but emigrants and covered wagons could be seen moving back and forth, mostly westward to Edwards County. Isaac doubted that they could survive the winter, even if they found land to claim, having arrived too late in the season to make the necessary provisions for severe weather.

ISAAC HAD KEPT a daily journal since childhood, and after neglecting to make entries for thirteen years, his renewed journaling focused on the weather, his agricultural experiments, the labor he exchanged with neighbors, and occasional local news. The margins of the journal were often decorated with sketches of designs for his inventions.

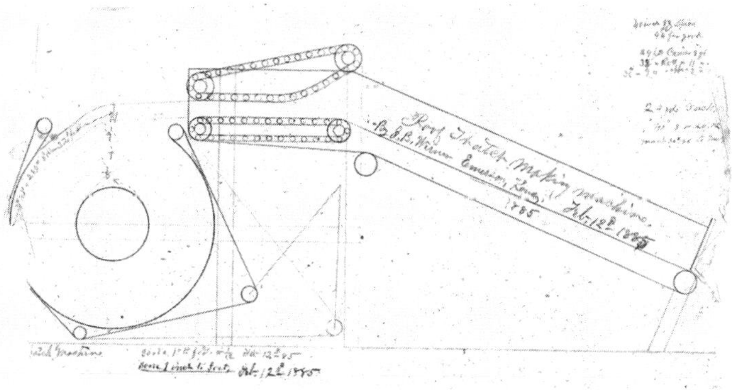

Drawing of Isaac Werner's design for a thatching machine using prairie grass, sent to Washington, DC. (The drawing of the belt to feed the grass into the machine is not shown.) The drawing was found inside Werner's journal.

A perfect example of his designing mind was his notion of using prairie grass as thatching material. He and his neighbors currently bundled grass and weighted it down with boards, but every strong wind unroofed their sheds. Having seen pictures of thatched roofs on cottages in England, he believed he could invent a thatching machine to cover the rural buildings of American farms with prairie grass. He developed a design[22] and began cutting native grass to use in his thatching experiment, working with urgency to harvest an adequate supply before cold weather made the grass too brittle.

Although prairie grass was beneficial for grazing, it was also feared by every settler on the prairie, having watched flames pushed by strong winds consume homes, crops, and animals. The risk could not be avoided, since embers carelessly left beneath the ash of campfires by others or lightning striking the ground could ignite dry grass miles away to start a raging blaze. Firebreaks might stop or slow the spread of the flames, but without a horse to pull a plow, Isaac was dependent on neighbors to plow firebreaks around his claims. Brothers-in-law Will Goodwin and Gus Gereke both had claims nearby, but they were working with their horses and plows away from home when Isaac noticed a threatening fire to the south. It looked bad, and Isaac used his scythe to cut grass around his house and shed until he was too exhausted to do anything to protect his trees. With arms trembling and strength spent, he made his way up his pinnacle hill[23] to see where the fire was headed, but even before reaching the top he could see the growing ferocity of the blaze.

Ugly orange flames shot high into the sky, their colors accentuated against the black and purple clouds of smoke raised by the burning grass. Trees and buildings were silhouetted against the glowing horizon, but the pulsating and wavering of the flames made it hard to identify exactly whose homesteads were threatened, although he thought he could make out Aaron Beck's timber claim and homestead in the dancing silhouettes before the flames.[24] The fire swept to the northwest, angling it away from his farm, and when it jumped the Rattlesnake Creek he tried to get some sleep. Several times during the night he awoke to be sure the wind hadn't changed directions to bring the fire back on top of him.

For a few days the prairie continued burning in the distance. Beck's had been spared, although the fire had traveled just to the southwest of their claims. Such a blaze within three miles intensified Isaac's desire for a horse. His neighbors plowed their common property lines too infrequently, he believed, and he could not afford to pay someone to plow around his house and the trees as often as he needed to feel safe. At last a little rain put the worst of the fires out, but wind from the northwest blew smoke from the smoldering grass back in his direction. On the prairie he could never be completely free from worry about wildfires.[25]

The first frost of the year blackened the peanut and tomato vines, and the box elder trees were turning yellow, making a pretty picture against the green catalpas. Box elders were fast growing, and settlers sometimes planted these less desirable trees just to get some quick shade or a windbreak. The catalpa trees were more beautiful, with their large, heart-shaped leaves providing pleasant shade. They also produced fragrant flowers in the spring, and Isaac enjoyed making catalpa bouquets for ladies who visited his farm when the trees were in bloom. As a boy in Pennsylvania he had taken trees for granted. In fact, they had sometimes been regarded as a nuisance when clearing fields. Many settlers on the treeless prairie grew melancholy, missing the beauty and shade of trees, as well as the wood for building and fuel. People would sometimes travel distances just to sit in the shade of a lone tree, even hugging the trunk affectionately.[26] Isaac was certain he would never again take trees for granted.

While Isaac focused on his timber claim, he watched other neighbors expanding their farms. Gereke had recently bought a pair of oxen for $175, and Goodwin was building a new dugout on his homestead claim just to the south across the Pratt-Stafford county line to make room for his younger brother Felix to move in with him. Isaac worried about neighbors entangling themselves in mortgage debt beyond what they would be able to repay.

His other nearest neighbors were the Vosburgh family, whose claims were northwest of his homestead.[27] Persis Vosburgh had claimed a quarter section as a single woman, and Jerome Vosburgh's family claimed a homestead just north of hers. It was convenient having nearby neighbors with whom he could exchange work, and sometimes he and Jerome hired out together, one day helping a man in Pratt County dip sheep in a heated mixture of lime and sulfur to protect against parasites. When much of the plains had been open range, three sheep trails had crossed the Kansas plains, used to drive sheep from the Rocky Mountains to eastern markets.[28] The earliest homesteaders had often raised sheep, grazing them on the unclaimed prairie, but as more homesteaders had arrived and crops were planted, sheep herding decreased.[29] A few men in both Pratt and Stafford counties had large herds, but most did not.

Isaac was particularly known for his carpentry skills, but he was willing to accept about any job, whether large or small, to earn cash or exchange his labor for work neighbors could do for him in return. Before dawn one morning, he walked to Gereke's place a mile east to help butcher a hog. Gereke, a decade younger than Isaac, had come to America with his parents when he was about ten years old, and now he had a family of his own, with three young children to support. His wife Mary was a sister to Goodwin, and the brothers-in-law worked together regularly.[30]

When the butchering was done, Isaac walked to Goodwin's place to help set the roof on Goodwin's new dugout. Goodwin had done some work plowing fireguards and breaking sod for him, so Isaac was glad to balance the ledger a bit by helping with the roof, although the heavy lifting made him eager for a good night's rest when they finished the job. The late autumn days were still warm and pleasant to work in the open, but the nights were cool for good sleeping. Unfortunately, Isaac had uninvited guests in his parlor when he arrived home on November 2: "We set roof on Will Goodwin's new dugout S. of me. (3/4 day 1.15) Eve found skunk in my parlor, annihilated him & family."[31] Without doubt Isaac must have slept with the windows open wide that night, despite the chill.[32]

Two days later he walked up to a neighbor's preemption house to clerk for the Clear Creek election,[33] probably hoping he and his clothes had aired out enough not to offend. Even before the land in his area had been officially opened for settlement, some people had arrived early to claim the most desirable property, especially land nearer the creek. The soil was likely to be better because of richer soil deposited by flooding in the past, and the creek provided a source of water, although those benefits were offset somewhat by the danger of future flooding. These settlers had assumed that the land they had preemptively claimed would eventually be opened for settlement, and when it was, they officially staked their claims.

When Isaac began his duties as election clerk that morning, he noted that there were sixty-eight men registered to vote, the majority Republicans. At the end of the day with fifty-six votes polled, only fifteen were Democrats. Clear Creek Township was larger than most in Stafford County, containing seventy-two square miles within a rectangular boundary twelve miles wide from west to east and six miles wide from north to south. An area that large offered 298 quarter sections available to be claimed as homesteads or timber claims. The Republican majority was not surprising, given the number of Union soldiers who had staked claims and followed the party of their old commander, Lincoln; however, there remained many homesteaders who had not yet registered. Perhaps the number of voters would grow as more homesteaders got settled into their claims, but for now political activity was fairly limited.[34]

Isaac's day-to-day contacts were usually limited to his nearest neighbors, but he was acquainted with just about every man in Clear Creek Township. John Garvin's claim was too far for frequent visits, but he had a fine barn large enough for community celebrations, and that allowed people throughout the township to gather for special occasions and get better acquainted. At a holiday party that Isaac attended in Garvin's barn, the host convinced Isaac to repaint his fancy buggy. Garvin agreed to establish an account at Doc's store, against which Isaac could draw, and using that arrangement, Isaac ordered a manual titled *Sign & Carriage Painting*—fifty cents in stamps for the manual and five cents for the postage. It was the beginning of a job Isaac came to wish he had never agreed to do.

Weather on the prairie was a severe taskmaster, having no sympathy for those who neglected accomplishing seasonal tasks at the proper time, and this December seemed particularly unsettled to Isaac. He knew better than to postpone minimizing the leaks that let cold into his house, and he also prepared for the cold temperatures by cutting up tough stalks of corn to use for fuel, still not dry enough to burn, but pre-cut for when they were needed. Newcomers to the prairie sometimes put off preparations too long, and he worried about neighbors, already complaining about frosted feet from the cold in their houses but seeming to do little to reduce the leaks. Too many of them were not well prepared for such weather, nor for the danger of worse cold yet to come.

CHAPTER 2

1885

Spring had finally shoved winter out of the way, and it was a pleasant time for Isaac's twin brother Henry to come by train from Pennsylvania for a visit. Much as Isaac hated asking favors, he had arranged for his neighbor Jesse Green[1] to take him to Larned to meet Henry. The Greens had moved onto the claim just east of Isaac's homestead, and Jesse needed lumber and a roll of Iron Board Roofing paper for the sod house he was building for his family. Jesse agreed to arrange his shopping trip for the date Henry was arriving, so he and Isaac could travel to Larned together in Jesse's wagon.

It had been several years since Isaac had seen his brother, and after a quick greeting they proceeded to the Larned Land Office[2] to transact the business that had brought Henry to Kansas, transferring Isaac's timber claim into Henry's name.[3] Jesse and Isaac did their shopping before beginning the long journey to Isaac's home.

Along their way were large areas of burned prairie, some the result of fires set intentionally by farmers who saw burning as the easiest way to clear the prairie, whether to begin breaking sod or simply to burn off old growth to get a better start for the new season.[4] Knowing how often those fires got away, burning everything in their paths, Isaac disapproved. He had helped battle a fire only a month before that a new settler west of the Beck place intentionally set in the midst of March winds. When the foolish settler lost control of the fire's spread, neighbors came with horses and plows, while others like Isaac used blankets, wet gunny sacks, or whatever they could find to beat back the creep of the flames.[5] That fire was stopped by midnight, but it had been the second serious threat for the Becks,[6] who were naturally anxious.

Henry Beckley Werner, Isaac Werner's twin brother. From the collection of Jim Werner.

Isaac had seen such fires burn out of control for miles, and even if burning off the mat of old dry grass rejuvenated new growth, he did not think burning was worth the risk of destroying homesteads and any spontaneous timber growth. Trees were precious things on the prairie, and just ten days before the fire near Beck's, Isaac had counted thirty-four hundred healthy, growing trees that he had planted since arriving on his 320-acre claims.[7] Isaac and his neighbors protected their homesteads by using horses to plow strips of bare soil around their claims to remove anything that could fuel an approaching prairie fire, but strong winds could push the flames across those firebreaks. As they traveled, Isaac explained to his brother the dangers of prairie fires and the importance of having a horse with which to plow the fireguards and widen them if fire approached.[8]

After their father's death, it was Isaac's brother Henry who assumed the responsibility of managing their father's estate, and Isaac had written Henry about his need for cash. His requests had been ignored, and Isaac was using his brother's visit to explain not only how a horse could help protect his claims against fires but also why it was needed to break more sod for crops.

That evening, comfortably settled in Isaac's kitchen, the brothers caught up on news about the family, Henry's own wife and child, as well as Emma's family in Reading, and Ettie's family in Abilene, Kansas, with whom their mother Rebecca was living.[9] If Henry questioned why Isaac had not visited their mother and sister, Isaac had two explanations—first, he lacked

(LEFT) Henrietta "Ettie" C. Werner Palmer, Isaac Werner's youngest sister. (RIGHT) Rev. Samuel Palmer, husband of Henrietta C. Werner, and brother-in-law of Isaac Werner. From the collection of Susan Davis.

the cash for a railroad ticket, and second, there was a genuine risk in his community of having claim jumpers take over his property in his absence.[10]

Recent challenges to claims had arisen when homesteaders, temporarily absent, returned to find someone had moved onto their property, claiming an abandonment.[11] On February 16 Isaac wrote in his journal: "Vigilence Meeting at Naron School House," and on the twenty-first he recorded "Eve 2nd meeting at Naron Schol house to oust claim jumpers. 60 present and 70 names on the list." A week later, Isaac described "about 60 out and also 3 of the jumpers. Rev. Smith, Rev. Nelson & Bails a very earnest and interesting meeting and talking till after 12 o'clock, affecting a sort of Compromise and tending to increase better general feelings among neighborhood." The meeting scheduled for two days later resulted in the failure of the claim jumpers to appear, but the final meeting on March 3 concluded with some success:

> A good 50-odd turn-out to hear final report of visiting committee to claim jumpers, Nelson, Bales & Herold, and express willingness to withdraw their contests. Long and general talk about P. Vosburgh

> suspended title—Campbell & Shat offering to sign a petition favorable. Also, statements on both sides made of Rice and Steinmetz land controversy. Standing committees were all discharged . . . none begrudging the meeting & its object, and great deal more peaceable accomplished than was generally expected[.][12]

Certainly sharing that experience with his brother Henry would have explained the risks of Isaac leaving his claim to visit his mother and sister in Abilene.

Isaac spent the next day showing Henry his place and introducing him to the neighbors. The wild plums were in bloom, and his trees were budding, making Isaac feel particularly proud of his farm. He enjoyed explaining to his brother how he propagated cottonwood trees from fifteen-inch cuttings. He had also planted box elders and catalpas, and he planned to seed a few Osage orange trees for use as fence posts as their hard wood did not rot easily. Osage orange trees took their name from the Osage Indians who used the strong wood for their bows. The nubby peel of the inedible fruit resembled citrus peel, but the green pulp inside was useless for anything but its own reproduction, although some believed it repelled crickets. The trees were also called hedge apple trees because of their use in planting dense hedges.

Native sand hill plum thickets grew on his land when he homesteaded, but the bushes were nearly impossible to transplant unless he happened to get a parent bush with the taproot. Instead, he had selected seeds from the best plums to plant near his house, despite it being a slow means of propagating the bushes. Although the plums were a small fruit, with only a thin layer of pulp around the seed, Isaac looked forward to them every season, enjoying their sweet tartness. Settlers had learned to appreciate fresh fruit while it was available. Isaac's options were peaches from his orchard, sand hill plums from the native bushes, and melons from his garden. On occasion, his delight with the first fruits of the season resulted in his eating until he gave himself a bellyache.

After showing Henry his farm, the brothers set out on a walking tour to meet Isaac's neighbors. Isaac's life was crowded with friends, acquaintances, correspondents, and encounters with famous people. He referred to friends with their given names and nicknames. The less intimate the relationships the more formal the references, generally using the surname for business acquaintances and well-known public persons. Occasionally, as men sometimes do, he also used the surname of male friends, and conversely, addressed women formally as a sign of respect, even when he knew them well. As for the close neighbors to whom he introduced his brother, most were greeted with their given names.

They began at the dugout of Will and Felix Goodwin,[13] just across the county line to the south in Pratt County, before going to Jesse's homestead just east of Isaac's home to meet his wife and children. They walked further east to Gus Gereke's place but missed seeing neighbor Joseph Mayes whose home was nearby. They circled back west to visit Isaac's newest neighbor, Isabel Ross, who had moved into her sod house only the week before. Her claim was just to the east of Isaac's timber claim, and they angled across its corner to admire his young trees on their way to George and Nancy Henn's place to the north.

The two brothers had nearly completed a circle around Isaac's claims, with their last stop being the Vosburgh claims to the northwest. Jerome Vosburgh had come to Kansas from New York with his wife Ann and their four children, and his older sister Persis had also staked a claim. Single women were eligible to claim homesteads, and many did.[14] When Jerome's wife died, Persis stepped in to help her brother with his children. Some neighbors, who coveted her claim, argued that Persis no longer maintained the separate household necessary to prove up her homestead, but Isaac supported Persis. Had Persis been Jerome's bachelor brother claiming an adjacent homestead, rather than his unmarried sister, Isaac doubted that anyone would have objected. Persis had her own home, ran her farm, and the fact that her brother and nephews helped was no different from brothers who worked together on their claims, in Isaac's opinion. A few weeks earlier, Isaac had helped Persis write a letter to "Washington about further information concerning her homestead case."[15]

Having made a complete circuit around Isaac's land, the two brothers headed a mile west toward Doc and Susan Dix's house, where the Emerson Post Office and a small store were located. Neighbors were often found there in the evenings, having come for their mail and a little shopping. After some visiting, it was dusk by the time the brothers returned to Isaac's house.

The next day, Isaac repaid Jesse for the trip to Larned by helping with the roofing, while Henry walked to the post office to make arrangements to travel back to Larned with the mail carrier the following morning. Later, the brothers worked side by side in Isaac's house garden, hand plowing around the peach trees. There was probably no better way to have spent the final hours of Henry's visit, working together as they once had on their father's farm. Early the next morning they walked to Emerson, and as Isaac watched

Henry climb onto the mail coach, he must have wondered if he would ever see his twin brother again.

HENRY HAD NOT AGREED to supply money from their father's estate for Isaac to buy a horse, so Isaac set about finding work for which he would be paid in cash. Several days in early February, he had built Moore's house[16] down in Pratt County, with a full day's wages of $1.50. He might have built Mrs. Ross's soddy, but after hearing all of her "architectural opinions," he was glad to let someone else get the job. He did dig her well once the soddy was built, however.

Another neighbor, Jake Baker,[17] who lived north of the Henns, asked Isaac to be his agent while he went to the Indian Territories to the south. Most of the men who had staked claims around Isaac were married, but Jake was a young bachelor and seemed less settled. Isaac hoped he would keep his trip short, with some of the neighbors all too eager to use any absence as an excuse to assert an abandonment of a claim.

After several weeks of taking jobs in an effort to save money for a horse, Isaac had placed most of those wages on accounts for work neighbors had done for him. No closer to buying the horse needed to increase crop production, his hopes now rested on the thatch-making machine he had designed. His computations of necessary materials to build the machine were more weighty and costly than he had expected, but he was not discouraged. He had compared the cost of thatch roofing with the cheap wood shingles that would be most equivalent, and he estimated a savings of about half, which would encourage sales among settlers.

For now, his big ideas were being funded by little projects, and the worst job he had got himself into was painting John Garvin's buggy. Repairs and paint removal delayed the actual painting until March, and it was two more months before the final varnishing began. Garvin had grown picayunish about the cost, and the compromised price left neither man happy, although the quality of the finished product raised no complaints. Like everything Isaac did, perfection was the only satisfactory result.

His incubator invention, made from wooden coffee boxes in which coffee had been shipped to Doc's store, was a great success. Repurposing was essential on the prairie, and very little material of any sort was wasted. As chicks hatched, Isaac added more eggs, marking them with letters when they were put into the incubator to identify owners of the chicks when the eggs hatched.

Jake Baker returned on May 12, and by then Isaac had hired someone to plant Jake's oats. His relief over being freed from the agent's responsibilities was brief, for within three days another neighbor, Charles Shattuc,[18] contested the claim, saying Jake's lengthy absence was an abandonment and that hired labor having planted Jake's oats made no difference.[19] Acquiring title to a homestead required the claimant to build a dwelling and live on the claim for five years while cultivating the land, requirements intended to prohibit absentee owners from registering a claim but hiring others to do the work in the owner's absence—in effect, becoming land speculators rather than settlers. Jake's burden of proof was to bring witnesses to establish that he had done those things, with Shattuc's counter evidence intended to dispute that proof. As Jake's agent, Isaac was caught up in the dispute. On Sunday, June 21, Jake and his two witnesses, Isaac and Jesse, traveled all day to reach Larned for the land contest scheduled to begin the next morning. Travel and time in court kept Isaac away from his farm at the busiest season of the year, which he deplored in his journal:

> June 22 . . . Fair like to loaf about Larned, by 11 A.M. examination of us witnesses commenced & not got quite through by 4 P.M. closing hour. Much disagreeable loafing around
>
> June 23 Some cloudy & misty morning, further examining of witnesses, our (Baker) side only by noon got about done, leaving decision in 'status quo.' P.M. completed our shopping . . . & started out about 7 miles by dusk homeward. Stopped at English family.[20]

A month later on July 30, Isaac noted that Jake had "loaded up his tent & things at Greens & moved down below Iuka temporarily."[21]

Summer was always busy for farmers, and Isaac stayed active helping neighbors and tending his own small plots. Without a horse, he knew financial independence would remain out of reach, making success of the thatching machine even more important, and he worked out details of its design through the summer. On August 8, he sent a "letter to Wm Simms & to Fred A. Seamann, Washington, about patent ability [*sic*] of my Thatching business & with sketch enclosed."[22] Their reply validated the soundness of his plan. Before the approaching cold weather made the grass too brittle, Isaac cut and stored a supply of grass in his shed, ready to complete the machine and experiment with the use of native grass as roofing material for pioneer farms.

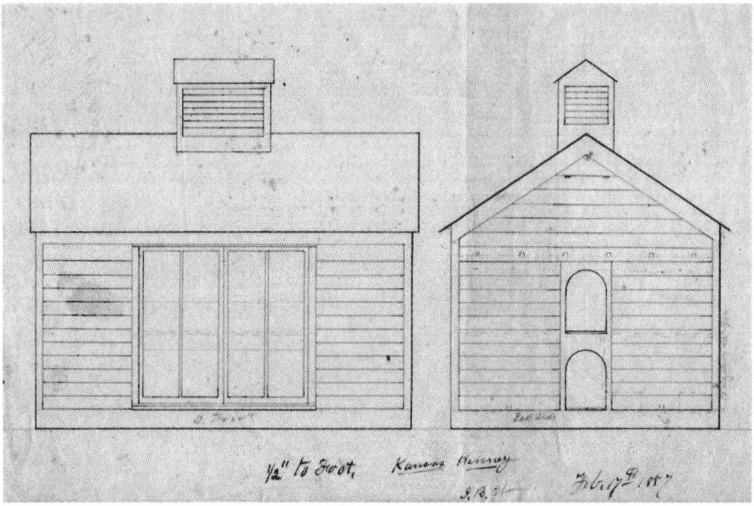

Isaac Werner's drawing of his hennery, found inside of his journal.

Undeterred by the trouble his previous trip to the strip had caused, Isaac's restless friend Jake decided to take a trip to Iowa while the judge's decision was pending. Isaac accompanied Jake to Great Bend to meet the train and brought back Jake's three horses and wagon, loaded with about five hundred feet of lumber Isaac had bought to build a hennery. Two of Jake's horses were loaned out to other farmers, but he loaned his favorite horse, Joe, to Isaac. There were many jobs that Isaac accomplished by having Joe, and one job was his road tax obligation. Men forty-five-years old and younger were required to do unpaid road work a certain number of days each year in their township as a road tax, and with Joe's "horse power," Isaac and five of his neighbors spent an entire day filling a few bad holes on the road west of Vosburgh's, satisfying the annual township road tax obligation of all the men.[23]

A paying job for Isaac was offered when David Carnahan,[24] a neighbor to the northeast, received the contract to build the new schoolhouse and asked Isaac and Will Goodwin to help. Excerpts from Isaac's journal entries throughout the month of October document the progression of their labor:

> October 20 . . . Helped Carnahan at school house (put pulleys into window jambs . . .
>
> 22 . . . I all day at school house, made window strips; Goodwin at siding up W., Carnahan making window frames . . .

23 . . . all day at school house . . .

24 . . . We 3, Carnahan, W. Goodwin & I at siding up school house . . .

26 . . . I on foot up to school house, all three getting little later start than usual . . . me siding up E. & N. sides, nearly done, few boards yet on N. side . . .

27 . . . to school house soon after sun rise . . .

28 . . . little windy from N. most the day to do satisfactory shingling . . .

29 . . . Morning up to school house and by sun down had it done, shingled, (one day scant) . . .

30 . . . We up to school house, Dilly and I at ceiling all day, Carnahan beating & Goodwin priming outside.[25]

After long work days during most of October, Isaac's journal entry of December 6 reported, "Yesterday school house building accepted by directors, of Carnahan pleased with the job etc. School to commence to-morrow."[26] After settling wages with Carnahan, Isaac finally had some much needed cash.

The schoolhouse job had interfered with some of Isaac's usual preparations for winter, and one job in particular demanded prompt attention. Crickets had spoiled the taste of Isaac's well, and drawing out all the water hadn't helped. Before the ground was frozen, Isaac and his neighbor, Joseph Mayes, spent four days of digging to a depth of thirty-nine feet for water, and Isaac declared the work worth it when he drew his first bucket of clean, fresh water.[27] A dependable well made him feel better, with winter ahead.

Isaac awoke December 23 to the finest mirage he had seen in the seven years he had lived on his homestead. St. John, sixteen miles away, and Leesburg in between, could both be distinctly seen, somehow elevated above the curve of the earth to sit on the horizon as if they were much nearer.[28] Having returned Jake's horse Joe, Isaac used the day's spring-like weather to walk to St. John to pay his taxes.

Although there were sundry entertainments in celebration of the holidays, including a dance[29] on Christmas Eve and a great dance Christmas night at Garvin's barn, Isaac chose to stay home. The uncharacteristically mild weather of late December was so unusual that it seemed almost ominous, and Isaac wondered whether Mother Nature's next trick might top even the incredible mirage.

CHAPTER 3

1886

Winter was hard on both humans and animals, and Isaac Werner scattered corn in his peach orchard for his half-tame flock of quails. He had a particular soft spot for birds of all kinds, never hunting them. The prairie chickens generally kept their distance from him—and no wonder, since their numbers had been greatly reduced from hunting. Isaac measured the seasons by watching the ducks and geese fly over, and he knew when to expect the arrival of each variety of songbird in the spring.

Ironically, Isaac was also partial to cats, despite their tendency to stalk his songbirds. Before going to bed on January 8, he checked on the box of three-week-old kittens in the kitchen. The old mother cat was out of the box, and the four kittens mewed hungrily when he bent down to pet them. Their eyes were open, but they crawled clumsily over each other, nibbling at his fingers as if they expected to find milk. He put the mother cat back into the box to keep her kittens warm and went to bed. If she would not stay with them, he knew they could not survive the cold, even inside the house.

The following day began with what Isaac called "about worst blizzard in 7 years."[1] The rattling of his house at dawn awakened Isaac to a blizzard with the temperature at eight degrees below zero. He spent the day indoors, grateful he had hauled in extra cornstalks to burn. Although the blizzard subsided the next night, the temperature had plunged to eighteen below zero. He was disgusted to see the old mother cat curled up next to the stove, out of the box where she should have been keeping her kittens warm. All four seemed dead, but he wrapped them in a towel and built up the fire in the stove, attempting to revive them with its warmth. He was only successful with one kitten, but he warmed the bedding and returned the mother cat to care for the surviving kitten. The ground was too frozen to bury the dead kittens until a thaw, but he covered them deeply with snow to keep coyotes and skunks away.

He felt fortunate to have no livestock, for the hardship of the blizzard was severe, especially for stock on the open prairie.[2] The temperature by evening was minus nineteen degrees, and Isaac had to revive the kitten again. He moved the box closer to the stove and added more rags for the kitten to burrow under if its mother continued leaving it alone. He hoped her need to reduce the pressure of full teats would force her to return frequently to her lone kitten.

When he awoke the next morning it was still brutally cold, and he was relieved to see the mother cat nursing the kitten. By the following day, he had seen no sign of his "flock of pet quails," although he continued to keep corn out for them, just in case. For several evenings there had been sundogs, and that evening a particularly pronounced trio of bright orbs hovered at the horizon, the sun in the center, and at the same height on either side, a pair of smaller mock suns, blushing pink on their sides nearest the sun. Isaac believed that such a phenomenon forewarned of treacherous weather; however, some Native Americans believed that sundogs were evil stars trying to kill the sun.[3] In a way, both were about the same thing.

When he checked on Isabel Ross that same day, he noticed she was burning more cornstalks for warmth than he allowed himself, so he asked two neighbors to help him load and haul three wagonloads of stalks to her, along with some fodder for her cow. As they worked, the talk was mostly about the blizzard. One neighbor had lost forty-seven head of cattle, and another lost about eight hundred sheep. People had brought cows into their homes to keep them alive, especially if they had only one milk cow. Reports were already reaching their community about the devastation further west of them, where large herds of cattle were grazed on open prairie. Cattle had scattered in search of shelter, and it might be weeks before the numbers killed could be determined.[4] The men helping haul cornstalks told Isaac of bad news closer to home: "Quails reported found around froze to death, likely my flock suffered ditto during late severe blizzard, none reporting now several days."[5] He stopped putting out corn for them.

Most prairie houses were not well insulated, and livestock had little or no shelter. High winds accompanied the snowfall and extreme cold, pushing snow into drifts as high as eighteen feet. Places near Isaac recorded even colder temperatures than what his thermometer had registered, and newspapers reported cattle and horses frozen to death in stables.[6]

Isaac stopped going for his mail due to drifts from the blizzard still blocking the trains. He needed to stay close to home anyway, tending fires in his basement day and night to keep the potatoes and other produce he stored there from freezing. The earthen insulation that usually moderated the cellar temperature was inadequate with below-freezing temperatures for this long. He worried about the stored produce intended to feed him through the winter, provide seed potatoes for his next crop, and generate income when they were sold as seed potatoes in the spring. Outside, rabbits were doing so much harm to his hedge plants that he began feeding them corn to keep them from gnawing the trees.

Plants, animals, and people suffered, and one neighbor who lived alone froze to death a few days after the blizzard. The old man's death led to a cruel joke on young Frank Curtis when neighbors staged a mock arrest, charging Curtis with breaking into the man's house. The boy nearly skipped the country in fright, and although Isaac sympathized with the boy's fear, he had brought the joke upon himself by lying about entering the old man's house.

As the weather moderated, David Carnahan asked Isaac to help build a coal house and improve the privies at the school, and other neighbors called on him for construction and repairs. It seemed that milder weather had motivated everyone to undertake projects they had put off during the worst of winter, and Isaac was the beneficiary of the extra work.

In addition to the building activity, a meeting was held at the schoolhouse to discuss getting a railroad, the community feeling at a disadvantage without a local railroad to ship or receive freight. William Campbell stepped forward to lead the effort. Most tracks ran from east to west, but some connecting lines and spurs going north and south were also laid. The previous year the Arkansas River and Western Railway Company had proposed a rail line from Hutchinson to Kinsley, seeking bonds at $4,000 per mile.[7] With nearby communities getting rail lines, Isaac's neighbors hoped they might locate a railroad company planning a north-south route connecting larger towns that could be induced to pass near their community.

The relationship between early settlers and the railroads was a love-hate one:

> Like most nineteenth-century Americans, farmers were enthusiastic about the arrival of each new railroad that promised to further 'open up the country' to new towns and new markets. But the farmers' euphoria at the appearance of the new rail line inevitably turned to bitter resentment. The farmer in the West felt that something was wrong with a system that made him pay a bushel of corn in freight cost for every bushel he shipped.[8]

Although communities were eager for railroad service, the quest for regulation of rates was ongoing. Nevertheless, the community decided to pursue getting a local spur, and Campbell, Ben Webber, and Doc Dix were appointed to investigate.

The schoolhouse served many purposes beyond its use for educating children. In addition to community meetings like the recent railroad meeting, it was also the site of religious services, and one evening Isaac went to the school to hear a farmer-clergyman born in England but now living in Garfield up in Pawnee County. Isaac's general indifference toward church attendance was not a reflection of his childhood training. In fact, his family's attendance at the old Hain's German Reformed Church had been as expected as the rising of the sun. Isaac had begun drifting away from regular attendance by his mid-twenties while living in Rossville, preferring to spend the one day a week when his drugstore was closed reading or enjoying exercise in the fresh air. It wasn't a matter of turning away from God but rather dissatisfaction with those preaching His word, whom Isaac often found to be dull at best and hucksters at worst. He preferred to read his Bible and study at home, using the volume of *Cruden's Concordence*[9] in his personal library.

The threat of prairie fires was another reason that staying close to home was prudent, and fortunately, Isaac was at home when fires that started in the sand hills to the southwest drifted north toward neighbor Persis Vosburgh's land. He joined neighbors fighting the flames, but the fire swept through Vosburgh's timber claim and headed northeast toward the Henns. A shift of wind out of the north drove flames southward, sparing the Henns but blazing a path directly toward Isaac. He recorded in his journal how it "flew roaring Southward going over and through everything over my sandhill and set two fodders & hay stack on fire and then my shedding. [I] saved the implements till it got too hot to go near it, about 5 good loads of roofing grass piled in it made an awful heat & lasting several hours. Wind being in our favor or could not have saved the house."[10] An hour after dark, fires glowed all around him, but his property was no longer threatened. In his desperation to save as much as he could, Isaac had blistered his face. Although neighbors who had arrived to guard against spreading embers insisted Isaac go to bed, his blistered skin kept him from sleeping.

The fire had destroyed his hopes for the thatch-making machine, leaving him even more dependent on good crops. The stored prairie hay had ignited so quickly, and surely would have done so had it been a thatched roof, making saving anything inside whatever building it covered nearly impossible. Isaac realized that prairie buildings roofed with the dried grass would be an even greater fire risk than the cheap wooden shingles most farmers currently used, and no doubt his neighbors had also seen that risk. There would be few customers for native grass roofing, even if he chose to pursue his idea.

As he surveyed the devastation to his farm, Isaac felt grateful he had no family to suffer this loss with him. Although having a wife to nurse his burns would be a comfort, he refused to allow himself any regret or loneliness when there was work to do, nor could he allow the pain from his burns to keep him in bed, and the next morning he was out planting potatoes when Jake Baker arrived.

Their friendship had cooled over blunt words exchanged about Jake's absence from his claim, Isaac criticizing Jake's tardy return and Jake implying that Isaac could have done more to protect his claim. Jake's lengthy absence had resulted in the judge declaring an abandonment and recognizing Shattuc's claim to the land. Now Jake was finding work until he could decide what to do next, and he had come to borrow Isaac's windlass and ask for help digging a well at another farm. The winch-like apparatus allowed one man to dig at the bottom of the hole, filling a bucket with dirt. Another man at the top could winch the full bucket to the surface, dump the evacuated soil, and lower the empty bucket to the bottom to be filled again. The money Isaac was paid for digging wells was an important source of cash. Jake seemed oblivious to the fire's damage and Isaac's burns, and needing the wages more than ever after the fire, Isaac said he would try to help. However, the next morning his face was so swollen and delicate he could not go. He spent most of the day indoors, cutting seed potatoes for planting.

Despite the blowing sand and ashes for several days after the fire, and without regard for his burns and disappointment, Isaac could not ignore potato planting season. He had also decided it was better to have a share of someone else's crop as income rather than watching his ground lie idle, so he had rented some land to Jesse Green for planting oats on shares.

The failure of his thatching machine venture meant no future revenue from a roofing business, nor from manufacturing thatching machines, nor from selling the patent. What he raised, and his share from the rented ground, would determine the success or failure of his farm. Isaac decided that buying a horse to clear more prairie for crops was his best hope, even if it meant borrowing the money. He began shopping and sought the advice of Ben Webber, whose knowledge of horses he respected.

Except for occasional short-term credit extended by merchants, Isaac had managed to stay out of debt, and he hated the idea of borrowing money, likening it to stepping into quicksand. He spent hours studying his accounts and running figures, trying to find some way to make his farm a success without incurring debt. The financial understanding Isaac thought he had made with his mother and siblings when he came to Kansas was proving to be complicated and disheartening, with ongoing correspondence asking for working capital and maintaining the accuracy of their transactions.[11] Isaac's brother Henry's visit had made it clear, however, that no money would be advanced for a horse.[12]

Potato planting was interrupted in March, not by weather but rather when delivery of seed potatoes he had ordered did not arrive because trains were stalled by striking workers.[13] Isaac stayed busy, awaiting settlement of the strike, planting his own potatoes saved from the previous year and the varieties he had already received. It was just another setback beyond his control, and he was not alone among other farmers feeling discouraged about their prospects. Money was becoming unusually close and tight.

After trying two horses, neither of which had handled plow or wagon well, Isaac found a horse he could afford. He described the transaction in his journal: "Eve up to Frank Gullet and engaged his mare at $115. He to pay horse bill, we to finish trade next day." An acquaintance named Gullet[14] had run up a stable bill in St. John that he could not pay, and rather than letting the stable seize his little mare for the unpaid bill, he had sold her to Isaac. Gullet, Isaac, and Green went to St. John to finalize the transaction, and what freed Gullet from his stable debt bound Isaac to the first encumbrance of his homestead. He described the transaction in his journal: "I took loan at $350 at 10 percent and straight on my homestead for 5 years, interest due every six months. Frank Gilmore doing my business."[15] He hated owing money, but he believed this necessary evil could be disposed of early with increased production from his land. That prediction proved overly optimistic.

While in St. John to purchase the mare, Isaac observed the impact the new Atchison, Topeka & Santa Fe Railroad was having on the town.[16] He described in his journal what he had seen on April 19:

> A grading outfit of some half-dozen wagons, [with] some 12 spans of horses & several 2-wheel scrapers, all loaded on road towards Larned or beyond to do R. R. grading, all completely equipped with men, necessary shelter, and tools. Grading was completed past St. John, headed toward Macksville and Casody, nearly a hundred new buildings put up there this spring in anticipation of new R. R. Everyone wild. St. John booming with new business firms one after the other, now some half-a-dozen groceries, some 5 dry goods stores, 3 drug stores, some 4 feed stables, . . . 1 harness [shop], 2 good hardwares [stores], ½ doz eating houses, etc. pretty well most kinds of businesses represented.[17]

It was a puzzle to Isaac how the town of St. John could support all of them.[18] Even outside of town a similar rush to expand could be seen, new rural buildings and fencing of pastures visible everywhere—most likely, he guessed, built with mortgaged money apt to take the borrowers under. Macksville and Casody,[19] dual communities built on opposite sides of the approaching railroad tracks, were also expanding at a fever pitch, both communities racing forward to be the one that prospered and survived.[20]

Uncharacteristically, Isaac had bought the mare he named Dolly Varden without trying her. He hitched her to a wagon, gradually seeing what she could do, and she did fine. The next day he hitched her to a small plow, and the mare worked well. By the third day he had her plowing the tree row, assured that he had a gentle mare that would do just what he needed.[21]

Despite his initial reaction to the female homesteader settling next to his timber claim, Isaac had come to respect Isabelle Ross's courage in claiming a homestead on her own, especially after learning what had brought her to that decision. About three years before homesteading, Ross had been a married woman with four young children.[22] Because of her husband's ill treatment of her and the children, she had taken the drastic step of filing for divorce.[23] There were allegations and counter allegations, she claiming that he beat and cursed her and the children, and he claiming that she was a neglectful mother. The proceedings dragged on for nearly a year before a divorce was granted. What was known about the divorce came from gossip and the legal proceedings, including allegations that her husband had forced their children to drink a concoction he called a "blood purifier" but which consisted largely of whiskey. She had intervened when the mixture made her children sick, and her husband had kicked her and severely twisted her arm, all of which was described in the court records.

Isaac felt sorry for women like Mrs. Ross, many of whom found no means of escape. He admired her for having the courage to risk social condemnation and financial hardship to remove herself and her children from their situation, and fortunately she lived in Kansas, where women had an equal right to men in claiming custody of their children.[24] She was also fortunate that Isaac often did chores she could not do for herself. In exchange, she, and sometimes her children, helped him with tasks that could be done by hand in his potato operation. If his help sometimes exceeded what she did in return, he did not begrudge her that.

With or without help, handpicking bugs off his potato plants often proved inadequate, and Isaac felt the need to resort to Paris Green to poison the bugs. The emerald-green powder was a highly toxic combination of copper II acetate and arsenic trioxide that had been used to kill rats in the sewers of Paris, France. That use, combined with the powder's color, resulted in the commonly used name of Paris Green, and it was a popular poison for sprinkling on the potato leaves to kill potato bugs. Farmers knew that it was a poison, but the risks from exposure may not always have been sufficiently appreciated. The farmers as well as the French artists mixing Paris Green for the pigment to create the brilliant greens of Impressionist painters did not always take adequate care in handling it.[25] When Isaac's supply of the sand-textured powder ran low, he went in search of more.

There was no Paris Green in Iuka, so he traveled the short distance to Pratt Center, the newest of the three towns vying for the county seat. Pratt Center owed its existence to investors who had apparently exaggerated the number of residents, for it gained the nickname of "Dog Town."[26] Although the town had grown considerably since then, the joke about those investors counting the prairie dogs to reach the number of residents they claimed hung on. Finding no Paris Green there, Isaac headed east two miles to Saratoga, an industrious prairie town located on the Ninnescah River, beside which Cooper's Mill and the Ninnescah Milling Company were built. The town was laid out around a square, and with the Clarkson brick kiln to supply bricks, there were several brick structures in Saratoga, specifically a two-story schoolhouse, a livery stable, a hotel, a city hall opera house, and some private homes. In addition, among the wooden buildings were grocery and general stores, restaurants, butcher shops, two bookstores, a dressmaker, milliner, as well as a jeweler, pool halls, barber shops, and a soda fountain in one of the drugstores.[27] There were many things to distract Isaac during his trip to Saratoga, but no Paris Green. Disappointed, Isaac headed home and tried to stretch his small supply, mixing a teaspoon per gallon of water. He splashed it on the vines with a wisp, a sloppy business and not very efficient, since the diluted solution proved too weak to kill the bugs.

As a former druggist, Isaac must have known the dangers of handling poisons carelessly, but he admitted in his journal that he had "extemporized best I could under circumstances towards my own exterminating commenced splashing potatoes with Paris green solution, teaspoonful to gallon but seems slow to kill them. . . . Needing my Solution stronger than a teaspoonful to large (2 gal) pail, nearly a teaspoonful to gallon seeming nearer proper dose for effective soak, after some practice one can get along quite rapidly[.]"[28]

Tending his potatoes, Isaac watched railroad surveyors mark a preliminary line across his property, anticipating rail service from Stafford to Greensburg. The surveyors' line only cut across a small wedge of the southeast corner of Isaac's timber claim; however, the proposed tracks[29] would slash diagonally through the center of his homestead, posing an inconvenience to farming and the risk of fires started by trains. Isaac supported getting rail service to their community, but he hated to see his property molested.[30]

Only recently having acquired a horse, he had not yet acquired all the necessary equipment, and occasionally he borrowed neighbors' machinery. Their neglectful care nearly always meant he needed to make some repairs. The same neglect and abuse could be said about their treatment of animals: "Many of the worked down horses about giving out & pink-eye prevailing about country, many dying," he wrote on June 26.[31] Neglect and overwork caused deaths sooner than was necessary, and it made no sense to Isaac to sacrifice an essential animal, paid for so dearly, through careless treatment.

Early Saturday morning on July 3, Isaac heard anvil shooting at Macksville, the loud ringing sound the traditional means for calling out "Celebration." The ringing was capable of being heard at Isaac's home, a distance of fourteen miles. The local blacksmith was usually the one called upon to shoot the anvil. Shooting required two anvils, each weighing one hundred pounds or more, with about half a pound of black powder secured to the base of each. With one anvil base facing upward, a fuse then laid on the powder and a second anvil placed on top, base to base, the fuse was ready to be lit to ignite the black powder. The eardrum-aching explosion would send the top anvil soaring 150 feet or more into the sky, ringing as if pounded by some heavenly smithy.[32] Not only was the birth of the nation

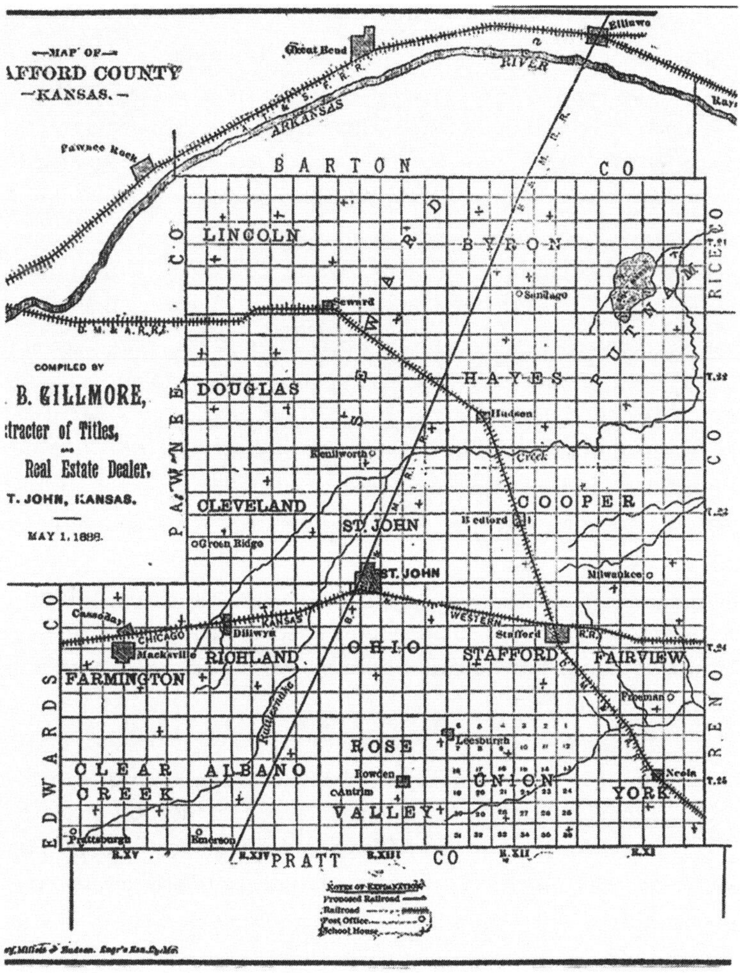

Stafford County Map of 1888 showing the proposed rail line crossing both of Isaac Werner's claims, the homestead in the southwest corner of the section abutting the Stafford-Pratt County line and the timber claim directly above in the northwest corner of the section. *County Capital*, June 8, 1888.

being celebrated on the fourth but the first excursion train was to run from Macksville to Hutchinson through St. John, whose depot was complete, as were the switches, the well, and the water tank, with fireworks to celebrate on both the fourth and the fifth.

At the end of the week Isaac made his first shopping trip to Macksville, still in search of Paris Green. None was to be found there either; however, he was impressed with what a trading metropolis Macksville was becoming, even attracting a few "spreeing" track hands. Isaac returned home and ordered some Paris Green from Dix's store, something he might have done in the first place to save all his wasted trips to surrounding towns.

Having encountered his neighbor Jesse Green at the post office, Isaac learned during their walk back to their adjacent claims that the family was moving. Maggie Green's widowed mother had died, making her home in Pratt Center available, so the Greens had decided to move into town with their five children. The two men had shared work, but more than that, Isaac had also felt a closeness to Maggie and the children. He dreaded their move.

Another neighbor asked Isaac to serve as a witness for making the final proof on his claim. Now having a horse to feed, Isaac was busy raking wild hay, so his neighbor helped finish that job to allow Isaac time to attend the hearing in St. John. Isaac wondered if he would lose another neighbor, since so many discouraged farmers were selling their claims and moving elsewhere once they received the titles.

Having gone into debt to buy Dolly, Isaac was trying to think positively about his farm with a horse to open more land and assist with things he had been doing by hand. Yet, he could not help but worry as his September 20 journal entry revealed:

> Under somewhat discouraging financial prospects, $13.00 in pocket and $17.00 interest to start off . . . doubtful about chance to borrow some in town without something to Mortgage. Gillman accommodating me with $7.00, what I needed, [and] refusing my note or interest. Bought New York draft in 1st National Bank for $17.65 in favor of Warren & Harrison, Emporia, Kansas, mailed same. All goods I wanted offered at each store what ever I wanted, money or no money . . . discovering I had better credit that I expected or asked.[33]

For a man who had shunned debt for so long, his pride about merchants' willingness to extend him credit seemed an ominous reversal.

While in town, Isaac bought a new wagon and loaded it with lumber for the hen house he was planning, all paid for on credit. Missing chickens had made Isaac feel more urgently the need of a hen house. For several months he had heard no coyotes howling at night and had concluded most of them had left the area. The missing chickens changed his mind.

Raising chickens was proving more challenging than anticipated. Chicks with only fuzz for insulation easily froze, and while warming in the oven

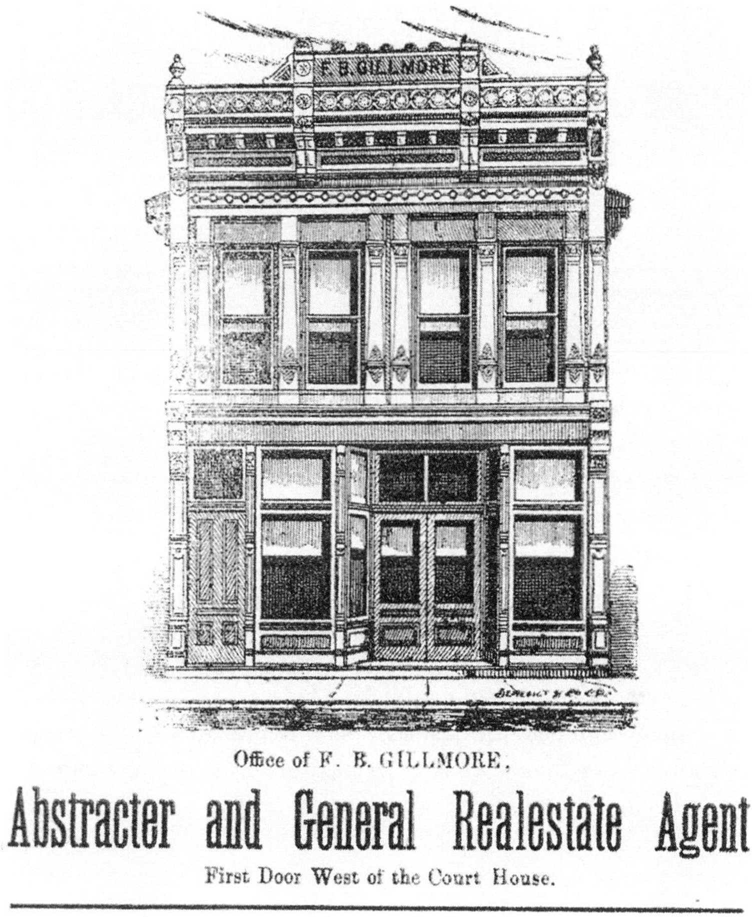

The office of F. B. (Frank) Gillmore, from whom Isaac Werner borrowed the money to buy his horse Dolly and farm implements, a loan that created Isaac Werner's first significant indebtedness. *St. John Weekly News*, October 11, 1895.

might revive some, it was clear that they needed better shelter. On the side of his shed he built a ten-foot-by-ten-foot hennery to protect against the skunks and coyotes slinking around. However, despite his work, one night a skunk got into the new hennery. Isaac killed it with a hammer, but not before it had killed his pet out of the whole flock. He made his hennery more skunk-proof and constructed an elevated roost for the chickens.

Not only was the October chill bad for chicks, Isaac realized that kittens were nearly as susceptible, unless he provided a warm place, and they had an attentive mother. Everyone knew that Isaac was partial to cats. His choosiness about who got his kittens when he had a new litter had become a neighborhood joke, most farmers regarding cats as little more than disposable mouse catchers, easily replaced by the next litter of kittens. Isaac expected the kittens he gave away to receive at least some sort of shelter, and he didn't care if people found that sentimental.

On October 24 Dolly foaled her first colt, which Isaac named Jimmy. He attended them until he was sure his mare could manage. Jimmy's birth represented a positive step forward for Isaac, a future with two horses of his own to work his fields.

Neighbors did little celebrating on Thanksgiving, everyone too busy getting ready for winter. Feeling somewhat caught up with work, Isaac used Thanksgiving evening to write a letter to E. M. Shelton, Professor of Agriculture and farm superintendent at Kansas State Agricultural College in Manhattan, Kansas, asking about separation between differing varieties of potatoes to avoid crossbreeding.

As 1886 drew to a close, Isaac and Doc were discussing the difficulty of making a decent living on the farm. Doc admitted he was thinking of moving into town where his daughter Mable could attend a full school year and he could gain the advantage of establishing his medical practice before other doctors came to compete for business. Now two of Isaac's best friends, the Green and the Dix families, were anticipating leaving the community to move into Pratt City.

CHAPTER 4

1887

Winter, when a farmer is less pressed by work, gave Isaac Werner time for reflection. Almost a year had passed since neighbors had discussed getting a railroad, and he had watched surveyors measuring for a spur line across his property. Why shouldn't the community consider organizing a town? Sometimes towns sprang up near a river or around the local post office or a small store, but railroad towns were developing without any natural features to explain why one community prospered and another did not. Isaac decided to propose organizing a town at the next Clear Creek Literary meeting.

Literary societies could be found in most communities.[1] Some met to discuss books, art, music, or even to perform plays. Others were concerned with specific causes, like Prohibition, whereas some programs shared personal reminiscences or ideas. Refreshments and friendship were enough for other groups.[2]

In the case of Isaac's local Clear Creek Literary, there was an "editor" who determined the subject of the meeting, which was not necessarily of a literary nature, as Isaac's purpose for attending made obvious. He proposed a small country slaughter and packing house as the nucleus for a town, recording on January 7, "I out on foot seeing neighbors about the neighborhood slaughter & packing house, etc. in fact try to start the nucleus of a little country town in accordance with our surrounds now of other distant

R. R. towns, evident we should help ourselves. Ordered meeting to discuss same in school house eve Jan. 10th."[3] Interest in promoting a town was so strong that a series of meetings were held, with the corners adjacent to the school proposed as potential town sites. A blacksmith who lived near Livingston claimed to have already bought the lumber to build his house as soon its site was certain. Everyone liked the idea of a local blacksmith, unlike the slaughterhouse suggestion, which had not received much support. Ultimately, fifteen people signed their intent to take stock in the town company.[4]

Along with investigating a town company, the idea of partitioning Clear Creek Township began to circulate. The current township was seventy-two square miles, and as more people populated the township, a division creating two separate townships of thirty-six square miles each gained momentum. The locations of the existing post offices and schools would leave each township with both facilities if the township were split, the Prattsburg Post Office and School #70 to the west and Emerson Post Office and School #33 to the east. With two six-by-six mile townships, elected officials would know all of the residents they represented, and labor to satisfy the annual township road tax would be performed on roads and bridges actually used by the men doing the work. It seemed like a logical decision; however, interest in the division seemed to have more support in the east half than in the west. Isaac wrote in his diary, "A rising vote taken to divide present Clear Creek township, 24 for and 9 against, part of those 9 from W. part," adding another journal entry a few days later: "Evening 'Refutation Meeting' in school house attended by about 45 as to diverse rumors."[5]

Isaac made time to participate in these and other community matters, but his priority was the success of his farm. At last his tree farm was producing young trees large enough to market, and on his trip to Larned to deliver orders, Isaac also peddled seed potatoes in the Prattsburg community in Edwards County. Most homesteads there looked impoverished, and he found few buyers to the west. Another day, he took three wagonloads of rain-freshened prairie hay to Pratt Center where payments for hay were higher because of workers on the Rock Island Railroad coming through the town. He was impressed by the many new buildings going up along Main Street, with foundations being dug for several brick businesses.

Although business took him to the nearby towns, he did not like to be away from his farm too often. Prairie fires remained a threat for the community, and Isaac spent much of his time plowing fireguards. In the midst of dust blizzard conditions one day, Isaac noticed a fire four miles to the west.

He had learned the importance of taking precautions when fire threatened, and he pulled his wagon out of the shed and moved Dolly and Jimmy onto the green rye patch. The shifting wind conditions caused him enough concern that he "went into house, commenced packing up things to carry out doors in a hurry and did carry some out prepatory for a 'burn out' as much as I could. Finally the Western folks got the fire out."[6] Evening temperatures brought a light snow blizzard, and although there were fires to the south, nothing burned locally. It was frightening to imagine fighting a fire in such blizzard winds.

As seasons changed, Isaac kept even busier now that he had a horse, but that had meant incurring more debts for needed equipment. He wondered if worry might be the explanation for unexplainable bouts of poor health such as he had never known. How optimistic he had been just a year ago when he had first gone into debt to buy Dolly, thinking he was borrowing enough extra to get the implements he would need. How confident he had been that with a horse he could become more productive on his farm and quickly pay off the mortgage. Instead he had signed one note after another with ever higher interest rates, and he could see no likelihood of paying all of them off any time soon. Many of his neighbors were facing the same economic realities, and there were days when he felt defeated by things beyond his control. The last thing he needed was worry about his health.

When a toothache returned to swell his cheek, Isaac took to his bed, using the time to write a letter to *Kansas Farmer* in Topeka, edited by William A. Peffer. Peffer had been a teacher, a soldier for the Union, and a lawyer before beginning his career as a newspaperman, learning his craft at several small town newspapers before becoming the editor of the *Kansas Farmer* in 1881.[7]

Isaac believed in the importance of sharing ideas to improve agriculture in the region, and he often wrote to farming publications. Even when money was tight, he continued his subscriptions and read the articles faithfully. He also corresponded regularly with Professor E. M. Shelton at Kansas State College, writing that morning for advice to improve the quality of Kansas-grown potatoes. The professor's reply a few days later, that watery potatoes were the result of premature ripening caused by heat and drought, offered no advice for remedying the problem.

Isaac had begun traveling further from his farm in search of better potato markets, and on one trip he sold most of his potatoes to a railroad bridge camp. He decided to venture as far as Sun City further to the south, where the soil was less suited for growing potatoes. Seeing the more rugged terrain on his journey tweaked Isaac's always curious mind, as he imaged the geological past of the region, later recording his thoughts: "Curious country around here. Once a flat country but gullies started & washed by ages & frost crumpling projecting rock flatten bluff sides down to gentle sloping & now green grass covered."[8] Even more satisfying than his geological musing was selling his potatoes for $1 to $1.25 a bushel and his corn for fifty cents. Isaac had borrowed a mule to help Dolly pull the load, and the long, arduous trip made him feel an even greater need for a second horse of his own.

A few days later, by chance he arrived in Iuka during a horse sale, and by evening he had negotiated the purchase of a grey mare with a roan colt for $125, with the note given to the seller due December 31 at 12 percent interest. Not only was a mortgage on the two horses retained by the seller, but Isaac had also used his homestead again as security. The good news was that Dolly and the new gray mare he named Jule worked well together, after getting used to each other. Except for the debts, Isaac felt he was making advancements toward a successful farm.

In contrast, several families in the west part of the Prattsburg community were considering giving up their claims. The *Casody Mirage* wrote, "Prattsburg: The Oregon fever has struck some of the citizens. . . . many others want to go to Oregon as soon as they can dispose of their sand piles here. . . . We want to see everybody stay and help to build up this country, which is far ahead of anything west of the Rockies."[9] Crops had been poorer around Prattsburg to the west, but it saddened Isaac to see homesteaders giving up on Kansas.

As some of Isaac's neighbors considered leaving Kansas, Elizabeth Bacon Custer was expounding on the beauty of the prairie in her book, *Tenting on the Plains, or General Custer in Kansas and Texas*, released in 1887. Elizabeth had been a military wife, not a homesteader, and she had not faced the same struggles confronting farm wives, but she described her 1867 arrival at Fort Hays with her husband, Gen. George Custer, as "a wild sense of freedom that takes possession of one in the first buoyant knowledge that no impediment, seemingly, lies between you and the setting sun. . . . Oh, the joy of taking in air without a taint of the city."[10]

Most of Isaac's closest neighbors were sticking on their claims, including the Goodwin brothers, Will and Felix, with whom he had often shared work. When he began mowing and raking hay with the Goodwins' younger brother and brother-in-law, he assumed the same working agreement would apply, and they did not discuss rates before beginning work. Upon completion of the work, there was no disagreement about the number of days worked nor the price of $1.50 a day for a man and a horse. However, when Isaac assumed the usual rate of $1 for a mowing machine and rake, the young men expected $1.50 and he acquiesced. Only the fee for Isaac's hay rack, wagon, and forks remained to settle, but they insisted that no fee was owed for those things. Lacking a prior agreement, Isaac conceded to their accounting, but voiced his irritation in his journal: "A good hay rack and wagon and forks, all in complete working order, no charges to whoever fool furnishes them! These seem the modern basis of settlement in such matters."[11]

Concerns about money never completely left his mind. With others in the community installing windmills, Isaac stopped work one afternoon to hear a windmill agent's sales pitch. The calculated cost of $240 for what Isaac needed convinced him that incurring more debt for such an expensive purchase was unrealistic, as appealing as it seemed.

Where his neighbors found the money for such improvements to their farms Isaac had no idea, but he certainly could not understand wasting money on gambling. Despite his admiration for fine horses, he didn't join in the neighborhood excitement when a challenge race was scheduled to be held on the north side of the schoolhouse, with the winner to take home $200. Jake Baker had been boasting that his horse Joe would win, but when the race was run, Jake suffered the loss of both his pride and his entry fee. Joe trailed the winner by fifty feet at the finish.

As winter approached, Isaac's potatoes were his only bank account, and he sorted and stored them like a banker counting his money and putting it into a vault. He took some of the money from his potato sales in Sun City to St. John to pay debts owed merchants, and he inquired at the bank about a second note. Apparently too many farmers were "double and triple bleeding" their farms as security, and he did not secure a loan.

In the November elections, there were seventy-four men voting in the first Albano election since the division of townships. Isaac was on the ballot for town clerk, but he lost by one vote. He claimed to be well satisfied with his defeat, having "enough at home to attend to let alone bother with petty offices." However, the sting at losing seemed apparent in that evening's journal entry.

The booming town of Pratt Center had also been handed a loss. Following a long history of legal and illegal maneuvering by contenders for the county seat, Iuka retained the title. Because the events were happening in Pratt County rather than Stafford County, Isaac knew only the outline of the complicated legal and political tricks.[12] Pratt County itself had been illegitimately established in 1873 by a small group of scammers submitting the requisite six hundred signatures to organize a county when there was hardly a handful of residents living there.[13] Fraudulent or not, Pratt County came into existence.[14] The precedent of chicanery continued in the race between Saratoga and Iuka for the county seat. The enumeration of misbehavior was long and complicated, but neither town could claim clean hands. When the governor had come in September of 1878 to help resolve the matter of Pratt County's legitimacy, and to determine whether a county seat was even necessary, a welcoming party from Iuka met his train at Great Bend with a delegation of citizens and a brass band. Somehow, the entertainments of the day in Iuka resulted in the governor never traveling the few miles to Saratoga; yet, he named Iuka the temporary county seat while the irregularities involved in the establishment of the county itself were sorted out.[15]

It was said that Iuka gained the advantage because it was more centrally located, which may or may not have been what truly swayed the governor. After the northern boundary of Pratt County was moved south six miles,[16] Iuka's geographic advantage was diminished, and although the county itself was recognized, the selection of a permanent county seat was delayed when petitions from both Iuka and Saratoga contained so many irregular signatures that both petitions were invalidated and no permanent county seat was chosen.[17]

Saratoga had become quite a prospering town, and Iuka had lost its claim of having the central location;[18] however, to complicate things, a third town had joined the race. With the legitimacy of Pratt County resolved, a group of businessmen from McPherson had decided to create a town, and they joined Iuka and Saratoga in the race. Their financial and legal skills were more sophisticated than the farmers contending for the county seat in Saratoga and Iuka, but their tricks were no less shady, despite perhaps a fancier veneer of legal maneuvers.[19] They seized the title of Pratt Center for their new town, based on the change in the county's northern boundary.

Farmers who had broken the sod for fields and built homes and barns before their land had been opened for settlement, intending to gain title when the land was eventually available, occupied the same land the investors had chosen for their town. A legal battle erupted, and although the Kansas attorney general sided with the farmers, they were eventually displaced, partly by their own lack of legal sophistication, and partly by the businessmen's dishonesty sheathed in legal formality.[20]

During the months and years the towns battled for the county seat, Isaac followed the news. Each delay left the county seat in Iuka, and Isaac wrote in his journal on November 11, 1887: "Pratt County seat decided in favor of Iuka again, and election matters on the simmering down order." He was definitely wrong about that.

Eventually, it was Pratt Center that was chosen as the county seat. Iuka accepted the decision more easily, many residents and businesses having gradually moved into Pratt, sometimes taking their structures with them. The fight between Pratt Center and Saratoga had been more bitter, and a few stalwarts believed their community could survive. Ultimately, the death of Saratoga was inevitable.

Five years earlier, Stafford County also had dueling towns seeking the county seat, the leading candidates being St. John and Stafford. Election Day April 5, 1882, was intended to determine the location, but it was Mother Nature who stole ballots when a tornado carried away the ballot box in Stafford. The polling place and many other buildings were damaged or destroyed, but despite several people being injured, no one was killed. The impossibility of determining the voting in Stafford resulted in a special election on April 14, and although St. John received more votes than any other town, it did not receive a majority. Four days later, after a third election, St. John was chosen as the county seat, and matters in Stafford County were resolved with very little rancor among communities.[21]

ON AN UNUSUALLY FINE autumn day, Isaac joined four neighbors in meeting their annual road tax labor by filling in approaches to the bridge across the creek near Webber's Mill. Isaac felt more satisfied doing work on roads and bridges he was likely to use in the new Albano Township, rather than when he had labored in the west part of Clear Creek Township where he rarely traveled, although he had freely put in his road tax obligation wherever needed before the township had divided.

It was his nearer neighbors with whom Isaac had formed closer bonds, including his adjacent neighbor Persis Vosburgh, whom he had come to know quite well. She was born in 1834 and had never married, and although she was only a few years older than many of her neighbors, they had picked up the habit of calling her Aunt Persis, as her brother's children did. She was about to leave for New York State to visit relatives. With her absence and two friends discussing moves to Pratt County, Isaac was feeling rather abandoned by his closest neighbors.

Perhaps his sense of loneliness was greater because he wasn't feeling well. His back had been aching for several days, and he wasn't sure of the cause. Something certainly seemed to be affecting his kidneys. Well enough to write some letters while he rested, he sent the *Kansas Farmer* a report about his tree royalty and included a description of a seed corn revolving screen separator he had designed; to his brother Henry he repeated his unanswered requests regarding financial matters; and to a woman named Ellen, whom he was now writing more regularly, a personal note.[22]

He spent Thanksgiving Day alone yet another year, noting in his journal: "Everybody busy with their work, little thanking for short crops and hard times." Isaac remained in a despondent mood as he spent the last day of November writing letters. He had gone to Emerson, hoping for a reply from Henry to both of his prior letters, but there was none, and he was forced to borrow five dollars short-term from Doc Dix. He wrote a third letter about family finances to his brother.

Receipt of the forty dollars he had been expecting from Henry came the day after horse dealer Sam Jones had visited to collect on the note Isaac had given for the gray mare Jule and her roan colt. He mailed Jones a postal order, paid debts and taxes in St. John, and used the rest of the money to settle a few small debts owed neighbors, one of which was at least a year old.

As usual, Isaac noted Christmas on his calendar but spent it alone, tending to odds and ends that couldn't be done once snow fell. On a miserably cold December 29 he and Charles Shattuc helped Doc Dix move to Saratoga. It had been a year since Doc first mentioned to Isaac moving into town,[23] but the decision had finally been made and Isaac was losing perhaps his best friend in the community. Doc would still make trips to his farm, but their regular chats would decrease. When they finally reached Doc's new home it was well after dark, but they carried their load inside before falling into exhausted, chilled sleep amidst the crates and barrels. The next morning, Isaac and Shattuc paused in nearby Pratt Center for some shopping and the chance to ride the new streetcars that had been running for a week. Traveling home, they were forced onto the rough sod to escape the slippery, thawing roads, and they finished their journey by moonlight, under "cigar-roll" clouds.

As 1887 came to a close, Isaac did some work indoors, but most of the day was spent sitting by the fire, reflecting on how he could continue to keep his creditors at bay long enough to save his struggling farm. His memories

Isaac Werner's friend and physician, I. H. "Doc" Dix. Courtesy of the Pratt County Historical Museum.

of the past year were nothing more than columns of numbers, most of them written in red ink. He knew of no parties in the neighborhood, people hunkering down in their homes to face the hardships of the year ahead.

CHAPTER 5

1888

Isaac Werner bent over his kitchen table in the winter half-light, two books in front of him. One was a thick, leather-bound journal the size of those found at the courthouse for recording land transfers. The other was a notebook small enough to carry in his pocket. His head moved back and forth between the two books as he made notations on a sheet of paper, turning pages of the two books slowly, sometimes flipping back and forth to reconcile entries between the two sets of records before writing something on the new document. Although it had seemed like a good idea to keep his financial records in his daily journal when he began, Isaac had never imagined when he made the early entries that he would borrow so much money or be forced to carry debts for so long. He had begun using the small notebook to carry with him when he went to town to conduct business so he could jot down payments as they were made. Now he needed to reconcile exactly how many outstanding debts he had and whether all his payments had been properly credited.

There were notes owed banks, credit accounts with merchants, informally documented loans from neighbors, notes given to businessmen, ongoing labor exchanges among neighbors, and the endless family transactions that sometimes made him so frustrated. It had become more than he could keep track of in his head, and he spent the day getting everything down in an organized way to start off the new year. Clearly needing cash to retire at least some of his indebtedness, Isaac decided it was time to sell the forty acres of timber he and his brother Henry owned in Le Sueur County, Minnesota, and he wrote Henry to urge the sale.[1]

The note he had given Frank Gillmore to buy Dolly was due, and he had come to town to discuss renewing the note yet again. Each purchase he considered while in town seemed almost unthinkable, but he needed buckets and ropes for his new well, and he was hopeful the fresh water might help him feel better. Hard work, worry, and weather were wearing him down, and a bilious spell had increased his concern about his health. Perhaps fresh water from the new well would be healing.

Many farmers were more entangled in debts than he was. A New York moneylender had come to Pratt Center, getting 6 percent per month on a note with a four-month term and two cosigners from a farmer so desperate for cash he agreed to pay interest of 72 percent per year.

As Isaac was working on the new well curb, the swelling of one of his fingers began to bother him too much to ignore, and by the next morning he could do almost nothing with that hand, his entire body aching. For the next three days he poulticed his finger,[2] but rather than improving, the swelling moved into his hand and the achiness worsened. The Green family had moved into Pratt, but Isaac had become well enough acquainted with his new neighbors, the Bentleys, to ask if he might sleep on their lounge or in a rocking chair until his health improved. They made him feel welcome, and he rested there, poulticing his finger two or three times daily until he was finally well enough to return home. He knew that he would never forget their kindness. Having lost over half the month of February nursing his sore hand, Isaac eventually returned to doing what work he could, his finger improving but requiring careful use.

When the battle for the Pratt County seat had finally been settled in favor of Pratt Center, many Iuka residents and merchants simply moved into Pratt, but Saratoga seemed determined to survive only two miles away, with their mill, many fine businesses, and the same railroad passing through both towns. Isaac wondered whether the election might cause Doc Dix to move his family and his medical practice from Saratoga into the new county seat.

Isaac had always appreciated the importance of sharing ideas with neighbors, but he had begun to believe that cooperation beyond individual communities was necessary if agriculture on the prairie were to succeed, and he wrote Congressman S. R. Peters and Professor E. M. Shelton at Kansas State College about his idea. In his journal he recorded the ideas he had shared:

> While eating my breakfast conceived the idea of some competent man to go through the country and inspect each ¼ section of land, its Surface Soil & its sub-soil, and classify them by number or letters, according to the predominating elements of soil. Then implements could be devised to work most satisfactory just those different soils, and that would afford a basis to work on and continue improving, thereby soon elevate the standard of agriculture and saving large sums of money from being expended in useless tools.[3]

He was convinced that this information would be helpful not only to farmers but also to implement manufacturers.

As another way to advance agricultural ideas beyond his local community, Isaac decided to promote what he termed the County Agricultural Society, through which the professionalism of farmers could be elevated by coming together to study, as well as sharing each of their own successful methods. He submitted a newspaper article to the new *County Capital* about organizing the society, and editor John Hilmes invited him to continue submitting articles to the paper.

When the day for the first County Agricultural Society meeting arrived on April 14, only three people appeared despite all of Isaac's promotion among farmers and town merchants. He was about to leave when more men began arriving, about as many businessmen as farmers. At least they made a start, and on the day of the final organizational meeting a few weeks later, about thirty men gathered in the courtroom to elect officers and draft bylaws and other rules.[4] It was a good group leading the organization, although Isaac felt more farmers should have been interested enough in the goals of the group to have attended.

Although Isaac chose to voice his public comments to farmers in a positive way, his personal opinions about the inferior methods employed by some farmers were revealed in his private journal: "I for my part getting disgusted to look on such faded styles of farming for this droughty country, if no better methods be resorted to, bankruptcy will continue to stare into the face of every one trying to continue such farming."[5] Rather than publicly ridiculing those farmers, however, he hoped the County Agricultural Society might be able to help them improve their farming.

The newly elected County Agricultural Society president, Joseph A. Cooper, lived in Cleveland Township in the western part of the county and was one of its most respected men. He had served during the Mexican-American War in the 4th Tennessee infantry, afterward becoming a planter in Tennessee. With the outbreak of the Civil War, he had joined the Union Army as a captain with the Tennessee infantry, advancing in rank to leave the service as a brevetted major general. In 1879 he came to Kansas to farm. He was at least two decades older than most of his neighbors, adding the weight of his years to the high regard in which he was held. He had married his wife Mary Jane when he was fifty-two and she was twenty-two, so he was raising a family late in life. Cooper's leadership was a good beginning for their group.

WITH SPRING'S ARRIVAL Isaac turned his attention to the familiar work of his farm with renewed energy, buoyed by his enthusiasm for having brought farmers throughout the county together to share ideas. Ten years after his arrival in Kansas, Isaac now had enough cottonwood trees that he could use some of them as posts for light fencing. With groves of his own trees to sell, and trees he could use on his farm, Isaac deemed his tree farming operation a success.

Despite his debts and disappointments, Isaac was doing better than many farmers.[6] One sad case close to home involved Fred Weeks, who illegally disposed of mortgaged property. After his arrest he convinced the local constable, David Carnahan, to release him to raise money for his bond. Instead of appearing for trial as promised, Weeks absconded, with law officers in pursuit, and in ten days he was returned for trial. Somehow the Bentley family was also responsible for his debts, and except for property left in their hands by Weeks's creditors, they were divested of nearly everything except their land. Isaac worried for his friends, and his concerns proved justified. Although Mrs. Bentley had hoped to stay on her place, despite the ruinous obligations relating to Weeks's debts, the Bentleys decided to rent to a man named Hacker and make a new start in Las Animas, Colorado. Isaac hated seeing them go.

Adding to his sadness was learning that Persis Vosburgh had died in Moravia, New York, while visiting family. Less serious, but still continuing bad luck in the community, a prairie fire burned Lou Clouse's plum patch and "hog-back,"[7] the only good luck being that it spared his buildings. The fire had spread further into the next day, reaching the corner of Carnahan's place before it was stopped.

With neighbors moving, suffering loses to their claims, and in one case, dying, Isaac tried not to be discouraged. Although his new year's bookkeeping had made it clear that it was questionable to incur further debt, Isaac continued adding equipment for his farm. He had hoped to buy a one-horse Rockford drill; however, after learning that the factory was sold out, he settled on a Keystone drill. Still unsure about his decision, he decided to conduct a test measuring the performance of his Keystone against a Rockford, and he borrowed Charles Waters's drill for the test. Not everyone took care of their equipment as well as he did, and Isaac was annoyed to find that the Rockford drill he had borrowed needed an overhaul before it could be used. Once he got the Rockford in proper working order, he determined that his Keystone performed comparably well. Isaac returned the borrowed drill the following day, taking it back in better condition than when he had borrowed it.

Plowing around his young trees to keep thirsty weeds from stealing all the moisture was an ongoing job, and as he worked on May 9, Isaac noticed clouds gathering to the south. For the first time he saw a twister, which he described in his journal as "a tapering white sock hanging down, slanting from clouds, and in a mere streak connecting down to ground, raising the dust at times, then rising and vanishing, and moving on down again and renewing the dark dust funnel."[8] He watched in fascination, the twister never seeming to head in his direction. In the following days he found himself looking to the sky more often, watching for twisters in every cloud that resembled those that had harbored the tornado.

THE *COUNTY CAPITAL* NEWSPAPER continued to publish articles about the agricultural society Isaac had organized, and when the group met to adopt the charter and bylaws and to elect directors, they gave a vote of thanks to owner-editor Hilmes. The progressive role Hilmes played in Stafford County was repeated across the nation, although he may have been in the forefront of the growing number of Populist journals and newspapers.[9] Whereas Hilmes never faced violence, other newspapermen did, in the form of fires that destroyed their shops, break-ins that damaged their presses, threats and attacks, and in the case of one Texas editor, murder. Despite such dangers, the Populist press played an invaluable role in the movement. The Progressive articles authored by Isaac and published by Hilmes described the benefits of "a united effort on the part of the farmers."[10] In one particular article Isaac urged: "Many of you farmers think and no doubt for good cause that you are taken advantage of by . . . men generally who engineer the corners on your productions, say and virtually dictate how much you shall take for your toil and labor. In an institution like the agricultural society, you can council together, defend your own interests and assert your own independence."[11] In short, Isaac was at the forefront of cooperative efforts in his county. He found himself in a more reflective mood as he labored on his farm, settling into a familiar pattern of seasonal work, similar crops, and soils he knew increasingly well. He battled the same weeds and pests by inventing new ways to combat each challenge, made improvements to his property, and broke more sod each year, beginning to accept that the hardships were unlikely to ever be entirely overcome. On May 23, 1888, he wrote in his journal: "My 44th birthday. General feelings this spring along tells me I must be getting about that age. Feel more like taking things moderate, let them come as they will."[12] His thoughts of marriage and a family occurred less often, like something seen in his future for so long that it had passed by unnoticed, an opportunity lost. He could find no explanation for the bilious spells, the more frequent achiness, headaches, and back pain that was situated deep within rather than caused by strained muscles or spine. He attributed everything to aging. Yet, his years as a druggist could not help but make him occasionally wonder whether there might be some other cause. Successes and disappointments created a familiar rhythm to his days, the staccato of good moments and the underlying rumble of the bad.

THE ROBBERY OF the Pratt County National Bank made Isaac wonder if hard times had driven a desperate man to criminality. The bank cashier had turned the day lock on the safe to quickly go across the street for the mail, and in his brief absence the bank was robbed. The bank president had his office in a conjoined building, and it was suspected that someone waiting to see him had watched the cashier leave for the mail and, with no one present in the bank, had used the opportunity to enter unnoticed, open the safe, and remove $4,016.[13]

Ironically, considering the hard times, the special June 8 issue of the *County Capital* declared that Kansas held great economic promise for everyone—farmers, businessmen, and investors—describing the land's superior quality and the potential of coal and "other subterranean resources" awaiting discovery. Oversized advertisements from St. John's leading real estate dealers filled the pages, seeming to explain why Hilmes's newspaper would publish such extravagant claims.

Isaac turned to the back page to see if any local news was included and was pleased to read an open letter signed by nine citizens of Prattsburg, including two women, who wished to join the County Agricultural Society. There was also a notice that "I. H. Dix has moved to Pratt to resume the practice of medicine," having made his decision to abandon Saratoga and build his medical practice in the new county seat. However, the primary subject of the local article on the back page was Isaac himself. The article claimed that his several varieties of potatoes planted from those he had saved from the previous season were "admired by everyone that sees them," continuing, "Some of the old settlers think that I. B. Werner's half section should be called 'Forest Farm' as the 18 acres of trees scattered over it, only four and eight years old, give it that appearance with such charming surroundings." The local reporter had not resisted teasing Isaac a little, concluding, "We think the rooster of the sand hills ought to take some fair damsel under his wings."[14]

Apparently, his neighbors had not given up on Isaac finding a wife, but he seemed to have accepted that he would have no children of his own, and only his brother's son, Charles, would carry on the family name. It was a great disappointment to Isaac that his invitations to his nephew the past several summers had been ignored each year. Initially, he had extended the invitations as much as an opportunity to get acquainted with his nephew as to have his help, but as he opened more acres for crops and his health declined, he truly needed a summer worker. When Charles ignored his invitation yet again, Isaac decided to employ the son of his old friend, A. B. Greene in Danville, Illinois. Having young John Green to help with weeding and harvesting at the right time might result in producing better crops to compensate for hiring a full-time worker. When Isaac found Greene's letter at the post office, alerting him that his son John was arriving that very day, it was too late to travel to St. John to meet the train. Returning home, he met the young man walking up his sand hill. Finding no one waiting for him at the depot when he arrived, he had caught a ride with one of Isaac's neighbors part of the way from St. John, with directions to walk the rest of the way to Isaac's farm.

The luxury of having a full-time extra hand was everything Isaac had hoped. Often, he and John worked side by side to make short work of things that would have taken Isaac all day, and it freed Isaac to help his neighbors or to accomplish different tasks that needed to be done at the same time. Although having help did not avoid problems that Isaac had faced during previous years, it did allow him to attack them sooner. Chinch bugs still infested some of Isaac's corn, drought still burned his crops, but his fields were less weedy, which helped crops get the moisture instead of sandburs and sunflowers stealing it first. The two men were getting little sleep at night, not only from the heat but also from bedbugs biting them, so John cleaned everything and oiled the bedstead to try to be rid of the bugs for a while. As they worked, they often saw covered wagons heading east with settlers who had finally given up.

During the summer, Union Labor Party (ULP) speeches were being made at surrounding schoolhouses and, without John Greene, Isaac could not have taken the time to attend as he did. Isaac was among the thirty-five men who gathered at Emerson School to organize a ULP club. Women were also joining the growing ULP clubs in the area, but very few Republicans were to be found at meetings.

Local newspapers that had generally supported the boom economy when things were flourishing had changed their perspective that summer, now reporting that farmers had been duped by what one Kinsley newspaper editor called "the silk-tie crowd."[15] With poverty stalking the country, the ULP movement was attracting farmers who believed banding together gave them the power to confront this "silk-tie crowd" of bankers, monopolists, and politicians.

Even nature seemed to defy farmers. The drought had made everything dangerously dry, and the very night that Isaac and John had carried the last of that year's potato crop into the cellar, King & McKibben Livery Barn in Belpre had burned to the ground. The origin of the fire was unknown, and reports were that there was no insurance on the building or its contents. Several horses and a mule team belonging to Henry Laird, as well as harnesses and buggies, were lost in the fire.[16] The loss seemed particularly cruel to Laird, whose cattle ranch had been practically burned out the previous April when the Chicago, Kansas & Western Railroad had started a prairie fire. The Laird Cattle Ranch was the largest in that county, and the fire had taken the house, barn, cornfields, and livestock, with an estimated loss of $4,000 and only $1,000 covered by insurance. The agent for the railroad had arrived quickly to settle the damages, but cash rarely compensates completely for such losses.[17] The Laird family certainly did not deserve a second calamity in August.

There was some good news, however, for the *County Capital* proudly printed news of the receipt of the County Agricultural Society's charter, certifying that "this corporation is formed to encourage general agriculture, horticulture, floriculture, forestry, and the display of farm products fine and fast stock."[18]

Whereas the *County Capital* reported Populist news, the *St. John News* reflected the Republican perspective and mocked the ULP, writing that "two Union laborites have stopped taking the News and now depend upon borrowing it." The August 23 *St. John News* made a specific attack on Macksville resident, John Askew, claiming that he "openly declares . . . that the anarchists executed in Chicago a year ago were martyrs of a holy cause.[19] No one but an ignorant blatherskite will make such an assertion, yet Mr. Askew claims to be one of the high muck-a-mucks of the Union Labor party."

The Chicago case to which the *St. John News* made reference was the famous Haymarket Square case of May 4, 1886. About a thousand laboring class men had gathered not only to urge their demands as workers but also to protest police brutality. While the mayor was present, the meeting had remained orderly, but when he left, a detachment of police, led by Capt. John Bonfield, rushed to Haymarket Square to disburse any demonstrators who remained. Because the very demonstration evidenced the animosity between the laborers and the police, a combustible situation was not surprising. Someone threw a bomb, and both policemen and civilians were killed and wounded as a result, followed by deaths and injuries from the resulting gunfire. The investigation never determined who had thrown the bomb, but several defendants were found guilty and hanged, while others remained imprisoned. It was apparently these men that John Askew had spoken up for in some way. Men who were never shown to have thrown the bomb or to have engaged in a murder conspiracy had been executed. It was an angry time in America, with other clashes involving working-class laborers, and the Haymarket Square case had become symbolic of that greater class conflict.

The mocking of Askew and the defendants in the Haymarket Square case by the *St. John News*, as opposed to the articles published by Hilmes about ULP meetings and farmers coming together in the County Agricultural Society, clearly differentiated the social and political sympathies of the two local newspapers. It was Hilmes's *County Capital* to which Isaac subscribed. He was not only a contributor to the *County Capital,* but occasionally and surprisingly he was the subject of an article, such as "Champion Potato Raiser," which described Isaac's potatoes as "the nicest home grown potatoes we have ever seen this year."[20] Unfortunately, Isaac's corn was so burned by the heat, and the leaves so tattered by winds, with only a few ears on the stalks, that he salvaged what he could by cutting it up for fodder.[21]

Local enthusiasm toward the ULP seemed to grow with each meeting, and a challenge discussion at the Albano Schoolhouse brought an overflow crowd of about 150 men and women. Latecomers were forced to listen from the outside through the open windows. When the ULP convention was held in St. John a few days later, a straight Union ticket was nominated, without merging efforts with the Democrats. William Campbell was nominated for state representative, and his maiden political speech given at the Albano Schoolhouse two nights later was well received. However, Isaac sensed resentment in their community, feeling that the "mossbacks" of both old parties disliked the political challenge of a new party. Just as the term "mossbacks" came from the idea of a creature so old and slow that moss had grown on its back, old-fashioned politicians and voters seemed to Isaac to show the same sluggish unwillingness to accept new political ideas.

Isaac welcomed new ideas, since the current situation for farmers was not working. However, he wanted to learn more about the ULP to understand how an organization that seemed to be more associated with factory workers could represent the concerns of farmers. Campbell's farm was in the southwest corner of the section just northeast of Isaac's timber claim. If Isaac cut across Isabel Ross's homestead, the distance was even shorter and took only a few minutes. He decided to walk to Campbell's house one evening to discuss how the ULP could help farmers.

Campbell's opinion was that the combined efforts of all laborers, whether factory workers, miners, railroad employees or farmers, could wield more political power together than any group could by acting alone. Isaac questioned whether laborers and farmers had enough in common to unite politically, but he liked the words on The Knights of Labor's seal: "That is the most perfect Government in which an injury to one is the concern of all." Campbell believed that the ULP offered a political organization that could nominate electable candidates who would work from within the government. Too often farmers had voted for Republican or Democratic candidates who failed to keep their promises once they were elected. The formation of the ULP was intended to correct the political imbalance of the wealthy and powerful by bringing all laborers together in one political party.

At last, the months of having John Greene's help came to an end, and when they went together to St. John, they arrived early enough to attend the Democrats' rally at the rink among a crowd of about seven hundred, at least a third of whom were women, listening to what Isaac described as "Millionaires and Monopolists getting the butt end" of the speakers' criticism. Isaac slipped away to borrow fifteen dollars from the 1st National Bank to make a partial payment of $20.05 to John for his nearly four months' work. Watching the young man board the five o'clock train for Illinois, Isaac did not regret the expense of having help for the summer.

A few days later, Isaac was back in St. John, having been asked by Ben Webber to serve as a witness to prove up Ben's claim. Judge Dixon heard the testimony, and afterward Isaac and Ben lingered in town to listen to political talk. Isaac thought the general "mud scooping" being done by those who considered themselves respectable citizens was a disgrace.

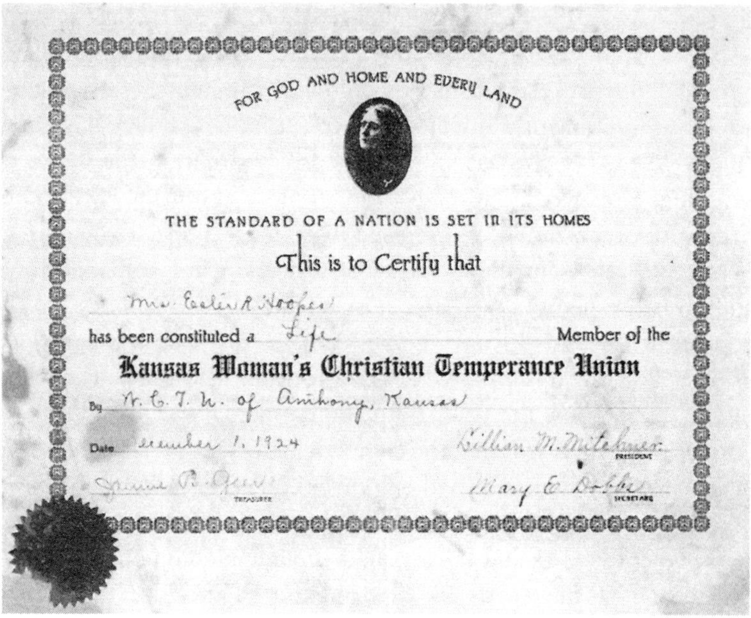

FOR GOD AND HOME AND EVERY LAND

THE STANDARD OF A NATION IS SET IN ITS HOMES

This is to Certify that

has been constituted a Life Member of the

Kansas Woman's Christian Temperance Union

By W. C. T. U. of Anthony, Kansas

Date 1924

PRESIDENT

TREASURER

SECRETARY

Women's Christian Temperance Union membership certificate. Collection of Helen Carr Wewers.

Some of this slandering made front-page news in the *County Capital*, and Isaac realized he had not heard the worst of it. A political feud between neighbors Campbell and Carnahan had divided the community. As the ULP candidate for state representative, Campbell had been accused by Carnahan, a Republican, of immoral character. In rebuttal, Hilmes reminded readers of Campbell's military service for the Union, adding that even today he "endures the pains sustained from the bullets of the enemy."[22] Several personal testimonials in praise of Campbell were also published, with some affidavits pulling no punches in specifically identifying the source of the slanders as Carnahan. Despite the efforts to refute the slanders and to expose Carnahan's motives, it was unlikely that most Republican voters would read the *County Capital*, as they generally got their information from the *St. John News*. There was genuine concern whether the political wounds within the community would heal after the election.

Prohibition speeches were part of the political season, and one evening Isaac went with several neighbors to Davison School to hear Blanche B. Hazelett deliver a Prohibition speech. Isaac thought the young woman did "a first class job," even using magic lantern views to illustrate her words.

The schoolhouse was crowded, and several Prohibitionists delivered short talks, but Isaac felt that Hazelett, whom he guessed to be about twenty-three, was the most sensible speaker of the lot.

According to the newspaper, Hazelett was running for county school superintendent on the Democratic ticket. Reading her published credentials, Isaac was impressed. She had been educated in Chautauqua County, New York, and had taught one year there before coming to Kansas to teach a year in Osage County. To her credit, she had returned home to New York to assist her widowed mother in the care and support of two invalid family members, after which she served as private secretary to Mary A. Woodbridge, the well-known Women's Christian Temperance Union leader. She had returned to Kansas following a meeting with staunch Prohibitionist and Kansas governor James St. John, after whom the Stafford county seat was named. She served as bookkeeper for the St. John & Marsh Lumber Company in Hutchinson, until being transferred to Stafford in 1887. In recent months she had resided in St. John with the new dentist, Dr. McCann, and his wife, spending the greater part of her time lecturing and organizing for the Women's Christian Temperance Union. Single women of her caliber were rare, and Isaac took notice.

Isaac still owed a half-day's labor toward his road tax, so he went to a bridge north of the schoolhouse to help two neighbors scrape dirt on the levee. In a moment of distraction, he failed to get completely out of the way of the scraper as it was dumping dirt, and sprained his ankle. He knew how close he had come to breaking his leg when the scraper struck him, and he thought how ironic it would have been to have broken his leg the last half-day's work owed as a man under the age of forty-five. There would be no more road tax labor owed by him, he thought to himself, as he limped around on his sore ankle—at least one benefit of growing older.

In St. John for a ULP rally, Isaac skipped lunch and the procession to get a front row seat at the rink[23] where Mary Elizabeth Lease was speaking. The room filled up quickly with an audience of nearly a thousand people. For four hours, Lease lived up to her reputation for political oratory. The November 1 *County Capital* reported, "Mrs. Lease, the well-known U.L. oratoress [*sic*], addressed the largest number of voters that ever assembled in the St. John Opera house . . . [delivering] the most instructive political speech, that had been made at St. John during the entire campaign." Also published under the headline "Campbell's Neighbors Speak!" was this statement: "The stories spread abroad by D. S. Carnahan and others, and as published in the St. John News, . . . are simply a mass of falsehoods gotten up solely for the purpose of injuring him politically," signed by fifty-five of Campbell's closest neighbors, including Isaac.[24]

Caught up in the ULP political excitement, Isaac decided to travel to Stafford City about twenty miles away the day before the elections. Not having visited there for seven years, he enjoyed seeing the improvements made since then, and he was delighted to find Miss Hazelett among the public speakers. He estimated five hundred people had gathered in the hall, some two hundred or so women.

The next morning, with a large turnout expected for a presidential election year, he and the other Albano Township election clerk got to the schoolhouse early. Despite several hotly contested races, the day passed peaceably, and toward closing of the polls, Lou Clouse arrived with his violin and played for the crowd that had gathered. Seventy-seven votes were polled, with forty-two for Campbell and thirty-two for his Republican opponent in their race for state representative. It had been an unfairly nasty race for his friend Will Campbell, and Isaac was relieved to have it finished. In addition to Campbell's victory, the local offices were swept by ULP members.[25]

When at last the national election results were reported, the reason for the delayed outcome was clear. The incumbent, Democrat Grover Cleveland, received 5,534,488 votes, or 48.6 percent of the popular vote. The Republican challenger Benjamin Harrison received 5,443,892 votes, or 47.8 percent of the popular vote. However, it was Harrison who captured the election, with 233 electoral votes to Cleveland's 168. The ULP presidential candidate, Alson Jenness Streeter, had come in fourth with only 149,115 votes, well behind the Prohibition Party candidate, Clinton B. Fisk, who got about a quarter of a million votes. In the Kansas race for governor, Lyman U. Humphrey, the Republican, won overwhelmingly.

THANKSGIVING NIGHT there was a dance at John Garvin's barn. For several days, Garvin had gone through the neighborhood buying about every fat hog there was, and he had shipped them out by train from Macksville the previous Saturday. As a result of those hog sales, many needy families had a little cash in their pockets and reason to be thankful. Isaac expected the dance would be a festive night, but he was content to sit at home by his warm fire.

The ULP enthusiasm leading up to the election had subsided, but about a dozen men at the Albano School decided to continue meeting every three weeks, alternating the location between the Albano and the Clear Creek schools. They chose Isaac to be their chairman. Despite their hopes for further ULP activity, without the excitement of an election, few others showed much interest. Despite some ULP success in their community, and "strenuous organizational efforts, the attempts to merge agrarian 'union Labor' with urban 'united Labor'" would never again be so successful.[26]

ISAAC'S ADMIRATION for Mary Elizabeth Lease, after hearing her speak, had motivated him to order a sample copy of her *Wichita Independent*, which was waiting for him one morning when he went to get his mail at Becks, the local post office having been relocated there following the Dix family's move to town. He decided to subscribe. Lease was a remarkable woman. She had come to Kansas in 1870 at the age of twenty to teach in a Catholic mission school, and soon married the local druggist. For about two years they prospered, but the financial panic of 1873 took everything, and they moved to Texas to start over. Ten years later they returned to Kansas to live on a farm near Kingman. By then, Lease had borne six children, four who survived infancy. She had become interested in women's suffrage and, through the Women's Christian Temperance Union, Prohibition. Studying law at home, she also published articles in the *Kingman County Citizen* in support of women's equal abilities to participate in male-dominated fields, obviously thinking of her own intention to be admitted to the bar to practice law. In about 1885 she and her family moved to Wichita, where she became active in politics.[27]

From his vantage point in the front row at the pre-election ULP rally, Isaac had felt privileged to observe Lease clearly. She stood nearly six feet tall, and her confidence could be seen before she ever spoke by the forceful way she walked to the podium, looking out over the crowded room with her fierce eyes, seeming to draw strength from their cheering. Her posture was almost military, although not a bit unfeminine, nor was the seeming strength of her body unpleasant.

Mary Elizabeth Lease, c. 1890–1900. Courtesy of Kansas Memory, Kansas Historical Society.

A willowy frame would have seemed misplaced to carry a woman with her powerful opinions, Isaac believed. Her voice had exactly the right tone, a rich contralto that filled the room with its resonance, without the need to shout to be heard. Her face was classically Grecian, an elongated oval shape with deep-set eyes flanking a long, straight nose, the proud head carried on a slender neck. Hers was a grace formed of steel, with nothing fragile about her. As commanding as her mere physical presence was, it was when she began to speak that her absolute charismatic power emerged. Unafraid to be dramatic and emotional, she could bring a crowd of a thousand to hushed anticipation with a whisper, and raise them to their feet with her verbal assaults on monopolies and Wall Street. It was written about her that "she could recite the multiplication table and set a crowd hooting and hurrahing at her will" and though the description was written by one of her detractors, Isaac would have found no reason to refute those words.[28] Lease was scheduled to speak again in St. John sometime in the new year, and Isaac was determined to be there, even if snow drifts blocked the roads.

He stayed busy getting his homestead ready for winter, also hauling fodder to Isabel Ross for her cow, and making room in his corn crib for three loads[29] of Mrs. Bentley's corn that renter Hacker brought over. The anticipated cold temperatures had not yet arrived, twenty degrees being about the coldest morning.

Feeling better about having things in shape, Isaac attended the Cane Meeting at the St. John Courthouse. The idea of raising cane sorghum to be processed into sugar had been around the area since the Pioneer Sugar Mill was started by John Bennyworth in Larned in 1880. Bennyworth had planted an entire square mile section to early amber sorghum and had urged other farmers to join the venture, getting the Central Arkansas Valley Sorghum Sugar Association incorporated and encouraging Larned business and political leaders to participate. A small plant had been built at Dundee, near Great Bend, and Kinsley had organized a company. Although neither these nor other ventures had been commercially successful, promoters continued to believe that technical problems could be resolved to make sugar a good source of revenue for Kansas farmers. Kansas senator Preston Plumb was instrumental in getting a $50,000 appropriation for the industry in 1884 and again in 1885, and in 1886 Congress appropriated $90,000 for a study of sugar technology in Louisiana, New Jersey, and Kansas. Although the secretary of agriculture opposed further funding, in 1887 Senator Plumb managed to get $20,000 allocated to sugar experiments in Fort Scott, Kansas.

The Kansas legislature passed "An Act to Encourage the Manufacture of Sugar" which paid a subsidy for products made from sorghum cane sugar grown in Kansas.[30] Isaac's neighbor Charles Shattuc now processed sorghum for molasses, but that was a simpler proposition from the refining of sorghum into sugar.

While he was in St. John, Isaac made a social call on Blanche Hazelett at the home of Dr. and Mrs. McCann. Of his visit, Isaac wrote: "Some pleasant surroundings and agreeable company to talk to."[31]

Isaac fell victim to a personal embarrassment, although he had been drawn into the situation innocently. A U.S. marshal had come to Albano Township to arrest Ben Webber, charging him with perjury. The charges arose out of the proof Ben made for his claim, for which Isaac had served as a witness. Unknown to Isaac, a rather complicated business scheme involved the land. Ben had traded three quarters of land for some horses. At the time, he owned only two quarters, although he intended to prove up the third quarter, which he in fact did. However, in order to prove up his claim Ben was required to make an oath that he had not bargained or sold, nor was he about to sell, the land he was proving up. Ben made that oath, despite his horse trade. The man with whom he had bargained informed against him, resulting in the perjury charges. Isaac had sworn honestly to the facts he was asked about in relation to the improvements and Ben's stewardship of the land. He had known nothing about the horse and land transaction, but it was an embarrassment to him anyway.

At last, Isaac's brother Henry had accomplished his part toward selling their land in Minnesota, and one evening Isaac found a registered letter waiting for him at the post office containing a draft for $374.50 as his share of the sale. The next morning, he left early for St. John, but with so many creditors to pay he felt as if he were only "paying up drips." He continued paying creditors until the money from the sale of the Minnesota land was nearly exhausted, but almost no one had been paid in full. He was entering the winter season feeling about as overwhelmed by his financial situation as he had before the money draft arrived.

What he was able to produce on his farm had failed not only to retire his debt but also to keep up with current expenses, and Isaac felt the need for new ideas. He was familiar with the Sorghum Sugar Mill promotions, but he remained uncertain. In the meantime, Hilmes had run lengthy articles on the venture in his newspaper, and William Peffer of the *Kansas Farmer* promoted the economic advantages of growing sorghum rather than wheat. Reputable authorities seemed assured that refined sugar production was the future for Kansas agriculture. None of the existing sugar factories had achieved commercial success; yet, sugar fever continued to infect nearby communities. Medicine Lodge had organized a company, Pratt was considering a sugar plant, and farmers in Coats had subscribed $20,000 toward a plant. Hilmes continued to insert articles about the sugar mills planned for other towns, suggesting that it was a possibility worth investigating for Stafford County. As far as Isaac knew, no one locally was pursuing the idea, and he remained skeptical.

Perhaps political efforts offered better ideas for farmers, so on a cold damp evening, Isaac and Will Campbell spliced their teams and went to the Clear Creek ULP meeting together. The meeting was called off when only four men came. Since the election, people had lost interest in politics. What Isaac could not have known was that the success of the ULP was already on the wane when it reached Stafford County. After a national peak of seven hundred thousand members in 1886, membership had begun to decline, and its popularity would not be repeated.

A milder evening's temperatures enticed Isaac to attend the Christmas Eve party in Garvin's barn, joining a crowd of about 250 neighbors, but by Christmas morning, ice covered the grass and trees, and Isaac rushed to prepare himself and his animals for a cold and disagreeable spell. He injured his foot cleaning out the stable and banking up his cellar for winter by stamping on the icy sled to keep the runners clean. Pain kept him awake that night; however, some remaining business matters in Pratt required his attention before the end of the year, which forced him to make a trip there. Particularly important was making a payment toward what he still owed Jones & Katterbeck for his gray mare Jule and her colt.

The trip did his health no good, and he saw out the old year from his bed, sick at his stomach all day. He had given this land a decade of his life, and for the first time he was beginning to realize that the dependable body of his youth could not continue to work at the pace he had labored in the past. He had kept his creditors at bay, but only by selling his Minnesota land, and he had brought in his crops, but only by hiring John Greene to help him do it. He had not claimed a homestead simply to survive, and spending the last day of 1888 sick in bed left him feeling little hope for the coming year.

CHAPTER 6

1889

Isaac Werner noted in his journal the eclipse that cast its strange shadow across the sun on New Year's Day, depositing a gloom across the land that seemed like a foreboding omen of things forever beyond man's control, of drought and hail and wind and pests that even the best farmer could not vanquish.[1] Even more disheartening were the debts and crop prices defeating farmers' best efforts. In St. John, very little business was being conducted other than loan negotiations and debt juggling, and Isaac was among those doing exactly that.

Not one to give up, Isaac was considering ways to escape the economic doldrums. On January 30 he wrote, "Past 10 days doing reviewing and reading in evenings of old favorite books, Grammar & Rhetoric, Elocution, etc., thinking of preparing to do something besides [farming]. . . . Women's rights interesting study for next several years to come & agitate."[2] He ordered a copy of *Extemporaneous Speaking* to hone his skills.

A few days earlier, Isaac had gone to the Emerson Post Office at Becks after his mail. He wrote in his journal, "Got my Patent from Larned land office for Homestead quarter executed at Washington the 9th day of June 1886, signed by Grover Cleveland and M. McKeane Secretary."[3] Such a delay in receiving his patent lacks explanation. Calculating from the date Isaac had matured his timber claim, he would have arrived on the prairie in the later half of the 1870s. Maturing a homestead claim took only five years, so the explanation for his delay in receiving the homestead patent is uncertain. His lack of a horse to travel to the land office in Larned in the early years or the fee to make the final application after five years on the claim may offer possible explanations, and the lack of his patent would certainly offer a reason for Isaac's reluctance to be absent from his farm.

While he was at the post office, he left some books to Beck folks to read. Schoolteacher Susan Beck shared Isaac's respect for education and stressed that responsibility to her son and daughter. Certainly, Isaac habitually turned to books for ideas. He had first read Adam Smith's *Wealth of Nations* as a young druggist in Rossville, when his perspective had been that of a merchant. As he read with a farmer's perspective, he better understood Smith's explanation that "What every thing really costs to the man who wants to acquire it, is the toil and trouble of acquiring it."[4] Now, as a farmer engaged in the "toil and trouble" necessary to acquire equipment, pay shipping, and earn working capital from the crops he produced, labor and cost seemed unfairly out of balance.

He was also reading Henry George's *Progress and Poverty,* although the Union Labor Party (ULP) had gone out of its way to exclude Georgism from its principles, preferring to work within existing social structures to create a better balance between the wealthy and the working classes, seeing Georgism as too socialistic and radical. The idea for which George was best known involved eliminating the ownership of land and replacing it with land rents that would be applied to the benefit of the entire community. The renter would have undisturbed possession and would not be taxed on the improvements he made nor on what he produced on the land. There would be several advantages to farmers under the land rent system. Land could be used as if it were owned so long as the rent was paid. Hard work and innovation would be rewarded, and wealth would become anything of value produced by human effort. The land rents would pay for government services now paid for by taxes, and tax collectors would be replaced by the fewer government agents necessary to collect the land rents. George insisted that the "single tax" or land rent would be more equitable, but Isaac saw a big problem concerning the prohibition against conveying or inheriting the land. Although it would reduce or eliminate speculators holding land as an investment toward future sale, that prohibition would almost certainly be objectionable to farmers. Although Isaac had no children to whom he might pass his farm, he knew that leaving the land to their children was often the reason neighbors gave for enduring the current hardships. Without the

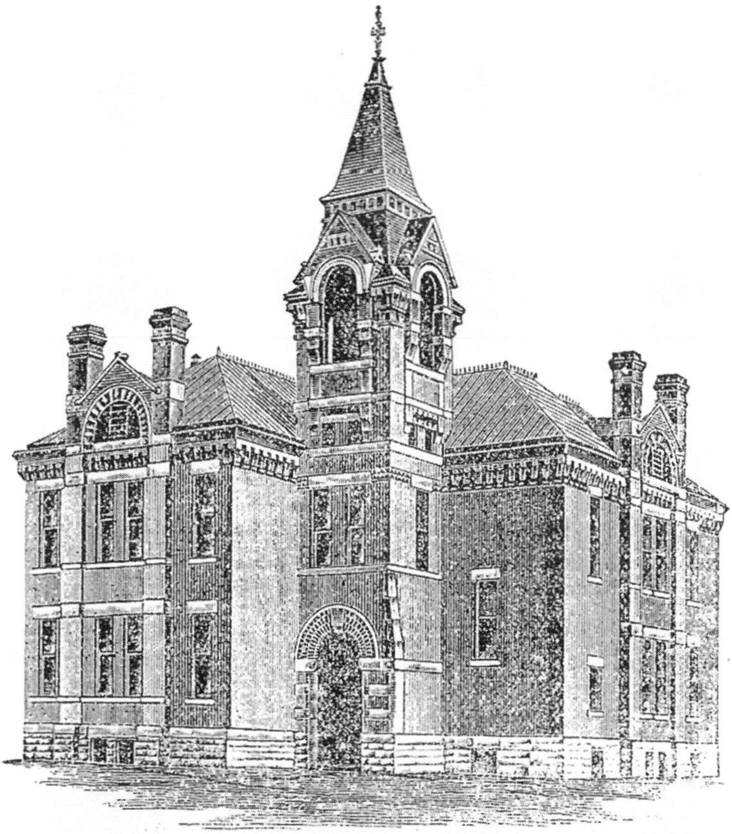

St. John's handsome brick schoolhouse. *St. John Weekly News,* September 6, 1895.

ability to pass the land to their children, many farmers would just give up. Isaac was willing to read George and other economic theorists,[5] in search of ways to confront what he saw as the current economic unbalance between laborers and the wealthy, even if some of their ideas were probably unworkable.

SOMETIMES ISAAC garnered ideas from unexpected places. He happened to be in town when Professor S. S. Hamill, an elocutionist, appeared at St. John's handsome brick schoolhouse, and Isaac stayed to attend the performance. Hamill's book, the *New Science of Elocution: The elements and principles of vocal expression in lessons,* advocated teaching elocution as both science and art, to improve not only public speaking but also everyday expression of ideas. Hamill was an entertaining performer, and he reinforced Isaac's belief in the connection between reason and communication.[6]

Isaac believed that too many of the speakers at local meetings expressed their ideas poorly, and it was hard to tell whether their comments were even worth hearing. That was why he supported the Farmers' Alliance's emphasis on education of farmers including training members to express their ideas more coherently. In January, he had ordered *Extemporaneous Speaking* from Martyn College of Oratory in Washington, DC, for himself, and a few days later, at the Alliance meeting, he distributed their catalogs to members.[7] Isaac built a bulletin board for community notices on the Pratt-Stafford county road, posting as his first notice the upcoming Albano Union Labor Club meeting.

When the evening for the meeting arrived, he dressed in the suit he had not worn since coming to Kansas, intending to add dignity to his function as chairman, but despite the notice he had posted, only seven members appeared. A ULP meeting at Clear Creek School was scheduled for the following Saturday, and with forty-one registered members from that area, he hoped for better attendance.

Although community efforts were important to Isaac, he could not ignore his own farm. His creative mind explored more than just planting and tending crops, and ways to improve machinery were a constant motivation. As with many of his inventions, Isaac had been allowing a design for a three-horse cultivator to percolate at the back of his mind until rather specific plans had taken shape. He believed his familiarity with the sandy loam soil of their area would allow him to design a superior machine, and he hoped to find the time and money to build a prototype.

Winter not only gave him time to read and reflect on his ideas, it also freed him to attend programs in town. Since first hearing Mary Elizabeth Lease speak at the ULP rally, Isaac had looked forward to hearing her speak again, particularly after receiving a letter from her. On February 19, despite the cold weather, he bundled himself in layers and used a veil over his face to endure the trip to St. John to hear her scheduled speech about Ireland and Irishmen, although other country folks stayed home. Before an audience of about sixty, Lease began by talking about "Women's Suffrage and her manuscript on the history of Kansas women," soliciting contributions for the project. Because he shared her interest in advancing women's rights, Isaac enjoyed hearing about her suffrage project, but he also enjoyed her scheduled topic, which he found "splendid from beginning to end."[8]

Unwilling to face the cold in darkness, he spent the night with W. C. Betzer, a former country neighbor who had moved into St. John when he reached his sixties. His wife Julia left the two men talking politics until after one o'clock. Despite Isaac's eagerness to start home early the next morning, his host was still talking. "[Finally] got away from old Betzer," Isaac wrote in his journal, "(his only fault, he needs a Westinghouse Air Brake to stop him from talking when he gets started)." Traveling home the next morning he could not help thinking how fortunate Betzer was with a younger wife to look after him as he grew older. It was another example of older men of his acquaintance who had married younger ladies late in life.[9]

Although he and Betzer had discussed many Progressive ideas, one thing they had not discussed was the Albano town project that Isaac had proposed for his community. Enthusiasm for his proposal had waned, so Isaac was surprised to read in the *County Capital* that "Kansas City Capitalists have bought the land adjoining the Albano town site and expect in the near future to erect a brick business block with a general store, Post Office, a public town hall, a local UL Newspaper, and all the necessary adjuncts for a thriving inland town."[10] Although Isaac hoped his idea for a local town had not died, he was unaware of any such offer.

The winter's cold had lessened day by day, and Isaac welcomed seeing the first wild geese flying north, a sure sign of spring. Everyone seemed anxious to plant something, and selling seed potatoes became Isaac's most successful business. He realized that each sale might eliminate a customer for the current year's crop and create a competitor in the marketplace, but he needed the spring revenue. Because few people had the space or the inclination to keep their own supply of seed potatoes through the winter, he believed they would continue as customers in future springs. If there were a glut on the local market when potatoes were harvested, he believed his town customers would still prefer the superior quality of his potatoes, and he could also market in communities where soils did not allow potato cultivation.

Isaac knew that as spring brought warmer weather, people would be busier, with fewer opportunities for leisurely chats, so he welcomed a visit from close neighbor Will Campbell. The relationship between the two men had deepened during the winter months as they had worked together on ULP records, and, that evening, their common political interests led to a discussion about the ideas in *Seven Financial Conspiracies which have Enslaved The American People*, written by Sarah E. Van de Vort Emery.[11] According to the author, before a movement can exist, people must be brought together by a common cause. "It [language] provides both visions of the future and an imagined past which will unify people. Language is central in drawing people together and in affecting their structural capacities to act as a class, for a uniform language can cut across racial and cultural boundaries." Thousands of copies had been distributed to laborers and her ideas were exerting significant influence. Among her detailed financial theories, her basic argument that "a nation's prosperity does not lie so much in the amount of its wealth as in a just distribution of that wealth among those who have produced it"[12] had resonated with Populists. Isaac was glad that he and Will had made the time to discuss Emery's ideas before spring work began, and he hoped she would come to Pratt or St. John to speak sometime in the future so that he could hear her in person.

For now, however, spring work demanded his attention. This year he felt particularly fortunate that his young horse Jim was at last old enough to work. Jim's training began by hitching him alongside the mares, Dolly and Jule, to drag the sled over grass to tire him a little before hitching him to a plow. April 15 was a proud day for Isaac, for he recorded in his journal that by afternoon Jim was "working as gentle as an old cow, no trouble at all, only wanting a chance to learn how and he is all right. Making me feel a little proud to be at it with three pretty stout horses[.]" That pride aligned with his continued work on the invention of his three-horse cultivator, which had gained enough attention for William Peffer to have published an article about Isaac's invention in the *Kansas Farmer*.

Isaac's correspondence with Populist leaders continued, and he received a letter from Mrs. Lease containing two pieces of good news. First, her health had improved, which would allow her to speak at the local July 4 gathering. Second, she had been admitted to the bar in Wichita. Isaac sat down immediately to reply to her letter.[13]

Isaac's involvement with the ULP brought occasional visitors to his farm. One couple visited to express their opposition to linking ULP with Prohibition,[14] but Isaac disagreed, believing that the goals of Prohibition and women's rights were consistent with those of the ULP. Prohibition was both a moral and a political issue, with drunkenness railed about from both the pastor's pulpit and the politician's podium. The people of Kansas had voted for a constitutional amendment in 1880, becoming the second state after Maine to include Prohibition in their constitution. However, the manufacture and sale of intoxicating liquors was permitted for medical or scientific purposes, and many citizens continued to find alcohol good medicine. Prohibition was enacted under the administration of Governor John Pierce

St. John, known for lacing his political speeches with moral and religious references, with prohibition one of his top goals. Kansans took great interest in the Prohibition movement and in the drinking habits of their neighbors.

May 23, an hour past midnight, Isaac confronted the arrival of his forty-fifth birthday, and although he was generally a sound sleeper, that night he was restless. Lying in the darkness he became nostalgic, whether because of his birthday making him more aware of the passage of time or because the recent news of the death of his favorite uncle had deepened his reflections on how quickly one's life passes. Isaac had carefully glued the clipping of his uncle's death in the margin of his journal: "Henry R. Werner died suddenly at his home at Wernersville, aged 84. Deceased had been enjoying his usual good health until Sunday, when he was stricken with apoplexy[15] and sank rapidly until his death." His Uncle Henry was the father of the two cousins who had joined Isaac in Rossville, Illinois, when he had lived there, his cousin Henry having been a business partner in the milling venture and his younger cousin Ezra having often entertained Isaac and other friends with his accordion. Perhaps because his own father had been dead for nearly twenty-five years, it had meant a great deal to Isaac just knowing that his uncle was still in Wernersville. Now, Uncle Henry was gone too.[16] The passing of his parents' generation meant that the keepers of the memories of his childhood were disappearing, and there was no family living near him to collect the memories of the life he had built in Kansas.

Never one to waste time, Isaac used the rest of the night to read a sample copy of the *National Economist*, edited by Texan Charles Macune, perhaps the nation's best edited journal of agricultural economics.[17] It was Isaac's first exposure to Macune, the man who developed the idea of a subtreasury plan involving government warehouses that would support low-cost loans to farmers as a means to gain more control over the marketing of their crops. Macune also disagreed with those Populists who were beginning to advocate free silver as the solution for the rural economy. Reading the positive ideas in the *National Economist* had taken Isaac's mind off the sadness of his uncle's death and his growing awareness of his own aging and his isolation from family.

It seemed an odd coincidence when only five days after that sleepless night, another event connected him to memories of his childhood home. He had heard the ominous thundering that rumbled over his farm without bringing rain. However, that storm front had brought a deluge into the Johnstown-Southfork area of Pennsylvania, only about two hundred miles due west of Isaac's old community. The heavens opened and dropped such a downpour that at about three o'clock the afternoon of May 31, a dam could take no more. It burst, and water roared down the Conemaugh Valley, engulfing towns and adding debris to the churning water. The wall of water and debris reached Johnstown, with a population of thirty thousand, where ninety-nine entire families were obliterated in the flood. The front-page story, published June 6 in the *County Capital,* carried the headline: "THE AWFUL CALAMITY, Thousands of People Find a Watery Grave." Because of the proximity to his childhood home, the tragedy felt particularly personal to Isaac.[18]

There were things that article did not tell. The dam and lake were part of an exclusive private resort owned by a group of wealthy steel, coal, and railroad industrialists, including Henry Clay Frick of Carnegie Steel. The integrity of the dam had been questioned by another wealthy man downstream, the head of the Cambria Iron Works, Carnegie Steel's chief competitor. Following the catastrophic flood, it became apparent that the failure of the dam was not an entirely unpredictable disaster. In fact, it appeared to be an extreme example of wealthy and powerful men acting irresponsibly with working men and their families suffering the tragic consequences.[19] The director of the U.S. Geological Survey, Major John Wesley Powell said: "Modern industries are handling the forces of nature on a stupendous scale. . . . Woe to the people who trust these powers to the hands of fools."[20] Such blatant disregard for others was apparent from the deaths of so many who had drowned because wealthy men disregarded warnings about their recreational dam. Their callous behavior was exactly why Populist speakers like Lease railed against the greed and social indifference of the wealthy. Having grown up in a valley community with a stream passing by his family home, Isaac must have imagined the horror of the flood more clearly than some of his flatlander Kansas neighbors.

THROUGHOUT LATE MAY and early June, Isaac recorded in his journal the gradual resolution of design problems with his three-horse cultivator, until at last he concluded: "I just feel all over like wanted to be out in field with a 3-horse machine and take revenge on weeds[.]"[21] Feeling optimistic about the implement's potential, he went to St. John to meet with a local dealer face to face for a discussion of the local manufacturing of implements. The idea of developing local manufacturing of farm equipment was one of the ways Populists hoped to avoid the market manipulation of large manufacturers. Isaac left the meeting with "new courage" that his plan might be possible.

While in St. John, he learned that the banks had suspended loaning money. Many of the merchants were in jeopardy from carrying too many customers on their books, and it was reported that Gloyd Bros. held delinquent accounts amounting to $7,000. Judging from the dark circles and weariness around merchants' eyes, Isaac believed many were suffering sleepless nights. Some had carried him on their books when he couldn't pay, and even if they had been slow to understand the connection between the financial stability of farmers and their own economic survival, Isaac sympathized with them now. Perhaps small businesses might be as mistreated by the power of the wealthy as farmers were. After all, they also purchased their merchandise from Eastern manufacturers and paid the railroads the same high rates that burdened farmers.

Entries in Isaac's journal throughout 1889 evidenced his continuing juggling of debt. On January 22 he had "seen Gillmore about the $106.00 due on 25th . . . and $100 in Thompson bank 1st mortgage . . . and in State Bank[.]" Six days later, he wrote, "I went to St. John got $230 of S. M. Burr on 2d mortgage on homestead ($350 for 5 years) to settle with Gillmore's $106, and $101 to 1st National bank reducing interest to 14% for one year. Deposited $56.10 in 1st National for Otterback & Jones, final payment and releasing mortgage on Jule & colt. . . . Business generally quiet save trying to borrow and paying debts." Entries continued in March, May, July, September, and November, each arrangement done to extend his loans rather than settle them.[22]

Even with his new perspective about the shared difficulties of merchants and farmers, Isaac felt more in common with his rural neighbors, who were beginning to think that acting together might offer solutions. A new farmers' organization had come to Kansas and many communities were organizing local chapters of the Farmers' Alliance. It had begun in Texas, started by the same Charles Macune who edited the *National Economist,* and the organization was beginning to expand to other states. Isaac and some neighbors decided to form a local organization, and although only seven men came to the organizing meeting, they elected Will Campbell president, Gus Gereke vice president, Isaac secretary, and H. M. Frack treasurer. Every founding member was given some office to perform, and Isaac believed membership would grow.[23]

Just as Isaac had anticipated, when potato harvest arrived there was a glut on the market, with the price for new potatoes at forty or fifty cents a bushel and continuing to fall. What he had not anticipated was that his former town customers were raising potatoes for their own families on their small town lots, having no need for Isaac's potatoes, regardless of their superior quality.

Not all losses could be anticipated. While working with the young tenant to whom the Bentleys had rented their former home, Isaac suffered an unexpected and unnecessary loss caused by the younger man, which Isaac recorded in his journal: "Frazee knocked Baldy's[24] right eye out with a stone, throwing at his worthless nuisance of a dog . . . Missed the dog but hit the colt's eye." Isaac did what he could to treat the injury, using a liniment of half lard and half turpentine, but the colt's eye was lost.

THE FOURTH OF JULY had become a traditional time in Isaac's community for people to put aside their labors and celebrate. This year the local alliance and ULP groups had decided to celebrate together, with Mrs. Lease as a speaker. On a pleasantly cool day, about twelve hundred people gathered in a shady grove to enjoy picnics and listen to speakers. The St. John brass band entertained, and prizes were awarded to winners of the sack race, the 100-yard foot race, and the biscuit eating race.[25]

At the time, Isaac believed Mrs. Lease had done an excellent job moderating her remarks, but her speech generated criticism. The dispute over Lease's speech lay in the purpose for which the Farmers' Alliance had been formed. The Alliance was not a political group but rather an organization in which Republicans, Democrats, or any other party's members could come together to support common interests. So long as that purpose was adhered to, the Alliance posed less threat to the old parties. However, with about two-thirds of the state's voters working as farmers, if they could be brought together to vote as a single block, neither Republicans nor Democrats would have enough votes to defeat Alliance candidates. The power of the two main political parties rested on farmers' divided political loyalties. If Lease's speech at the July 4 picnic had been a call for farmers to come together in a single political party, it was a threat to the establishment.[26]

Egged on by published notices in the *Stafford Herald*, the criticism of Lease, a ULP speaker addressing the crowd, reached the point that J. F. Guernsey chose to reply on the front page of the August 8 *County Capital*. He explained that both the ULP and the Farmers' Alliance had planned events without knowing of the other's plans, and upon learning of the conflict, they had decided to join in a united celebration. Lease had been engaged to speak at the ULP event and agreed to speak at the joint event, but her fee was paid by Guernsey himself, with no payment coming from the

ULP or the Alliance. He emphasized: "I understood then and I understand now that the Alliance is a non-partizan [*sic*] organization[.]" Guernsey's explanation may have been true, but it did not fully address the objection of the *Stafford Herald* editor. The issue was less about who had paid her speaking fee but more about whether her speech was political or merely patriotic.

Despite criticism by the old political parties and their hardcore adherents, a growing number of farmers were looking elsewhere for economic solutions, and the reason was obvious. Wheat that had sold for a $1.19 a bushel in 1881 was currently selling in St. John for around fifty cents. The U.S. Department of Agriculture knew that since 1883, corn, wheat, and other crops had been selling regularly for less than the cost of production. These financial realities had set the stage for the rapid growth of the Farmers' Alliance in Kansas by farmers tired of looking to the two old political parties for help. On August 14, 1889, Isaac wrote in his journal: "The day for 1st State Meeting of Alliance of Kansas to meet at Newton[.]" Isaac's brief entry was inadequate to indicate the significance of the day to farmers like himself.

The organization that Kansans and farmers from other states were joining initially formed in Texas, and the Farmer's Alliance had remained small for more than ten years. Its growth had begun in 1887, and by December of 1888 there were twelve states represented, with Kansas among them. The first convention of the Farmers' Alliance of Kansas held that fourteenth day of August had eighty delegates from twenty-seven counties. The state secretary reported that 470 sub-Alliances had already been organized, with a total membership of twenty-five thousand.[27] The Albano Alliance was among those 470 sub-Alliances, and Isaac was among the twenty-five thousand Kansas Alliance members. Republican and Democratic leadership had paid little attention to the Alliance in the beginning, but the growing number of its members was getting their attention.

Isaac supported the notion of the Alliance as beneficial for farmers, but he still had a farm to tend. Dry weather, thirsty corn, maturing potatoes, hay needing cut, peach seedlings needing to be watered and weeded, cricket-filled well water needing cleaning—a litany of useless chores with the prices where they were. Yet there was little Isaac could do but care for his farm and watch the sky for rain, for that is a farmer's way to survive. He continued to document his farming experiments in his journal and order books to be informed about economic and political matters, including Henry George's new book, *Protection or Free Trade*. No rain came. The stand of mammoth Cuban corn was so scattered and weedy that Isaac determined to let it go. The leaves on the early California corn were tattered by the wind. Only the corn on Persis's ground looked green and clean, but many stalks showed no ears yet.

Isaac was grateful for a new book to take his mind off his worries about the farm, and *Looking Backward* by Edward Bellamy did just that. He wrote in his journal: "Last evening read Bellamy's *Looking Backward*. . . . [I] had to laugh almost like a fool over Mr. Julian West sticking in his cellar sleeping room for over one hundred thirteen years . . . times changing so much for the better[.]"[28] Bellamy used the novel to describe a future world less competitive and less class dominated. His main character, a privileged young man, awakens to find a changed society living in a cooperative world. Bellamy's utopia captured people's imaginations, resulting in the formation of Bellamy Clubs around the world, devoted to implementing the socialist ideas described in the book.

Isaac's evenings were sometimes lonely, even for a solitary man. His books and his correspondence were his favorite ways to fill those evenings, and one evening as the early autumn weather made staying indoors by the fire desirable, he sat down to write a letter to his sister Emma. When he had first left home, his sisters had been regular correspondents, but now they exchanged letters only to share specific news. Emma's husband had advanced within the Philadelphia & Reading Railroad Company and was now the manager of the Southwark Foundry & Machine Company at Philadelphia, where he and Emma lived with their four children.[29] Ettie and Reverend Palmer were still living in Abilene, Kansas, with their two little girls[30] and Isaac's mother, but it might as well have been Pennsylvania for all that Isaac's impoverished ability to travel allowed. Even the exchange of letters with his twin brother had tapered off. Part of it was surely the distance between them and how long it had been since all of them were together. Some of it may have been the family financial arrangements. He probably was the financial failure of the family, but if only prices for what he grew would rise to a fair level again, things would be different. And, if only they could see his farm and hear the praise his neighbors spoke of its neat and pleasant appearance, perhaps they would be a little proud of him.

With no family nearby, he did have more time to donate to his community, and when the local ULP primary meeting was held at the schoolhouse on September 14, Isaac was selected as a delegate to the convention in St. John. He found the experience "quite an interesting time it was, especially to a novice." In an effort to defeat Republicans, Democrats had agreed to join with the ULP in selecting candidates. It did not go smoothly. Isaac wrote in his journal, "U.L. & Democrats locked for 2 hours on exchanging

Gen. James Weaver, 1892. From James B. Weaver, *A Call to Action: An Interpretation of the Great Uprising, Its Source & Causes* (Des Moines: Iowa Printing, 1892).

2 offices to democrats . . . finally U.L. got out of patience went ahead to nominate their full ticket. When Demos give in in a hurry and matters were compromised agreeably."[31] It was just the first example of how complicated it could be to join with one of the old parties in an effort to defeat the other old party.

Isaac continued to place hope in the benefits of educating farmers through the Alliance, but his involvement with the ULP had shown him the advantages of political efforts. The difficulty of the ULP trying to select candidates with Democrats and the question of whether the goals of the Democrats and ULP differed too much for those elected to represent both parties' goals once they were in office concerned Isaac. Neither had he entirely forgotten his concerns whether the ULP was the best fit for farmers.[32] Learning what leaders of the party thought was important to him. Although he never traveled more than a day's journey from his farm, Isaac was able to hear many well-known speakers, who traveled by train to towns across the nation.

Learning from a circular that Gen. James B. Weaver of Iowa was to speak in St. John, Isaac made arrangements to attend. Weaver was well known to farmers of the Great Plains, primarily as a prominent speaker for Populist ideas. What may not have been so well known by the crowds of people arriving to hear him speak were the things he had done that had nothing to do with politics, beginning when he was young. Weaver's parents had given up on Ohio when James was two and had moved with their thirteen children to Michigan, where farming again failed to support the family. They had moved their family to Iowa Territory when James was nine.

Experiencing his family's struggles had taught Weaver what it meant to eke out a living from the soil, battling weather and pests on the one hand and markets and bankers on the other. He brought that childhood knowledge with him when he spoke to farmers, along with other knowledge he had accumulated during his life. When he was twenty, he and his brother-in-law joined a cattle drive from Iowa to California, returning by way of Panama. He knew about blisters and sweat and exhaustion. He studied law and attended the Cincinnati Law School, and as a practicing lawyer he read *Uncle Tom's Cabin* by Harriet Beecher Stowe and became active in the abolitionist movement. He knew about justice. When the Civil War began, he enlisted as a private in the Iowa Volunteer Infantry Regiment, received a commission as a lieutenant, was promoted to major, then colonel, and by the end of the war was a brevet brigadier general, a rank earned through battlefield experience. He knew about discipline, self-sacrifice, and courage. He returned to Iowa and became active in Republican politics, until he began to perceive Republicans as controlled by business at the expense of farmers and small businessmen, and he walked away, joining the Greenback Party. It was on this party's ticket that he had been elected to the House of Representatives and had made a respectable but failed third-party run for the presidency. When he spoke about the causes that mattered to him, he spoke from experience and from the heart. Isaac could hardly wait to hear what Weaver had to say.

Weaver was to speak at one o'clock, following the morning Alliance meeting, and a crowd of about a thousand quickly filled the room. Weaver was fifty-five years old, still with a fine head of hair and a full moustache beneath his patrician nose. His expression revealed both weariness from the battles he had fought and confident courage that his cause could be won. His speech was filled with historical and literary references, to the extent that Isaac wondered whether some of Weaver's listeners were perplexed, but the room was silent and attentive as he spoke: "Many of the giant wrongs which [the American people] are seeking to overthrow are as old as the race of man and are rock-rooted in the ignorant prejudices and controlling customs of every nation in Christendom." Continuing, he said: "Capital possesses one thing which labor does not—ready cash. They will not hesitate to make the best possible use of it. But labor possesses that which capital does not—numbers." Weaver's style was not flamboyant, and he did not bring the crowd to their feet in frequent spontaneous cheers, but that night, Isaac wrote in his journal, "Made a very satisfactory speech to all present, very general and not much partisan but deep, simple, and truthful," underlining his words to emphasize his impressions of this respected man.[33]

Locally, Isaac's friend Joseph Towsley had been chosen as the ULP candidate for register of deeds. He had come to the Emerson School one evening with the intention of beginning his political campaigning at the Albano Alliance meeting. When rainy weather kept everyone but Towsley and Isaac at home, they adjourned to Isaac's for the night. After a brief political chat, their conversation turned to land rentals. Homesteaders had been prohibited from leasing their land, but now that most had matured their claims, many were doing just that. Towsley told Isaac he had rented all of his land, furnishing the team and implements for half the resulting crop. Isaac admitted his deal was not so good, having negotiated with Charles Shattuc to lease some of his land for wheat at one-fourth of the crop, with Shattuc paying all of the cost of planting, raising, and harvesting. Isaac had wanted a third of the crop for the same terms, but he was still glad he had agreed to the lease.[34]

Having heard several Populist speakers like Weaver and Lease, as well as having studied economists like Macune and Adam Smith, made Isaac a better-informed speaker than most people in his area. On the evening of October 23, a wagon filled with Albano Alliance men went over to East Clear Creek School to hear Isaac make his maiden political talk endorsing the candidates and the goals of the ULP. Facing an audience of about two hundred, Isaac bypassed the early reluctance of ULP to embrace some of the ideas of Henry George: "Oppression, Complaining, and Humiliation noticeable everywhere—Democrat, Republican, Sinner or any body else all unite that something needs to be done towards necessary relief, a dozen Mortgage foreclosures a day in our county is sufficient to alarm any honest man[.]" He finished by stepping to the schoolroom blackboard to calculate the impossibility of raising enough at current prices to pay the cost of producing the crop, the taxes, and the interest, with anything left to retire the principle or provide necessities for the farmer and his family.[35]

Only a few days after speaking on Georgism, Isaac delivered his first Alliance speech as lecturer at the Naron School in Pratt County, continuing to be active in the ULP as well as participating in the Alliance. Although he appreciated the respectful attention shown to his remarks, he was surprised by how little the Naron members knew about the very issues the sub-Alliances were being formed to confront.

Among the topics about which populist leaders expressed concern was land acquisition by foreign investors through foreclosures on indebted farmers.[36] November 1 was the date an English syndicate headquartered in Kansas City was reputed to begin aggressively foreclosing on farmers in several Western states, raising the image of worn-down American farmers, economically and physically broken like the Irish tenants working for absentee English landlords. Although the talk of this was commonplace, Isaac had seen no evidence that it was happening to anyone he knew, and he certainly knew more farmers than himself with mortgages on their homesteads. Surely, he thought, there must be something to the allegations, since the Kansas Republicans, Democrats, and ULP parties had all endorsed national platforms urging the passage of laws to limit or prohibit foreign ownership of land. These reports from trusted sources worried Isaac, but it also troubled him that he could see no evidence nearby to validate the reports. How could a farmer, whose travel was confined to a few counties, know what to believe?[37]

November 5 was Election Day, and once again Isaac served as township clerk on the election board. The results for this off-year election of local offices were mixed, the community seeming to follow personal loyalties rather than party allegiances. Isaac joined the family of his fellow clerk for midday dinner, impressed by the prosperity in horses, cattle, and hogs around the Loftiss premises and admiring the modest but tidy home Martha Loftiss kept for her husband and their four children.

Isaac lived in Stafford County, so that was where he voted and served. However, his claim abutted the Pratt-Stafford county line, and he had many friends and business connections in Pratt County. In fact, several neighboring farmers had land on both sides of the county line and exchanged work with one another. Isaac was respected as a speaker by groups in Stafford, Pratt, and Edwards counties. Consequently, he felt that it was important for him to be informed about ideas farmers were discussing in all three communities. A few days after the elections, despite below freezing weather, Isaac and Wes Logan attended the second meeting of the Pratt County Alliance. Over one hundred were present for the installation of officers and routine business, followed by informative discussions. Seeing the good use the well-informed Pratt Alliance members had made of W. S. Morgan's *History of the Alliance,* Isaac decided it would be beneficial to order circulars for distribution to Albano Alliance members.

Isaac had faith in the potential of the Alliance to help his community, and he was pleased that more women had been initiated. He did what he could to encourage better attendance, arriving early one evening with oil and a lamp so those nearing the school could see the welcoming light through the windows. Having William Campbell in their community, with his personal knowledge of events in the state capital at Topeka, gave members a first-hand awareness of what was at stake. That evening, Campbell described the deficient knowledge among his fellow legislators about financial matters affecting farmers, and he encouraged members to remedy that—whether through replacing the ignorant legislators or insisting that those legislators evidence a willingness to learn. When Campbell concluded, Isaac's lecture that followed was cut short; from "trying to tell too much important truth in one evening to a raw audience,"[38] Isaac believed.

He decided to form a separate local reform club, with those more willing to study and develop strategies at a sophisticated level. He invited nine neighbors to attend a meeting in his home, and although only Campbell and Frack came to the first meeting, they enjoyed a social chat until ten o'clock. When the group met a few days later at Joe Ferguson's house to designate offices among themselves, Campbell was chosen as president, Ferguson as vice president, Isaac as secretary, and Frank Stimatze as treasurer. It was an intelligent, progressive group.

The following Monday Isaac rose at two o'clock in the morning, taking care of his stock in readiness for going to Pratt with Logan to hear national lecturer Ben Terrell, a farmer from Gonzales County, Texas. By ten o'clock they were standing in Science Hall with about 150 people. Terrell was a man in his mid-forties, already balding, but with heavy brows and an impressive moustache that swooped down below his jawline in a way that accentuated his serious, somewhat sad-looking eyes. There was a dignity about his expression that added weight to his words. Isaac found his speech grandly effective, "because it was the truth and all practical."[39]

December arrived threatening snow, so Isaac hurried to Beck's for his mail ahead of the storm. A few of his neighbors seemed to have had the same idea and were lingering to talk. Their conversation was pessimistic, everyone admitting that financial pressures were getting to be more than they could endure. These were not greenhorns who had left some city job to try their hands at farming but rather men accustomed to being bone tired at the end of a day's labor, who accepted the uncertainties of rainfall and late frosts as part of the gamble that farmers face. It was the impossibility of getting clear of debt that discouraged them, with all their skill at farming defeated by poor markets. Some were talking about pulling up stakes, with Beck, Holbrook, Webber, Gullet, and Hingecliff thinking seriously about leaving their claims.[40] However, farming was what they knew, and little free land remained to claim elsewhere. With the markets for farm products depressed everywhere, there was no assurance that moving would make a difference. Instead of being cheered by a bit of social talk with neighbors, Isaac came home disheartened.

Gathering with other farmers still willing to seek solutions for their depressed economic circumstances was the only anecdote Isaac knew for such discouragement. A wintery evening's meeting of the Albano Farmers' Alliance was the best yet, with twenty-five in attendance. The subject for open discussion was how to get the St. John Milling Company to work with farmers to find a compromise on wheat prices. When the discussion concluded, the featured speaker for the evening was Isaac. His paper about the importance of educating members, which included a list of suggested reading material, had been published by the respected *Kansas Commoner,* and he had been invited to read his paper at the local meeting. [41] He urged members "to accomplish all we possibly can during the winter months, for when spring work commences we will have hardly time to think about anything else." Isaac concluded with his compilation of recommended books and newspapers. Several days later, Isaac's entire paper was published in the *County Capital*.[42]

Isaac was becoming a respected lecturer, and at the Clear Creek School on October 23, to a crowd of thirty or so, he spoke "for a good hour, and some still hungry to listen longer, and as some said could listen all night and not get tired."[43] Evenings like that made all the studying and work that he did for the Alliance seem well worth it, but it also made him impatient with members who neglected study and preparation.

A meeting to consolidate Farmers' Alliances with labor organizations had been held in St. Louis, resulting in a new name: The National Farmers' Alliance and Industrial Union. Their joint objective was not the creation of a political party but rather combining the efforts of their legislative committees to act in concert before Congress to lobby for shared legislative goals. Seven goals were adopted:

1. Abolition of national banks and substitution of legal tender treasury notes in place of national bank notes,
2. Laws to prevent dealing in futures,
3. Free and unlimited coinage of silver,
4. Laws to prohibit foreign ownership of land,
5. No taxation used to build up one interest or class at the expense of another,

6. Issuance of sufficient fractional paper currency to facilitate financial exchanges through the U.S. mail,
7. Communication and transportation owned and operated in the interest of the people, rather than private companies.

Social welfare programs were not requested. Like Isaac, most farmers and other laborers believed they were capable of succeeding on their own, if government policies did not favor the wealthy and powerful. It was buying implements from price-fixing monopolies and selling their products in markets manipulated by speculators that they blamed for the economy that failed working people. Isaac's efforts to find a small manufacturer for his three-horse cultivator was an example of what farmers sought, hoping not only for less expensive equipment to be the result but also for equipment better suited for their region. As for markets, the favorite targets for Populist speakers were Wall Street, trusts, and speculators, and Isaac agreed. He was certain that railroads should be regulated or replaced with government ownership if producers were ever going to be able to ship goods and produce economically. He wasn't so sure about free silver as the best economic remedy, preferring to continue reading what economists had to say on the subject. He was certain that wealthy men had too much influence in Washington, DC, and Topeka, and believed that if Kansas farmers were treated fairly, and if they continued to educate themselves, they could manage well enough.

During a trip to St. John to borrow money to pay creditors and make some small purchases for himself, Isaac ordered *Gronlund's Co-operative Commonwealth*. He also picked up *Duties of Sub-Alliances* leaflets and a pack of *McLean Almanacs* for local Alliance members. Sadly, he learned that Frank Loftiss's wife had died, and her funeral was to be held the next morning. Isaac joined in the procession of about twenty-five teams making their way to Neeland's Cemetery for Martha Deldora Loftiss's burial, the memory of his lunch with the family on Election Day still fresh in Isaac's mind.

Alone on Christmas Eve, he found himself thinking about young Martha Loftiss, only twenty-six years old, leaving behind four children, one barely two months old. Hard times like these seemed to fall most heavily on women and children,[44] and he was almost glad he had not brought a wife with him to endure the misfortunes that were the common lot of so many. Advertisements for patent medicines claiming outlandish cures with illustrations of haggard women filled the newspapers. The almanacs he had brought

Weather was so important to farmers, but almanacs predicting weather patterns for the coming year were largely guesswork. The cover is written in English, but the content inside is in German, an accommodation for non-English-speaking immigrant farmers.

home contained Dr. McLean's recipes for a variety of maladies. Most of the ailments men and women on the prairie were suffering could have been cured by decent food, adequate shelter, and a rest from their labors.[45] He had often written in his journal about the drafty homes of newcomers to the prairie, and on more than one occasion he had gathered up his tools to make neighbors' homes more secure from the elements. He had even taken some of his own supply of cornstalks and cobs to Isabel Ross when he feared she was running low on fuel to burn, as well as adding brush to the roof of her stable to protect her cow against the weather. He was a thoughtful neighbor.

ISAAC'S COPY OF *The Co-operative Commonwealth in its Outlines: An Exposition of Modern Socialism* by Laurence Gronlund finally arrived. The author had been born in Copenhagen, Denmark, where he studied law at the University of Copenhagen before coming to America. After his arrival, Gronlund earned his living teaching German until he was admitted to practice law in Illinois.

Isaac did not see himself as a socialist, although many of the ideas he was reading were regarded by others as socialistic. He agreed with the Alliance position that farmers needed legislation to modify the economic structure of the nation and limit the power of the wealthy; however, farmers on the prairie, accustomed to helping one another, did not see planting cooperative fields as particularly unusual. He had heard that Edward Bellamy's *Looking Backward* was based primarily on Gronlund's concept of the Co-operative Commonwealth, and having found some of the ideas in Bellamy's novel worth considering, Isaac was curious to read Gronlund's book.

As Isaac understood it, Gronlund took the position that all Progressive societies tend as a matter of natural evolution toward a "New Social Order, a Social Democratic Order," which he called "the cooperative commonwealth." Gronlund believed that this "natural evolution" could be guided but not stopped. Isaac agreed with the author's criticism of the "mad chase after wealth" as a destructive force, harmful to any society in which it gains control. Among the many volumes in Isaac's library was Gibbon's seven-volume set of *The Rise and Fall of the Roman Empire*, and Isaac empathized with Gronlund's concerns that if left unchecked, the power of the wealthy could lead to a collapse of society such as that seen in the fall of the once seemingly invincible empire of Rome.[46]

As he laid Gronlund's book aside, Isaac looked forward to sharing some of what he had read with friends gathering to celebrate the holidays at the regular Albano Alliance meeting to be held that evening. He decided to dress up for the occasion and was pleased by the number of compliments he received upon his arrival. Although it was Christmas, it was also their regular meeting, with Alliance business to be conducted, and Isaac had carefully prepared some financial remarks for the occasion. He had hardly begun when he was cut short, and despite the reassurance he received from his chagrined supporters, he was embarrassed. Back home that night, he tried to blame his treatment on shallow folks who had arrived expecting only to celebrate. Still upset the next morning, he discussed resigning as secretary when his friend Will Campbell visited. Having concluded that was the right decision, Isaac spent the following day "straighten[ing] up Alliance books, ready for delivering over [at] next meeting and get[ting] rid of a thankless job." It raised his spirits to attend the oyster supper at Ice Stimatze's house that evening, joining about twenty-five guests to enjoy good food and conversation as they saw out the old year a few days early.

ISAAC WAS NOT a nonbeliever. He had been raised in a religious family, in a community in which the old Hain's Church had been the center of society from the earliest days. One of his sisters was a minister's wife, the other the daughter-in-law of a minister, and he utilized *Crudon's Concordence* in his own Bible study. His library contained other Christian books, among them Henry Ward Beecher's *Life of Jesus Christ*, and John Milton's *Paradise Lost*. He was impatient with ill-educated, long-winded preachers whose sermons delivered little spiritual substance. However, what he currently found most objectionable were clergymen who used their influence to mislead congregations about nonspiritual subjects; in particular, he objected to those preachers who were speaking against the Alliance, parading their opinions as divinely received truth.

Some accused the Farmers' Alliance movement of usurping the role of religious faith, but a contrary perspective was that the Alliance simply shared similar Christian principles of feeding the hungry, healing the sick, clothing the naked, and following the Golden Rule. In short, the Alliance "transformed religious traditions for its own political purposes."[47] Whether that was viewed as a positive combining of efforts or a mutual hostility about their competing roles varied.

Isaac spent New Year's Eve at Will Campbell's home, discussing how to confront the plague of personal mortgages that farmers could not escape, a financial entrapment from which innocent women and children suffered as much or more than the men who struggled to support them, so many women dying in childbirth and so many sickly babies.

Men like Isaac and Will realized that more was needed than increasing crop yields. The Alliance's goal of educating farmers was important, and bringing urban laborers and farmers together in an organization to lobby legislators might also be helpful. If churches spoke against the Alliance, or even went so far as to speak favorably of their particular favorite established political parties, that was another impediment. So long as the two old political parties held the balance of power, they had shown little interest in listening to smaller political parties like the ULP or to lobbyists speaking for farmers and laborers. The steps taken so far were only a start, and more ways to confront wealth and political power had to be found. His closing journal entry for 1889 reflected his concerns for the need to avoid antagonism among those trying to resolve the same inequities: "Thinking a good deal over the 'decline' and final ending of Alliance movement, religious prejudice and accompanying ignorance the father of its decline. Common Sense Societies (excluding religious fanaticism entirely) in demand to prosper."[48]

CHAPTER 7

1890

Convinced that farmers needed to exhibit a willingness to study and an openness to new ideas, Isaac Werner worried that many of his neighbors showed too little effort in both regards. The January 20 meeting at the rink in St. John, called to discuss organizing a county exchange,[1] attracted about one hundred, "most of them crowding around the stove, more restless and disorder that else, nothing much done towards organizing County exchange, too much ignorance and variance of views, no united action for want of state organ to drill in thinking[.]"[2] The large crowd seemed more interested in gossiping about the sugar mill debacle than discussing the business for which the meeting had been called. The same newspapers that had supported the development of the sugar industry were now ridiculing towns that had voted bonds for sugar mills, especially since the discovery that one of the companies showing success was actually "salting" its product with refined sugar to improve the quality. When the *Newton Republican* called the people of Pratt County "serfs" for voting bonds, a local man responded, "Let me ask in the name of common sense what right the press of Kansas has for denouncing the people for doing the very thing that they have been recommending."[3]

Isaac's belief in the importance of a well-informed membership, able to read and study issues impacting the success of their farms, was so strong

THE PLUTOCRAT AND HIS TOY.

"The Plutocrat and His Toy." Populists felt that wealthy men controlled the content of the large newspapers, so they established Populist newspapers to publish their own news stories. Populist cartoons often appeared in these newspapers. *County Capital*, November 26, 1897.

that on January 31, he "mailed [a] letter to L. L. Polk, our President, on educating members."[4]

It was difficult for a farmer to sort the nonsense from the valid ideas, and Isaac supplemented his reading from local newspapers with books by Populist leaders, currently reading William S. Morgan's book, *History of the Wheel and Alliance and the Impending Revolution.* The engraving of Morgan at the front of the book showed a rather handsome but surprisingly young-looking man with a moustache that, it might be suspected, had

William S. Morgan, author of *History of the Wheel and Alliance and the Impending Revolution,* whose signed photograph Isaac Werner had glued inside the cover of his journal.

been grown to add a few years to his appearance. His ideas, however, seemed quite mature, especially his opinion about the Farmers' Alliance's involvement in politics: "[These non-political organizations] . . . seem not to know that politics is the vital force of capital, the holy religion of combinations of wealth and corporate monopoly. . . . The average Congressman fears nothing but the ballot, and respects nothing but well-directed and ably-conducted political action." Regarding the press, Morgan wrote: "Newspapers that look to corporations and election committees for the greater part of their support . . . will pander to the policy and interest of those whose patronage they most enjoy. . . . [T]he seeds of error they succeed in sowing are left to germinate among the generations yet to come."[5] Isaac had always considered the importance of educating young people, but the impact of newspapers on future generations may never have occurred to him.

In the course of following Populist news in the local *County Capital,* Isaac learned that his friend Ben Webber had gotten into another mess. A tradesman in St. John and a traveling cigar salesman had entered into a swap of ponies for cigars, and Ben had been entrusted to hold the local man's span of ponies[6] in escrow until the cigars were delivered. Instead, Ben bought the ponies directly from the cigar salesman, and with Ben's money in hand, the man absconded without delivering the cigars. Understandably angry, the owner of the ponies assaulted Ben and was arrested and taken to jail in Hutchinson because he had been unable to pay the fine for fighting. Title to the ponies was now in dispute.

Sometimes Isaac doubted whether enough of his generation had the good judgment to avoid foolish mistakes like Ben had just made or like some members at the Farmers' Alliance Christmas Meeting had shown in ignoring business in order to start celebrating. Yet watching young scholars bent over their books at the schoolhouse, trying to learn as much as they could in their shortened, winter sessions, always gave him hope for the future. Schooling ended for most country children with the eighth grade, at least four years less than Isaac had received. Somehow, most of them managed to learn a great deal. Children in town, who were not needed to help with planting in the spring and harvesting in the fall as farm children were, attended longer school terms. Isaac believed that both the country and city children were the region's best hope for the future.

He was proud of the leadership Kansas had shown in higher education. Early political efforts to encourage education in the agricultural areas of the nation had eventually led to passage of the Morrill Act in 1862 to establish "land-grant colleges," which were mandated to teach practical agriculture, science, and engineering without excluding classical studies. The act was intended to provide working-class students with a liberal, but practical education. The Hatch Act of 1887 authorized federal funds to establish agricultural experiment stations administered by the land-grant colleges. Professor E. M. Shelton, with whom Isaac corresponded, was the first director of the agricultural experiment station at Kansas State College. A particular mandate was given to these experiment stations for studying soil mineral and plant growth, ideas that aligned exactly with Isaac's own. Whereas Michigan and Pennsylvania had earlier state land-grant institutions, and Iowa was the first legislature to accept the provisions of the federal Morrill Act, it was Kansas State College that actually became the first federal land-grant college on February 16, 1863. Isaac saw that as evidence of the progressive nature of Kansas. He wrote to William Morgan and Professor Shelton to suggest using local Farmers' Alliances to collect soil samples, crop information, and weather statistics to assist experiment stations.

Isaac missed having the Bentley family nearby, but their hopes of returning to their claim someday had been abandoned, and Mrs. Bentley came back in February to retrieve the last of the belongings left in their house.[7] Isaac transported the Bentley's belongings to the Macksville train station, and as he and Mrs. Bentley unloaded the crates and boxes onto the station platform and said their awkward goodbyes, the two friends understood they would probably never see each other again. He left her waiting for the nine o'clock train.

Not every farmer struggling to survive had someplace else to go for help or a fresh start. Some Alliance members were in desperate situations, with months left before any crops could be raised or garden produce harvested. Isaac wrote letters to state Farmers' Alliance president Clover and local county Alliance presidents suggesting loans "to buy groceries and blacksmithing for . . . weaker brothers" until another crop could be raised. Without assistance, Isaac warned that these neighbors would either starve or be forced to give up their claims.[8]

Yet, the hard times had not made everyone lose their sense of humor. An unsigned story appeared in the February 20 *County Capital,* describing a joke played on an unnamed man, but everyone in Albano Township knew that Isaac was the subject of the joke. As he often did when he read a book with ideas he found relevant, Isaac had shared ideas from *Looking Backward.*[9] The correspondent wrote:

> At a recent public Alliance meeting, one of the single members expatiated quite extensive on the advanced ideas contained in Edward Bellamy's *Looking Backward*, and especially the period when it would be proper for the women to propose to the men. Since that meeting the marriageable ladies of that neighborhood have decided to help the coming of that period by auctioning off the gentleman among themselves . . . or make him agree never again to open his mouth about *Looking Backward.*

Isaac chose to ignore the joke.

He was restless, continuing to play with the idea of joining "a cooperative country . . . Sinaloa or Waukesha Colony the main subject of study."[10] The term "cooperative" was used in various ways. In addition to the business cooperatives where farmers organized to market their own produce, there were the informal agreements among neighbors sharing labor and expenses to plant cooperative fields. Sinaloa in Mexico, and Waukesha in Ohio, were colonies in which private ownership did not exist, a far more extreme idea.

In mid-March, Isaac and William Blanch began plowing a "co-operative tator patch" with Blanch's mules. Without really deciding yay or nay about joining a cooperative colony, Isaac had fallen into the familiar spring work of selling his seed potatoes and planting another year's crop. Doing something, whether or not it proved profitable, was better than all the moping around he had been doing, and the idea of cooperating with Blanch with one field of potatoes was something new to try.

The cooperative idea of establishing local farmers' exchanges continued to be discussed locally, and when president Benson, the head of the Kansas Alliance Exchange, came to St. John to speak, a crowd of nearly two hundred gathered to listen. Other states were ahead of Kansas in that effort, but making the exchanges work was difficult, with banks reluctant to loan money for operating capital.

Isaac's interest in cooperative colonies continued, and one day as he and Blanch were working, a representative of the Sinaloa Colony in Mexico arrived by buggy at Isaac's farm. The man had brought photographs as part of his promotion, which Isaac found interesting: "Such a strange looking country to me, with its scrubby, semi-tropical vegetation and its natives[.]"[11] Both Isaac and Blanch subscribed a twenty-dollar share in the Kansas Sinaloa Investment Company before the man left.

The Topolobampo Cooperative Colony in Sinaloa was the dream of Albert Kimsey Owen, a railroad surveyor and civil engineer who was sent to Mexico's west coast to look for harbor sites where ships might connect with railroads. He discovered Topolobampo Bay near Los Mochis, Sinaloa, Mexico. Having lived for a time in his youth at the utopian colony in New Harmony, Indiana, Owen visualized a cooperative colony operated under principles he called "integral co-operation." He devised a system based on credits rather than cash. Settlers were expected to renounce private wealth and adhere to a rigid schedule of eight hours of sleep, eight hours of work, and eight hours of culture and entertainment. The first colonists had arrived in 1886, about four years before Isaac saw the results of their labors in pictures taken by the colony's official photographer, Ira Kneeland.[12]

It was almost as if the possibility of escaping to the Mexican utopia gave Isaac new hope and energy for working his own farm. Within a few days Isaac had sold nearly all of his seed potatoes, the only ones remaining having been spoken for. The days had a predictable pattern for spring—the same crops and field work, the same strong winds blowing off roofs and displacing young plants and newly planted seeds, the same prairie fires started by fools. Yet instead of making plans to sell or lease his claims and move to Sinaloa, Isaac began planning improvements to his farm.

Making improvements required capital, however. When banker George H. Burr stopped by Isaac's farm one afternoon to propose a loan of $700, Isaac declined. With what he already owed Burr secured by his farm property, he realized that the banker might have offered such a large loan in anticipation of an unavoidable default, making the proposition merely as a way to acquire the farm at foreclosure. Whether Isaac's suspicion was credible or not, he was relieved to have declined increasing his debt.

When he awoke one morning to find his young roan horse Baldy "cold dead by fodder stack and Jim keeping him company," the temporary enthusiasm he had been feeling was dampened. Yet it was his nature to keep going, and so he "[b]uried him and prepared to fence off cane piles, as said to kill horses after much freezing, too much indigestible stalk shell in it."[13]

Isaac's correspondence with Mary Elizabeth Lease had continued, and a recent letter from her described how busy she was with nightly speaking in Wichita. Her fees seemed to be providing a good living, but her speaking also provided desperate farmers with a powerful advocate for their cause.

Another strong source of Progressive advocacy was a newspaper published in Winfield, Kansas, *The American Nonconformist and Kansas Industrial Liberator*. Commonly known as the *Nonconformist,* brothers Henry, Leopold (Leo), and Cuthbert Vincent edited and published the paper.[14] They declared that it was the "people's paper," more concerned with political principles that mundane local news. The Vincents gained a reputation as radicals when they published articles defending the men arrested in the Haymarket Riot, as well as crusading against monopolies, championing the rights of colored men, and supporting women's rights and suffrage. They did not, however, support Prohibition. Lease had begun selling subscriptions to the *Nonconformist* at the close of her lectures, and Isaac was a subscriber.[15]

The political activism advocated by the *Nonconformist* appealed to farmers who believed more was needed than the idealism expressed in the Farmers' Alliance and Industrial Union Declaration of Principles. Although the Alliance's political committees did lobby Congress, it was not a political party. Their approach was more idealistic and self-reliant, stressing education and the personal character of members. Their goals were:

1. To labor for the education of agricultural classes in the science of economical government, in a strictly nonpartisan spirit.
2. To develop a better state mentally, morally, socially, and financially.
3. To create a better understanding for sustaining civil officers maintaining law and order.
4. To strive constantly to secure entire harmony and good-will among all mankind and brotherly love among ourselves.
5. To suppress personal, local, sectional, and national prejudices, all unhealthy rivalry, and all selfish ambition.

Later, an additional principle was added: "To exercise charity toward offenders, to construe words and deeds in their most favorable light, granting honesty of purpose and good intentions to others; and to protect the principles of the Alliance unto death. Its laws are reason and equity, its cardinal doctrines inspire purity of thought and life, and its intentions are peace on earth and good will toward men."[16]

Although the principles expressed by the Alliance were worthy, younger men, like Morgan and the Vincent brothers, were urging the power of politics. The Union Labor Party had succeeded in electing some candidates in the 1888 elections, but many members of the Alliance movement were beginning to think that a new, third party should be formed, with the primary constituency being farmers. The Vincent brothers were a strong voice for that movement.[17]

On June 12, 1890, eighty-four delegates met in Topeka, Kansas, to organize a state People's Party and to lay the groundwork for a nominating convention to select candidates for each of the state's seven congressional districts.[18] Although it was transforming itself into a political party, the convention delegates adopted the old St. Louis lobbying platform of the Alliance as the political platform of the new state People's Party.

Isaac followed that political news, but his personal concerns were more immediate, as his journal entry for June 20 reflects:

> I started with 25 bushels corn to St. John, tiresome trips to man and beast. Got 21 cents a bushel, borrowed $20.00 out of First National and paid my taxes (last day of grace). Real [property] taxes on my homestead $24.91, last ½ of Personal [taxes] $3.11 with first half $3.11 paid on Dec. 23rd. Makes my tax for 1889 about $32.10, or corn at 20 cents a bushel just 160 bushels of corn for me to live under such a liberal Republican rotten government, occupying a 160 acre proved up [farm] & 4 work horses and necessary implements, or one bushel of corn tax to the acre of land.[19]

The need to borrow money in order to pay his taxes on the last day was still on his mind the following night when he was elected assistant lecturer at the local Alliance meeting, feeling none too flattered, as there was "hardly anybody hankering for [that] office."

A CRYPTIC ENTRY in Isaac's journal on July 10 read, "Second refusal from Lena," followed by a reference to Vermillion County, Illinois.[20] It appeared that a long-distance courtship that his Kansas neighbors never suspected had ended for the prairie bachelor. Whatever his feelings were, there was no further mention of Lena, neither to his friends nor in his journal.

Wes Logan was one friend to whom Isaac might have been expected to share the secret of his long-distance romance, but when Wes came the next morning to alert Isaac to be on the lookout for a thief, apparently nothing was said about the refusal from his lady friend in Illinois. Local thefts had become a problem, and in communities where everyone knew their neighbors, the idea that someone they knew might be a thief was appalling. The thefts in East Naron Township, just to the south, had become so bad that old Bill Fisher[21] wrote about them in his newspaper column. Neighbors did not know whether it was one person or a set of thieves, but it had begun about a year before when a heifer was taken out of a pasture. People chose to believe the thief was a stranger, but during the winter L. H. Naron had a young horse taken from his stable, and whoever took the horse knew which bridle belonged to that horse when it was taken from among all the other bridles. After that the thefts began happening more often, until nearly everyone in East Naron had lost something. The neighbors had resolved to keep their eyes open for each other, and they hoped William Fisher Brown's newspaper column written under his pseudonym "Old Bill Fisher," would put more people on the lookout.

FOLLOWING THE ESTABLISHMENT of the Kansas People's Party in June, Pratt County had chosen their slate of nominees on July 15, and two days later enthusiastic crowds arrived in Pratt. Isaac had used his trip to bring a load of corn to town, and after selling it for twenty-five cents a bushel, Isaac joined the supporters filling the streets, "streaming into town from all directions, and by 9 streets crowded and procession formed over a mile long up Main Street, and wheeled back lead by St. John Band . . . 2 flying swings and some 8 stands, and several extra eating concerns opened, all hungry for dinner . . . some 3000 people in attendance."[22] A grass-roofed shelter offered shade from the hot sun for those gathered to hear Knights of Labor national lecturer Ralph Beaumont, a newspaper editor from Oklahoma City instrumental in leading people of his state away from a coalition with the Democrats, speak for three hours to a crowd estimated at between two thousand and three thousand people. Isaac admired the well-dressed crowd, particularly some of the attractive younger ladies, and he was especially pleased to meet one of the Vincent brothers of the Winfield *Nonconformist.*

While at the rally, Isaac noticed a man with an amateur photography outfit, and after introducing himself, he discovered that the photographer was Seth Blake, who lived only seven miles south of Isaac's homestead. A quick friendship formed, and the next day Blake visited Isaac's farm in his cart, bringing his camera with him. They got on so well that they began constructing a dark tent and exposed two experimental dry plate views of Isaac's farm. In the following days, his friendship with Blake continued, and Isaac's farm became a popular place for neighbors to gather to have photographs taken. Blake even photographed what Isaac called "the first Co-operative Tator Patch & Force at digging in Stafford County." Later that evening the men brought in about thirty bushels from Isaac's patch and began digging at Logan's and Blanch's patches.

Following Pratt County's example, people gathered in St. John for the Stafford County People's Party Convention, and Isaac and Will Campbell attended with two other neighbors. The first order of business was election of officers, interspersed with singing and cheering until after midnight. Food and beds were at a premium, and many didn't go to bed at all. When the session resumed at eight o'clock the next morning, unfinished business was quickly completed, and the convention to select the People's Party ticket for the county offices convened. Campbell was chosen for representative on the first informal ballot, and the other offices were filled in rotation, the proceedings harmonious. Isaac noted in his journal that on the historic date of the first People's Party Convention in Stafford County, the new corn was suffering and old corn was bringing twenty-nine cents a bushel, wheat sixty-seven cents a bushel, and oats twenty-three cents.

Not only were crop prices down, it was beginning to look like the worst droughty summer since Isaac had come to Kansas. No one ever expected the thirty inches of annual rainfall that real estate speculators had promised naïve settlers, and the truth was that rainfall fluctuated widely from year to year and area to area. What was unheard of, however, was the Arkansas River being completely dry, as it now was. Part of that was caused by the increase in diversions upstream, but part of it was also due to the drought, and seeing that riverbed dry made everyone anxious.

There was only so much that a farmer could do in such dry conditions, and one day, to take his mind off his worries, Isaac started reading a new novel, *Caesar's Column,* written by Ignatius Loyola Donnelly, an organizer of the Minnesota Farmers' Alliance.[23] Donnelly's imagination had led him to some outlandish scientific theories,[24] but it served him well as an author

Ignatius Donnelly, Minnesota Populist and the author of *Caesar's Column*. Courtesy Wikimedia Commons.

of fiction. His novel, set in the future, imagined what could happen if the inequitable disparity between the moneyed class and the workers resulted in a war. The story was intended as a warning that the "blind, brutal and degrading worship of mere wealth, must—given time and pressure enough—eventuate in the overthrow of society and the destruction of civilization."[25] The present day was not likely to produce a class war, but Isaac did find many interesting social ideas in Donnelly's novel, particularly the concluding pages describing the settlement created by farmers and other workers who had managed to flee the devastation of the futuristic war.

After putting the novel aside, Isaac was pleased to receive the news that the Belpre Farmers' Alliance had elected Maggie Byrne lecturer of their sub-Alliance.[26] He applauded the involvement of women in the People's Party movement, although they still lacked the right to cast a vote in state and national elections.

Returning from mailing a letter to the *Commoner* about establishing an Alliance manufacturing company in Kansas, Isaac learned of the death of his long-time neighbor Jerome Vosburgh. Too late to attend the funeral held at Gullet School, Isaac joined about forty others at Neelands Cemetery for the burial. He felt the graveside service had been conducted in a hurry, without much ceremony, neighbors anxious to get back to pressing work. It was not uncommon for services to be held the day after death, as Vosburgh's had been, but sometimes news passed by word of mouth was slow to reach everyone, and Isaac was glad he learned of his friend's death in time to pay his respects at the graveside.

A sad and humiliating notice of the public auction for unpaid taxes appeared in the August 21 issue of the *County Capital*, with twenty-four Albano owners and forty-eight Clear Creek owners named. Good farmers and honorable men were facing public auction of their farms if they couldn't come up with what they owed in real property taxes. If Isaac had been unable to borrow the twenty dollars he used to pay his taxes on the last day, his name might have been among them. He believed the disgrace belonged not to the hardworking farmers on the list, but to the system that made it impossible for farmers to make a living.[27]

Despite the financial difficulties stalking nearly everyone in the community, gambling could still be found. On August 23 in St. John, a much-needed shower flooded the streets, soaking everyone—including attendees at a horse race. Isaac's opinions were expressed in his journal at length:

> Horse racing and original package system getting disgusting. The majority of attendees got a good soaking, but could not soak near all the whisky out of some. Ben Webber, [the] Wilsons, and Ed Landes the leaders, and some trickery and dissatisfaction, quarreling and knifing, as usual. . . . [T]he thought makes one feel like such doing should be strictly prohibited by law. If some of those wretched could be served with photographs taken while in their stupid condition, some time afterwards, they might get ashamed to repeat such conduct afterwards.[28]

The explanation for drunkenness in a dry state rested upon a U.S. Supreme Court ruling in April of 1890 upholding the interstate-commerce clause that allowed liquor shipped into a Prohibition state to be sold one time only, so long as it remained in its "original package." Liquor dealers in Missouri used that ruling to open the market to Kansas, their dry-state neighbor. The results were "original package houses" and "Supreme Court saloons," with sales of liquor in whatever "original packages" the Missouri dealers could devise.[29]

The temperance movement had always been strong in Kansas. The ethnic-religious influence had a political impact—the Protestant English, Welsh, Scotch-Irish, and Scandinavian settlers most likely to oppose liquor and vote Republican, whereas the German, Irish, and Eastern-European immigrants,were more likely to be Lutherans and Catholics, willing to condone the prudent use of liquor and vote Democrat. There were also those who supported the Prohibition Party, a smaller but important political party that included other issues besides Prohibition on its agenda. The "original package" ruling resulted in a series of legal maneuvers between state and federal officials, but at the time of the horse race, it remained the law, and some places in the community apparently provided "refreshments."

The rain, as a good soaking always did, gave farmers new hope for planting, and spirits in the community rose a little. When Doc Dix came out from Pratt to visit, he convinced Isaac to try hog raising again, their deal being that Doc would buy the pigs from George Hall, and Isaac would provide the corn and labor to fatten them. On his way to Hall's place, Isaac went by Ben Webber's farm to collect the payment for the eighty bushels of Mrs. Bentley's corn delivered weeks ago. He had sold the corn to Ben at twenty cents a bushel—well below the current market price—and he was determined to collect. His demand for payment was again ignored.

Summer drew to a close and Isaac's days fell into their autumn patterns of marketing wheat, paying interest to avoid foreclosure, and sorting potatoes, many of which were rotted—not surprising, since he was still digging potatoes on August 25.[30] The distractions of photography and politics had hurt his farm.

The previous February, in support of the passage of the pension bill by the House, Campbell had published a stirring tribute to the Union veterans of the Civil War in the *County Capital.* Now, when the Senate refused to pass the bill sent over by the House, Campbell responded with another emotion-filled article:

> The men who once stood up like a wall of stone, no longer command the respect of Congress. We have given a service pension to the soldiers of all other wars, but the boys in blue must stand aside at the behest of Wall Street. . . . We have millions to loan to national bankers, without interest, but nothing for the men who wrecked their lives that this government might live.

Campbell closed with a warning to Republicans: "The fire still burns in the soldier's heart. . . and if they do not rise in their might, and teach those truckling huxters [sic] who now fill our national Congress a lesson, then I do not understand the temper of the citizen soldier of the U.S."[31] Many Union soldiers had settled in Stafford County and they had consistently voted Republican in honor of their old commander-in-chief, President Lincoln. With elections drawing closer, Campbell's message was a call to his fellow Union soldiers to step away from the party they had supported in battles and ballot boxes if the Republican Senate thought so little of their sacrifice as to defeat the pension bill.

AFTER A FEW DAYS of working at home, Isaac left for Larned with a wagonload of corn, arriving at dusk amid the novelty of electric lights. The next morning, he explored the town before selling his corn. Governor Humphrey was speaking in the Larned Opera House, and Isaac was curious to hear him.

Lyman U. Humphrey had been elected in 1888 with the greatest plurality ever given a Kansas governor, winning the majority in every county but two. Like most Republican politicians, he had served the Union in the Civil War, and part of the respect voters had for Humphrey rested on his remarkable military reputation. He had enlisted at the age of seventeen, and despite his youth had quickly been promoted to first sergeant, then second, and first lieutenant, serving in battles that were familiar names to every American, among them Shiloh, the siege of Vicksburg, the Battle of Lookout Mountain, the Battle of Atlanta, Sherman's March to the Sea, and the final surrender of Gen. Joseph E. Johnston's army. When Humphrey was mustered out at Louisville, Kentucky, in July of 1865, he was six days shy of his twenty-first birthday.

Humphrey's mother, widowed in 1853, could offer few financial resources to her two sons, and although Humphrey managed after the war to attend a term at Mount Union College, followed by a year in the law department of the University of Michigan, when his funds were exhausted he left school to go west, settling first in Shelby County, Missouri. He taught school there and assisted in publishing the *Shelby County Herald* while continuing to study law on his own. In 1870 he was admitted to the Missouri bar, and he soon moved to Independence, Kansas, where he founded the *South Kansas Tribune*. A year and a half later he sold the *Tribune* to begin practicing law full time, and in 1884 he joined other prominent men in founding the Commercial Bank of Independence, serving as its president. He had held a series of Republican posts before being elected governor, and he seemed unbeatable in the coming election.[32]

The election season was beginning to gain momentum, and in Pratt, Isaac heard one of the Vincent brothers from Winfield give a rousing speech to a crowd of about a thousand. Their newspaper continued to gain political influence as the Populist movement grew.

Hopeful that Ben Webber might finally have some cash available, Isaac took twenty bushels of corn to Ben's farm. However, he demanded to be paid for the eighty bushels of Mrs. Bentley's corn delivered months earlier before unloading what he had brought. Angry when Ben asked for further credit, Isaac refused, "teaching him (the drunkard and gambler he is) that his promises or personal bank checks aint money for me to unload without pre-payment."[33]

With the end of October nearing, political activity increased, and Isaac and Seth Blake decided to photograph People's Party rallies. Their first expedition began at Harter's Ranch, where the Livingston and East Albano sub-Alliances were forming for the St. John rally. They joined the procession as far as the St. John depot, but once in town, they hurried to take positions on the balcony of the Arcade Hotel to photograph the procession entering the square.

When the procession ended, people assembled to hear the first speaker, a "colored" man from Topeka, whom Isaac found to be "quite satisfactory."[34] There were more older men and women in the crowd, which Isaac interpreted as a sign of broadening interest in the People's Party. Having been given the honor of speaking last, Campbell was greeted enthusiastically as he sought to be returned for a second term in the Kansas House, this time on the People's Party ticket.

Still feeling the previous day's excitement of being part of perhaps the largest crowd ever seen in St. John, Isaac left with Stephen Frazee for Pratt at daylight, joining a crowd of close to a thousand gathered in the rink to hear Sarah E. Van de Vort Emery, the author of *Seven Financial Conspiracies which have Enslaved the American People*. Isaac was pleased that she had finally traveled to speak near enough for him to attend. He wasn't sure exactly what he had expected, but he was surprised by the woman's "plain, motherly way and distinct voice." Emery's matronly appearance and style lacked the flamboyance and drama of Mary Elizabeth Lease. Yet "in a plain, motherly way and distinct voice she commenced addressing crowd, holding them closely (despite the crying babies) for over 2 hours."[35] In this calm, motherly voice, she said, "From earliest times the one class has lived by tilling the sod, raising flocks and herds, delving in mines, working in wood, brass and iron . . . . The other class consisted of roving bandits, who under chiefs or leaders subsisted by swooping down upon and plundering the honest toilers." After elaborating on the bandits of old, she continued: "The civilized brigandage is carried on under more euphonious titles, and new methods of robbery are employed. Instead of 'robber king' and 'brigand chief' we have today the money king, the coal king, the cattle king, the railroad magnate, the telegraph monopolist and the lumber baron. Instead of spoils and plunders, we have interests, dividends, revenues and rents."[36]

With careful detail, Emery described the class inequities and how the provisions enacted by the founding fathers had been eroded.[37] Her explanations may have been too lengthy for the crowd to recall the details, but many of them were already familiar with the seven conspiracies from having read her book. She concluded her speech with these words: "History proves that nothing has been so disastrous to nations as the enactment of laws which favor the few at the expense of the many. There is not robbery so suicidal as that sanctioned by law; for it not only destroys the morality of the legalized robber, starves and kills the victimized masses, but it degrades the lawmaker himself to a level with the most notorious highwayman."[38]

When Emery stopped speaking, the respectful audience wore the exhausted expressions of those whose brains had been spent as surely as a runner's legs at the end of a marathon. When R. D. Jones of Odina, Missouri, followed her to the podium, the tired crowd began drifting away. His speaking was postponed until evening, when Society Hall was comfortably filled to hear Jones speak.

Back at his farm to tend to chores, Isaac's biggest achievement was finally getting twenty dollars from Ben for the Bentley corn.

Continuing their decision to photograph People's Party rallies, Blake and Isaac laid their plans for the Pratt rally like a military maneuver, arriving the night before to be ready to photograph the earliest crowds. Before people began to gather the next morning, Isaac shaved and went to Logan's gallery for a sitting, his first formal photograph in fifteen years. Then it was time to get the cameras rigged for the day. Isaac's assignment was to go over to the east side of town to photograph the Saratoga delegation and return quickly and set up for the parade. Using three cameras, Blake and Isaac, joined by a third photographer, took about thirty exposures. The *Pratt County Register* declared the day a complete success, with a crowd of five thousand, and eight hundred vehicles in the procession.[39]

The People's Party platform had been published regularly in the *County Capital* during the weeks leading up to the election, so no one could claim with any credibility that they were unaware of where the People's Party of Kansas stood.[40] Summarized briefly, the platform provided:

> LABOR. "Labor is the beginning of progress, the foundation of wealth, and the laborer is entitled to a good living and a fair share of the profits which result from his labor."

LAND. "The earth is the common heritage of the people; . . . [who are entitled] to a place to live and earn a living."

PENSIONS. "We favor a service pension to every Union soldier and sailor, and . . . that the depreciated currency in which they were paid should be made good . . ."

DEMANDS. We demand. . .

1. . . . the abolition of national banks and the substitution of legal tender Treasury notes in lieu of national bank notes . . .
2. . . . free and unlimited coinage of silver.
3. . . . laws as shall effectually prevent the dealing in futures in all agricultural and mechanical productions . . .
4. . . . laws prohibiting alien ownership of land . . .
5. . . . taxation, national or State, shall not be used to build up one interest or class at the expense of another . . .
6. . . . a sufficient amount of fractional paper currency to facilitate exchange through the medium of the United States mail.
7. . . . communication and transportation shall be owned by and operated in the interest of the people, as is the United States postal system.
8. . . . effectually prevent the extortion of usurious interest . . .
9. . . . a reasonable stay of execution in all cases of foreclosure of mortgages on real estate, and a reasonable extension of time before the confirmation of Sheriff's sales.
10. . . . effectually prevent the organization or maintenance of trusts and combines for purposes of speculation . . .
11. . . . salaries of public officials to correspond with existing financial conditions . . .
12. . . . adoption of the Australian System of voting and the Crawford system of primaries.

The last demand was a reference to changes in procedural election matters. The idea of using a preprinted ballot, with provision for voters to mark their ballots in secret, had originated in Australia in the 1850s, which explains the name used. The Australian ballot soon became known as a secret ballot, which became the accepted means for casting votes. The origins of the Crawford primary system can be traced to Crawford County, Pennsylvania, and was devised to avoid irregularities in the selection of nominees by intermediaries who might engage in bargaining or trickery during the selection process. Under the Crawford primary system, township voters would assemble to cast individual ballots for their preferred candidates, with the person receiving a plurality of all the votes cast becoming the designated nominee.

The People's Party rallies had definitely brought out the crowds, and the speakers had been quite satisfactory, but in Isaac's opinion no one could compare to Mary Elizabeth Lease. She had traveled all over Kansas speaking out against Senator John James Ingalls, making 160 speeches during the campaign season and exciting crowds like no other speaker could.[41] If Ingalls were defeated, Isaac believed that she deserved a great deal of credit for his downfall.[42]

Election Day in Albano Township dawned fair and pleasant, bringing out sixty-six voters, but at the end of the day, Isaac was disappointed by the mixed voting, despite the fact that most of the People's Party candidates won. Isaac was elected town clerk with thirty-five votes to his opponent William Frack's twenty-nine, a wider margin than Campbell received in his home township, receiving only three more votes than his opponent. All victories amounted to a scant majority of the sixty-six votes cast, leaving Isaac feeling that "prejudice and ignorance prevailing to too large an extent, all working in favor of the Money Power."[43] Nearly half of those who had voted returned in the evening to wait for the votes to be tallied, with most focus being on Campbell's race, which had been so nasty during the campaign. By eight o'clock everyone had headed home, the losers crestfallen and the victors subdued in their jubilation, given the slim margins.

Knowing the date when another group of settlers was departing from Enterprise, Kansas, for Topolobampo, Isaac experienced a feeling of melancholic wanderlust. One hundred sixty-five men, women, and children were leaving that day while he was left at home to ponder the hog market. Isaac and Doc soon chose a cloudy day to butcher the hogs. Isaac got three hundred pounds as his share, and computing half a bushel of corn a day for feed, it had cost him fifteen dollars to fatten them. Gaining three hundred pounds of meat at seven cents a pound, calculated as either cost saved from not having to buy pork or revenue earned if he sold the pork, he felt he had come out about even, if his labor was worth anything.

Isaac was angered when a neighbor chose a different way to feed his family. On a drizzly mid-November day, the neighbor rode along Isaac's tree rows in his buggy, shooting the half-tame quails Isaac fed. At Isaac's appearance, the man left without a confrontation but returned the next day. Isaac stopped work to pencil "No Shooting" notices for posting around his property.[44]

Around the same time, the entertainment of neighbors coming to Isaac's farm on Sundays for photographs had ended because Blake had failed to deliver the photographs already taken. Blake still continued to come with his equipment, but Isaac doubted that his neighbors would bother to sit for any more pictures until the existing exposures were printed.

Isaac had delayed traveling to St. John to return his certificate as township clerk and complete the paperwork necessary to serve bond for John Hilmes, but finally he arranged his work to be gone for the day. It was a severe hardship for farmers to risk going the security for successful candidates, but candidates running for office were required to secure others to post bond for them, should they be elected. These friends and neighbors did so believing they would never be called upon to compensate for any wrongdoings committed by their friends. Campbell and Ice Stimatze had agreed to secure the bond of $300 required for Isaac's own election as township clerk, and in turn, Isaac committed $500 toward the $3,000 required for Hilmes's election as probate judge.

The shared interest in politics was at the core of Isaac's friendship with Will Campbell, and the two men enjoyed newspaper descriptions of that 1890 Kansas election as "a Waterloo to the Republican party." Republicans had retained only two of the state's seven congressmen, and Senator Ingalls had lost after eighteen years in the Senate. The People's Party had won ninety-one seats in the state legislature, to only twenty-six for the Republicans and a mere eight for the Democrats. Yet, many were disappointed that the People's Party had not taken the governor's office as well.

Despite the election successes, a disturbing set of statistics remained. The 1890 census reports showed that 60 percent of the taxed acres in Kansas were mortgaged, a far greater percentage than any other state. The per capita private debt in Kansas was found to be four times more than that of the nation as a whole. With Kansans deeper in debt that anyone else, the newly elected People's Party candidates faced quite an economic challenge, and it would be difficult to implement reforms.

GRADUALLY, MORE HOMESTEADS in his community had been proved up, and Isaac had served as a witness for several neighbors. He obliged Isabel Ross in making the final proof for her homestead claim, and while in St. John he bought lumber for the corner book cupboard he had agreed to build for

This image of William Peffer was taken about 1905–1906, several years after he displaced long-serving Republican senator John James Ingalls. Senator Peffer was elected on the People's Party ticket.

the Alliance to hold their literature. He also attended a special county Alliance meeting that accomplished little except drafting demands for legislation to be sent to the newly elected senator, William A. Peffer.

Peffer had shocked a great many people when he displaced Senator Ingalls. Like Isaac, Peffer was born in Pennsylvania. He had begun teaching school by the time he was fifteen, but when news of the California gold rush reached him, the young man headed for San Francisco. Failing to make his fortune in gold, Peffer headed back eastward but stopped before reaching his former home state of Pennsylvania. In his early thirties, he enlisted as a Union soldier, advancing through the ranks from private to judge advocate of the military commission. He studied law during his service and was admitted to the bar when he was discharged, and after practicing for a few years in Tennessee, he moved to Kansas in 1870. There he started his career as a journalist, while continuing to practice law. Typical of many Union soldiers, Peffer was a Republican during those years, even serving as a presidential elector in 1880. After editing daily newspapers, he became the editor of the *Kansas Farmer,* the state's leading agricultural journal, with a wider circulation than any other newspaper in Kansas. Through the *Kansas Farmer,* Peffer became well-known among Kansas farmers for his early advocacy of organizing to work together for political and economic reforms. Isaac was not only a reader but had also been published by Peffer.

When Peffer put himself forward to replace the powerful Republican senator Ingalls, many outsiders thought of him as an unknown lawyer from Coffcyvillc, Kansas, and didn't believe he stood a chance of displacing Ingalls. Kansas farmers, however, knew him well, and the reservoir of respect that he had built over the years as editor of the *Kansas Farmer* carried over into the polling place. National newspapers began to pay particular attention to Peffer, not only because he had surprised many of them by defeating Ingalls but also because he made such an amusing and identifiable subject for political cartoonists. He was tall and thin, preferring to dress in a black suit with boots and hat, but without collar or tie. However, what most distinguished him was the long beard that covered him from beneath his nose and cheeks nearly to his waist. He was an obvious choice for a cartoonist who wanted an image to represent a Populist, and soon Peffer became a figure known to newspaper readers across the country.

Having a Populist senator in Washington did little to change hard times locally. Isaac sold fifteen bushels of wheat in St. John for seventy-five cents a bushel but immediately used that money to pay half of his land taxes. As the year drew nearer to a close, Isaac felt the tedium and tiresomeness of his trips to town, and he would have preferred to postpone that day's trip but for his neighbors' increasingly common practice of letting their half-starved stock out to forage wherever grazing could be found. The need for fencing lumber to keep the stray stock away from his feed stacks necessitated the trip.

December was particularly difficult for Isaac, specifically the arrival of the holidays. He tried to keep his mind on the Alliance social scheduled for Christmas Eve, but his dear sister Emma had died the evening of the twenty-first, and her burial was to be that day. Emma was only sixteen months younger than her twin brothers, closer in age to them than to her younger sister Henrietta, and she had often tagged along after her older brothers. At the time of her death, Emma and her husband William were living in Philadelphia, but her body was being brought to Reading for burial in the Charles Evans Cemetery. Isaac had never considered the possibility of losing either sister before his own passing. Emma left behind four children, her daughters ages seventeen and fourteen and her sons only nine and four, but the picture in Isaac's mind as he grieved for his sister was of the sweet girl he had kissed goodbye when Emma was barely older than her oldest daughter was now.

Isaac was not one to reveal his emotions. He was hardly able to acknowledge them to himself, although he carefully wrote the day and time of Emma's death in his journal when he received the news, and her burial was also recorded on its date. He kept busy that day, shelling corn in the hennery granary and completing the fencing around a feed stack. When evening came, he dressed for the Alliance social and went to the schoolhouse, telling no one about his own grief and noting with pleasure in his journal the crowded attendance and the "pleasant time to all, long to be remembered by old and young."[45]

He paid no special attention to Christmas Day, and he kept busy during the following days working on the schoolhouse bookcase and installing "dinner shelves for scholars." George Hall and his hand, Holbrook, called on Sunday afternoon, and he spent most of one day writing a long letter to his brother Henry. He did not want his correspondence with his two remaining siblings to remain indifferent, if he could help it.

Despite cold and dampness that numbed his feet and hands and darkened his mood, Isaac was forced to travel to St. John before New Year's Eve to meet with Harry Ross and George Burr about his debt. It was a discouraging meeting for both sides, Isaac already paying what he could and the creditors recognizing that among their many rural debtors Isaac was doing as well as the best of them and better than many. Ironically, the last day of the year returned to pleasant spring-like weather, as if fate had chosen for Isaac the glummest day for his trip.

There was no New Year's Eve party in the community, and had it not been for the Alliance Christmas social, holiday celebrations would have been only the poor affairs families could afford for themselves. The brightest occasion for the struggling farmers had been the 1890 elections, and the only reason for hope in 1891 that Isaac could foresee was what the men they had elected could wrestle away from the moneyed class to give laborers a decent chance.

CHAPTER 8

1891

Kansas women still lacked the legal right vote, but by 1891 their active participation in the Populist movement was becoming commonplace in Isaac Werner's community and across the state. In a letter to the editor of the *County Capital*, one woman chided the women who did not support Populism as sluggards: "Don't you think it is a disgrace to allow your fathers, brothers and husbands to advance so far beyond you? . . . Are you not ashamed to let such a mighty strife of capital against labor, go on, and on, while you sit supinely by and do nothing?"[1]

This anonymous woman's outspokenness reflected the prevailing attitude of women who were part of the Alliance. They did not have the vote but they had a voice they were free to use, and if other women were not joining in the Populist cause, women like this one believed that farmwives unwilling to play an active role deserved shaming. For Alliance women, survival of their farms was their highest priority and Populism was their best hope. Prohibition and suffrage mattered to many of them, but saving their farms mattered more, and they prioritized the Alliance. As one Kansas woman pleaded to those women who said they were too busy or too tired, "Let your supper dishes go unwashed once a week, and come out to the Alliance. . . . Let the outside world see that wives, mothers and sisters have an interest in home outside and beyond washing dishes, milking and making butter and the general run of work in the home of a farmer."[2]

Isaac's support for women's rights had been firm for many years, and having seen the role women had assumed in the Farmers' Alliance had only reinforced his opinion. However, not all women in the Alliance agreed with giving women the vote. Speaking to the Chase County Alliance, one wife urged women to "be a man's help, comfort and sweetest, purest joy," but not "to vote or dabble in politics."[3]

Some middle-class women in towns and cities understood the differences between their lives and those of struggling farm women. Annie Diggs, who lived in Topeka, tried to speak for them, but often their lives were too different for comprehension.[4] Diggs intended *The Farmer's Wife,* a magazine of which she was a co-editor, to "elevate rural homes to a middle class standard," but the pages describing "fashionable summer resorts, European styles, and urban luxuries" had no relevance for farm women interested in falling market prices for their crops and ways to feed their children as shelves emptied and cash disappeared.[5] Many urban women considered cost-cutting measures in their family's budget to determine whether their daughter could take piano lessons or whether they could replace an old rug with a new Brussels carpet. Even within their own towns and cities, they neglected advocating to improve working-class women's issues, such as "long hours, pensions, and other protective policies."[6]

Annie Diggs was a suffragist, Prohibitionist, and active speaker for the Populist movement. Courtesy Kansas State Historical Society.

Urban women seeking suffrage tried to work within the two old parties, particularly the Republican Party, but one essay reveals how far removed that party's perspective was from the role of farm women. A Republican male author mocked Mary Elizabeth Lease and praised the "real women, the women to whom we go home," for keeping "our morals and our literature and our speech clean and pure."[7] These Republican men emphasized women's moral superiority and maternal influence, calling the Republican Party "the party of the home." Democrats emphasized "men's patriarchal control over their households," and were generally opposed to suffrage issues.[8] It was no wonder that farm women and middle-class urban women often misunderstood one another's circumstances.

A SHOCKING BURGLARY ATTEMPT in St. John distracted the attention of county residents from all other issues. On Monday morning, January 26, county officers arriving at the courthouse to begin work discovered that an attempt to breach the vault in the county clerk's office had occurred. Details were not immediately available, but that did not stop the rumormongers from espousing their own theories.

By Thursday, when the weekly *County Capital* came out, more details were known. Treasurer Ed Landes and other county officers had arrived at the courthouse about 7:00 A.M., and Landes had discovered papers scattered over his office floor. The door to the safe had been blown open, as well as the iron door to the vault, and although drilling had been attempted, the safe inside the vault that contained about $16,000 had not been breached. Because of the focus on the treasurer's office, the initial investigation had overlooked evidence in the county clerk's office, where three holes had been drilled in the clerk's vault door. A set of tools, all sorts of bits, two dark lanterns, a type of acid, and a basket of gunpowder had been left behind in the treasurer's office in the burglars' haste to get away. Inexplicably, the thieves instead took the treasurer's record book, perhaps to throw suspicion on Landes. However, Landes thought he could replicate the contents of the stolen journals from stubs and other records in the unopened county clerk's vault.

Distracting law enforcement officers from their investigation of the burglary was the robbery at the train depot the following night. At about 8:30 P.M., the night operator and the dispatcher were alone in the depot. They remembered hearing footsteps outside but took little notice when a man entered, assuming he wanted to purchase a ticket or send a dispatch. Instead, they were ordered to get their hands up, and the man's revolver claimed more of their attention than the appearance of the man holding it. He demanded money, and when the few dollars in the first drawer did not satisfy the robber, a second drawer with sixty dollars inside was opened. The man departed with the cash, leaving his frightened victims unharmed.

Sharing the front page of the *County Capital* that week was an article reprinted from *The Leader*, a monthly newspaper published in Wichita,

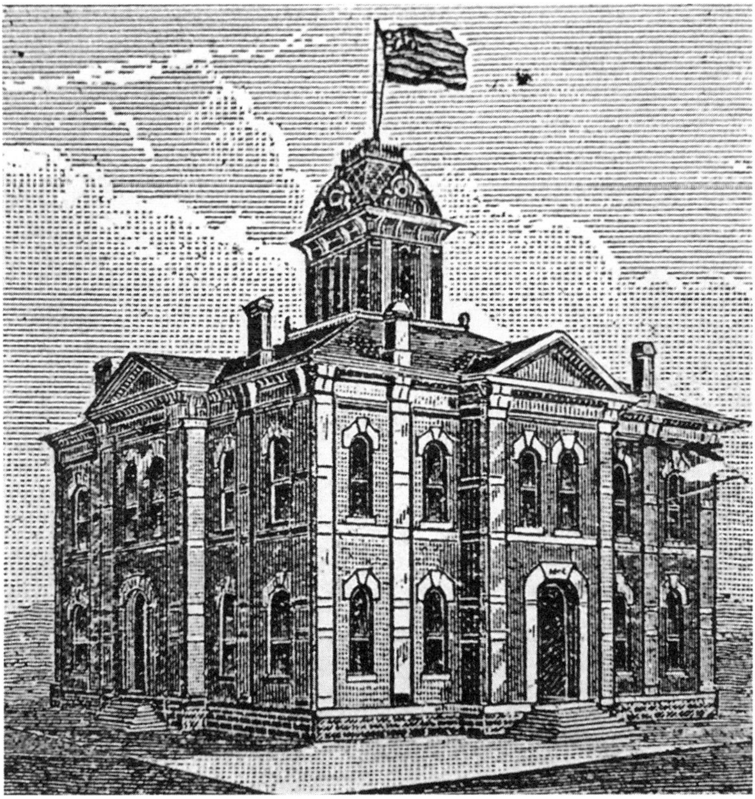

The beautiful St. John Courthouse, built by donations from the citizens of Stafford County. *County Capital*, June 8, 1888.

describing the benefits of a small town for rural communities to provide more self-sufficiency and less time wasted traveling to larger towns.[9] Isaac was the author, and he had used phonetic spelling to describe his rural utopia. Among Progressive ideas was the theory that it would be easier for illiterate and foreign-speaking workers to learn English if phonetic spelling were used in Progressive literature, and Isaac adopted the idea for his article to show its potential. He began by promoting cooperative reading clubs, which he believed would "soon lead to different cooperative communities . . . where farmers would decide upon starting the nucleus of a small town . . . under their own ownership and entire control, having their own store, hall for public meetings, elevator to store their own surplus grain, and slaughter house . . . besides minor industries deemed necessary in such localities."[10]

In addition to political efforts, some of Isaac's neighbors, particularly those who were Presbyterians, faced hard times by holding daily religious meetings at homes throughout the community. Clusters of a few wagons at certain homes could be seen most mornings. Describing what he had observed on January 30, Isaac wrote, "Yesterday at Ross's took it at first as a funeral gathering, some 4 wagons and teams congregated there A.M."[11] Some religious denominations had begun attacking Populism directly, calling it a "disease of lunatics" and "a great evil."[12] Others criticized Populists as having absorbed the "spiritual fire" that rightfully belonged to religion. Populists defended themselves by saying it was not religion but rather the actions and words of those who purported to speak for the churches with whom they disagreed, claiming that "churches distorted Christ, speaking more often in his name than in his voice." They pointed out that churches were ignoring the true role of faith by neglecting the needy and condoning usury, corruption, and industrial oppression.[13] Many also saw urban churches as "citified palaces.[14]

People were searching for anything that would relieve their current hardships, not only gathering for prayer but also meeting to discuss new approaches for just about every aspect of their lives. The day for the first County Reform Club meeting in St. John arrived, and because the idea for the organization had been Isaac's, it was not surprising that he was elected president, with D. M. Hunt, the county Alliance lecturer, chosen as secretary. After writing several letters to attendees, Isaac concluded that the group showed too little willingness to study reform ideas, so he chose to let the club die an early death. No further meetings were held.

Isaac instead turned his attention to his farm, where he had stored so much seed corn and other items in his living quarters that the basement ceiling was beginning to sag. He installed an extra brace for safety's sake, or as he wryly put it, "to avoid an unexpected second-rate funeral" if the upstairs caved in on top of him.[15] He did not entirely neglect his Progressive efforts closer to home, however, for he completed the book cupboard for the Alliance library and took it to the schoolhouse to install. His passion for books was beginning to take hold among his neighbors, and although the County Co-operative Club effort had failed, the local group Isaac had initiated was still active. Another of his articles had been published in *The Leader,* titled "Advanced Thoughts," advocating local reading clubs established to subscribe to the leading reform periodicals and meet in small groups to discuss what they read, which was exactly what he had started with his neighbors.[16] William Blanch and Stephen Frazee called on him to discuss future meetings and stayed to enjoy a literary time until midnight, talking politics, reform, and Shakespeare. Isaac would have been more than able to hold his own in discussing Shakespeare with his friends. As one journal entry of January 3 described, "I most the day reviewing books and Shakespeare, where several publishers combined in London to issue first complete edition and what reading that 1623 edition now is to us and our present mode of spelling, as abominable to what it may be in the near future with some proper effort."[17]

With nighttime temperatures still dropping below freezing, Isaac chose a day when the temperature rose to sixty degrees to walk the full half section of his homestead and timber claim, stepping off distances to estimate the amount of cultivatable land. Subtracting the acreage lost to roads and tree rows, he concluded he had 210 farmable acres, with eighty to one hundred best used for grazing and feed lots.

Days spent indoors because of feeling unwell were becoming more common, and Isaac used this time for correspondence and writing articles. Another article, this one titled "Better Farming," was published in *The Leader*.[18] The number of Populist newspapers and journals publishing Isaac's articles continued to grow. Because Isaac was chairman of a "Neck-tie Social" to raise money for the school and Alliance library, he had felt obligated to get out and make the arrangements, although he knew better. That decision lengthened his convalescence, and on February 15 he was forced to watch from indoors as Charles Shattuc's hogs rooted up his rye patch, searching for the few potatoes that had been missed when the crop was plowed.[19] Neighbors' cattle were also making free with his fields, leaving Isaac feeling that their stock fared better than his own, which he kept penned. Yet his health did not allow him to drive them away each time they trespassed. The next two weeks were a patchwork of sickness and attempts to work. For two days Isaac tried doing some listing[20] and even attended a special Alliance meeting called to discuss petty local stealing. That was followed by a day of considerable suffering, in which Isaac was plagued by chills and vomited bile. He missed the organizational meeting in St. John for a Mutual Protective Association, although there were reportedly about one hundred in attendance.

When he finally went to Pratt on February 26 to sell the last of his wheat and white corn, he learned of the suspension of payments by the Pratt County National Bank. The next day's *Pratt County Times* published an apparent effort to avoid a run on the bank, claiming, "The bank could no doubt have continued right along but good business suggested the course pursued and thus give ample time to realize upon the assets, of which there is a great abundance." Isaac must have felt sympathy for the bank's debtors, those cash-strapped farmers fearing being pressed for immediate payments of outstanding loans and foreclosures. The article added, "Depositors and all others will of course be paid every dollar. . . . The stockholders are worthy people, perfectly able to take care of the indebtedness if that should be necessary, which it will not." Particular assurance was directed toward the county, that "there is not the slightest danger but it will get its money in full."[21]

Isaac's health improved enough for him to resume work, but he tired more easily. When the Emerson Post Office moved from the home of Aaron Beck to J. S. Smith's place a mile north, likely due to Beck's recent stroke, the mail carrier's route no longer passed by the private box Isaac had installed. Changing his address to the Antrim Post Office in the home of the Gibbs sisters would be even further from his home, making the walking distance of either choice a real hardship as his stamina declined. Isaac was unsure how he would manage.[22] The sale of farm equipment at Beck's farm less than a week after the post office move more than hinted at the severity of Beck's stroke. Fortunately, the temperature rose to twenty degrees under a clear sky the day of the Beck's sale, and most of the neighborhood attended, tired of being cooped up by the weather. Items sold for fair prices.

This respite in the weather was brief, for a late snowfall soon left fourteen inches of snow on the ground. Isaac worried about his neighbors' stock, seeming to be nearly out of feed or being fed irregularly. Everyone was ready for spring, winter having reduced supplies for man and beast to serious levels. "Stock needs extra feeding and feed getting scarce and high, like cash itself," Isaac recorded on March 15.[23] He could not understand why the very people suffering the most under the current system did not recognize the need for reform.

By 1891 most of the land in Isaac's community had been settled. In recognition that free land was no longer needed to populate the prairie, laws changed, and the days of abundant free land were coming to an end.[24] The *County Capital* advised readers not to postpone proving up their claims, and the fees for making proofs at the probate judge's office were included in the article.[25] The former redemption law had also been repealed, although those already acting under the old law could complete their proofs. However, the *County Capital* warned against attempting to purchase the relinquishment to a timber claim, as those could no longer be refiled. Perhaps the government's decision to decline relinquishment conveyances to timber claims was related to the recognition that the ideas that "rain follows the plow" and "planting trees attracts more rainfall" had been proven untrue.[26] With most of the land already homesteaded, the published notice was more of a warning to those in the county who had delayed proving up their claims not to postpone securing ownership any longer.

Perhaps that warning to secure their land included some of the blacks who had settled in Stafford County. In general, Kansas had been welcoming to black runaways and freed slaves, but the fact remained that in the 1860s Kansas was a young state with fewer government resources to handle the huge numbers of former slaves that arrived in desperate need. These limitations had made their assimilation difficult, and some residents had been outspoken about their concerns, with others openly critical of accommodating these arrivals. In Topeka, F. W. Giles was overwhelmed by the 1879 surge of arrivals, with an estimated seven thousand blacks having arrived, and one hundred to three hundred more arriving each week. He had written, "Is Kansas a grand asylum for decrepit and destitute blacks?" However, by 1890 he complimented the ingenuity the new settlers had shown by finding ways to support themselves and becoming landowners. He also noted how well their children had succeeded in schools, competing with their white classmates at a comparable or higher level.[27] As for the Exodusters who had settled in Stafford County, many had remained, struggling to make a success of their farms, just like the immigrants from other countries who had claimed farms in the county.

Farmers whose claims were near Isaac's had experimented with cooperative potato fields the previous year, and they decided to repeat their potato venture.[28] As the men sorted seed potatoes in Isaac's cellar, they enjoyed some fun and joking to take their minds off the hard times. Nearly everyone remained short of feed for their stock, so animals suffered, and with the cold weather hanging on, fuel to heat homes was also running short. Those living in dugouts benefitted from the earthen insulation, and since Will Goodwin had never returned, Frank Stimatze was moving into the Goodwin brothers' abandoned dugout, becoming Isaac's neighbor just to the south in Pratt County.

After a discussion with Isaac about his efforts to improve corn production, John Hilmes concluded that Isaac was a "corn experimentalist," whose ideas deserved sharing in the *County Capital*. Isaac's piece on corn culture appeared on the front page, top center, just at the time farmers needed the advice for planting season.[29] He acknowledged that the previous year's crop had almost been a failure, but he placed the blame on farming methods, offering nine detailed recommendations to improve results. One thing was obvious about Isaac: his conclusions, once reached, were firm and specific.[30]

Alliance meetings were a place where neighbors not only studied and discussed political matters but also shared advice for improving their farms, and Isaac had come to believe a lower turnout of sincerely engaged members often accomplished more sensible business. He continued to donate his own books and pamphlets for the book cupboard he had built, and more members were studying from his books. In late February Isaac noted that he had "placed [a] cracker box full of sundry books 43 volumes, cost about $60 into District 33 book cupboard."[31] At one meeting, debate concerning which new reform literature to purchase occupied members until midnight, another indication of their willingness to learn.

The things discussed at meetings were confined to matters of direct concern to the members, like the wisdom of raising cane, concluding that it only paid to grow what was required for personal needs, the market not justifying raising more to sell. Members had also approved the Progressive idea of purchasing a barrel of coal oil from which members could buy small amounts without the penalty merchants imposed on small purchases. Isaac bought a five-dollar barrel in town and delivered it to George and Nancy Henn, whose soddy was in a more central location. The cooperative Alliance coal oil business would benefit everyone—if the Henns measured purchases accurately, collected payments at time of sale, and didn't tap the barrel for their own use.

Upon his return from the legislative session in Topeka, Isaac's friend Rep. William Campbell gave a brief talk at an Alliance meeting. Although everyone had been excited by the election of so many of the Kansas People's Party candidates in 1890, Campbell's remarks did not make what could be accomplished legislatively sound very promising.

George and Theresa Hall were among Isaac's closest friends. George Hall's parents were tenants of the Duke of Rutland in the village of Branston near Bevoir Castle, a charming English setting for a boy's youth that offered limited prospects when the boy became a man with a wife and two little daughters to support. George, his wife, and their daughters had joined his younger brother in Youngstown working in steel mills, doing the same work he could have done without coming to America. Soon after the birth of their son in 1885, George went to the railway station to buy tickets for his family as far as the money he could spare would take them. They reached Belpre, Kansas, and their last child, a third daughter, was born in Edwards County in 1888. Soon after her birth, the Halls moved onto a timber claim

George and Teresa Hall's Family. George and Isaac Werner developed a friendship through farming, but they also shared a belief in the importance of the Populist movement.

alongside the Rattlesnake Creek in Albano Township not far from Isaac's claims.[32] Their common opinions about farming and the Populist movement cemented their friendship. The Halls and other English-speaking immigrants had a language advantage in their new homeland. Although Isaac had come from Pennsylvania and spoke English well, his speech still bore the traces of the Pennsylvania-Dutch community of his youth.[33]

Albano Township was only one of the Alliance organizations in Stafford County, and Isaac had been chosen as a delegate to join about sixty other delegates from throughout the county for the quarterly Alliance meeting in St. John. For the first time, eight women were among the delegates, and for whatever reason, Isaac noted that the meeting was conducted with more discipline and respectfulness than usual. While at the meeting, he paid the dues for the thirteen members of the Albano sub-Alliance.

Although the community continued their activity as Alliance members, their efforts were doing little to ease worries about unpaid debts and the need for rain. The drought was worrying speculators too, who lacked their own crystal balls in which to find answers about prospects for the growing wheat. The volatility of the market seemed to defy logic. Some farmers were contracting for their stored wheat, wanting to tie down the price they would receive in case prices dropped even lower, whereas other farmers that Isaac knew were holding out for the market to reach a dollar, believing it would turn. Isaac found the speculation disgusting: "How the masses are imposed on through the big grain gamblers, just like so many children."[34]

A significant part of Isaac's farm was his tree business, but his "distant enterprise" with his brother had proven difficult. He had made a sincere effort after his sister Emma's death to revive cordial correspondence with his two remaining siblings, but their letters were mostly business dispatches.

Although Isaac rarely disclosed much of a personal nature in his journal, he admitted not only his regret about the waning sibling connection but also feeling "the decline of age coming on, tired and unwell in morning, have to rest [a] little to start in on day's work."[35] Isaac was an active man, not quite forty-seven years old. About a year before, when he had begun to feel significant changes in his health, he had ordered *The Two Hundred Year Club*, a book written by Edmund Shaftesbury, founder of the Ralston Health Club.[36] Shaftesbury believed humans could live far longer than they did at that time by employing his recommendations, primarily advice about diet and exercise, but also some pseudo-science ideas that he advocated. Isaac's efforts to follow Shaftesbury's program were recorded in his journal: "Should be fixed so as to comply in living more with 200 year club rules and indulge in suitable diet."[37] Advancing age no longer seemed to explain his declining health, but he had found no other satisfactory explanation.

Influenced by the success of the Kansas People's Party elections, the movement to expand beyond the state organizations to a national third party had gained momentum. A conference in Cincinnati, Ohio, had been called to pursue forming a national party, and at the local quarterly Alliance meeting in St. John Campbell had been chosen as their delegate to Cincinnati.

Support was not confined to Kansas, but it was particularly strong among farmers and reformers there, and newspapers reported that 483 Kansas attendees funneled into Kansas City, Missouri, to board a special train to Cincinnati. Among them was the St. John delegate, Campbell.[38] Banners at the music hall reminded attendees of their responsibilities: "United We Stand; Divided We Fall," "Nine Million Mortgaged Homes," and "Opposition to All Monopolies."

The convention was immediately confronted with the problem of deciding who to seat among the crowd of people wishing to be recognized as delegates. There were old Greenbackers, Edward Bellamy nationalists, Prohibitionists, proponents of the Georgisms of Henry George, and some whose reasons for attending seemed indefinable. The hotels were full, especially those affordable for the laboring class that comprised most of the delegates, and the first day's order of business seemed to be spent sorting out just who had come. Isaac read the newspaper accounts with interest, anxious to talk with Campbell as soon as he returned.

To understand the Cincinnati convention it is necessary to understand what had happened before delegates met in Cincinnati. The success of the state People's Party in Kansas had made it seem possible that a national party for farmers and other laborers could succeed, but several events had led up to that possibility.

A small group had been particularly eager to proceed, and among them were the Vincent brothers, who had the ability to promote the idea through their newspaper, *The Nonconformist*.[39] Another Populist newspaperman in Medicine Lodge, Kansas, Leon Beals, actively encouraged the national party idea as well.[40] The disappointing results of the Union Labor Party (ULP) in the previous election had made it seem that it was not the right organization on which to build a national party, and within the ULP a secret group of reformers eager to find a vehicle for a new national party formed.[41] This group was called the Videttes,[42] and they assisted the Kansas Alliance men in bringing together the small remnants of older organizations, the fading ULP, and the Alliance, which together could create a party large and powerful enough to challenge the old political parties.[43]

A large part of the challenge was unifying farmers from both the north and the south in order to create a party large and powerful enough to confront the two old parties. Scars from the Civil War remained, and that included whether blacks would be part of the new party.[44] Charles Macune's subtreasury idea to create warehouses, which would allow farmers the means to break the cycle of control by lenders,[45] was essential to southern farmers, including black sharecroppers.[46] This was key to the possibility of a national party.

A convention was held in Ocala, Florida, in December, following the 1890 Kansas state elections. Some in attendance were eager to form a third party immediately, but others disagreed, particularly those from the south. Two leaders emerged at the convention: Leonidas Polk and Charles Macune. William A. Peffer played a lesser role in Ocala because of poor health.[47] To resolve the differences between the north and the south, Polk suggested that paid lecturers spread across the country on an educational campaign to prepare the way for a third party. Because a platform had been agreed at Ocala, these lectures could speak on the substance of the party's goals.[48] The proposed platform and the success of the lecturers were important influences.

All of these steps had been taken before delegates reached Cincinnati, but some delegates remained uncertain about establishing a national People's Party. In Cincinnati, Ignatius Loyola Donnelly of Minnesota assumed a principal role, speaking for the group eager to form a third party immediately. Most Kansas delegates agreed with Donnelly, whose gift with words made him quite persuasive.[49] James B. Weaver was more cautious, countering Populists like Donnelly and Peffer. Weaver sought time to convince other Populists that "practical politics" were needed to combat the two old parties. Exercising a forceful counterbalance with almost military tactics, he sought more delay in order to promote his idea.

The lecturers arranged for at Ocala had focused particularly on southern farmers, who were less eager to form a national party. Polk's call for paid lecturers had included Populist superstars, including himself, as well as Kansans Jerry Simpson, Peffer, and Mary Elizabeth Lease. With the subtreasury plan included in the Ocala platform—something essential to southerners—Macune was also on board. Weaver had a different plan, and he wanted time to promote silver.[50] The important compromise formulated in Cincinnati was that the procedures to establish a third party were determined, a conference was scheduled for February 22, 1892, and the duties of the delegates were defined, but the Cincinnati convention itself did not establish the national People's Party. In that way both factions got part of what they wanted. The delay allowed time to educate those who were still uncomfortable with the idea of a third party, and it especially provided more opportunity to work with the southern Alliance.

Allegiances in the south were still impacted by the Civil War. Blacks voted with the Republicans because it was the party of Lincoln, but wealthy and influential southerners who had fought for the Confederacy despised Lincoln's Republican Party and voted Democrat. Whereas Progressives in Kansas had sometimes worked with the minority Democrats to achieve mutual goals, the reverse was happening in the south, where small farmers and black Populists worked with the minority Republicans. These party differences made it impossible to implement a unified national strategy.

Texas assumed more leadership in the south, and the subtreasury plan advocated by Macune was the best reform idea to recruit southern farmers. Learning to understand and appreciate the significance of Macune's subtreasury plan required leaders to educate farmers about the benefits for both north and south.[51] Breaking the selling cycle of southern farmers with mortgaged crops, which they were forced by lenders to sell immediately after harvest, was of more significance in the south, so Populist leaders there had been better trained to explain the subtreasury plan.[52] Under the existing situation, southern farmers selling at the same time caused prices to fall, grain dealers got the benefit of low prices, lenders took most of the sale proceeds, and farmers had to borrow to buy seed for the next season, resulting in a perpetual cycle of debt. In the north, farmers were also concerned with managing the sales of their unencumbered crops in order to reap higher profits with which to pay the mortgages on their land and equipment, but their debts did not all come due at the close of harvest. They had reasons to be equally interested in the benefits of Macune's plan, but the ability to manage marketing their crops was not as apparent in the north. Northern Alliance leadership had neglected training local leaders to understand and explain those benefits to their members. That distinction became very important in the political strategy of the People's Party.

Another distinction between the issue of debt involved the role of merchants. In the south, blacks and poor white sharecroppers dealt with storekeepers who abused customers with a two-price system. The cash price for merchandise was significantly less than the time-payment price, the markups for which could be 40 to 70 percent. Cash-strapped farmers would find it necessary to place mortgages or liens on their growing crops, and once they succumbed to that necessity, the cycle was nearly inescapable. Isaac signed notes for merchandise, but did not encumber his growing crop. While southern merchants grew rich, merchants in Isaac's community who extended excessive credit to farmers faced bankruptcy themselves.[53]

Bringing convention delegates from both north and south together was complicated not only by these differing regional prejudices and goals but also by these economic differences.[54] The convention left it to individual

"The Race Question Solved." The challenge of white farmers in the north uniting with black farmers in the south to present a united political effort was complicated by the opposition of some white farmers in the south. *County Capital*, July 31, 1891.

states to decide whether to nominate their own slate of state and local candidates like Kansas had done in 1890. However, the convention put in place all of the requirements needed to establish a national party at a specific later time, including agreeing to the party platform.

A national executive committee was created, with its chairman elected at the general session of the Cincinnati convention, and each state delegation was charged with choosing three delegates for a later meeting. These delegates would attend the February 22, 1892, conference to try to unify all the states. Even if complete unification failed, the executive committee was required to call a national convention by June 1, 1892, for the purpose of naming a presidential ticket. In other words, a third-party presidential candidate would be chosen at a national convention near June 1 regardless of whether complete agreement about all issues had been accomplished at the February conference. The Weaver faction could use the delay not only to recruit more people to the national People's Party but also to advocate for free silver, and the Alliance faction got an automatic default arrangement, with the steps in place for creation of the national party without further debate. The tactical maneuvers needed to move the creation of a third party to the national level did spotlight how difficult bringing all of the many factions and their differing goals together would be. Internal fighting seemed as much of a threat to the national People's Party success as resistance from the old political parties.

At some point, the term "Populist" had been adopted to identify those following this new political philosophy. Using the Latin word *populus*, meaning, "people," to create the word Populist, a new name was given to members of the movement.[55]

As the People's Party moved toward a national level, Isaac and his neighbors could not avoid considering how America had changed in recent decades. Perhaps they had given little thought to city workers and the laborers in windowless factories and crowded, unsanitary tenements until workers had begun to organize. Having become aware of the harsh working environments and unhealthful homes must have caused farmers to reflect on the differences between the lives of urban workers and rural laborers once they began trying to come together politically. Although a farmer's life was also hard, at least he had fresh air and nature's beauty. The open sky overhead, the prairie festooned with wild flowers in the spring, the annual arrival of his beloved birds, and the croaky chorus of frogs after rains were what made Isaac enjoy life. Even the drifts shooting sparks of light into the cold biting air after a heavy snow were beautiful in his rural environment. Cities blotted too much of nature out, stealing men's humanity by deceiving them into believing they were something different from the other creatures of the earth, whether the deception made them believe they were gods of wealth or beasts of burden. Both the abuser and the abused sacrificed a great deal of their humanity to the city.

ALTHOUGH FARMERS MAY have become more informed about urban labor, their own struggles remained their priority. In an 1891 statement, U.S. senator Peffer said "that the average net return on Kansas farms was only about

1% on their value and that that value was low and declining. If the farms of the state were put up for sale . . . they would not bring half the amount of the mortgages on then."[56] Stated differently by Peffer, "If a farmer had given a mortgage for $1,000 in 1870, he could have paid it with 1,050 bushels of corn. Ten to seventeen years later it would have taken, without interest, 2,702 bushels to have paid it."[57] No one understood that better than Isaac and his neighbors.

As for his own efforts, Isaac was finding hope in the success with his cultivator invention. When the ground dried enough, he began testing it, discovering minor details that needed adjusting and improving, and achieving more success than he had dared to hope. On his birthday, May 23, Isaac wrote in his journal, "My 47th birthday put in at a cultivator to revolutionize modern, miserable way of raising corn in Western Kansas."[58] Each day brought more refinements and some frustrations, especially when he ran out of bolts and suitable lumber, and had to improvise, but after a trip to Pratt specifically for materials, he replaced the makeshift parts with the proper bolts and lumber. On May 28, Isaac rigged the cultivator to hitch three horses for the first time, doing some preliminary scraping before taking it into the four and one-half acre piece north of the lane to do the "first 3-horse, 4-row cultivating in Stafford County, to the best of my knowledge." It took a bit of time for Isaac to get the shovels adjusted just right, but before stopping, he had cultivated eight acres. That night county president E. J. Westgate and county lecturer D. M. Hunt came to speak at the Albano sub-Alliance meeting, and Isaac mentioned his three-horse cultivator idea to them and invited them to come see it, if they had time.

The visit by the two men the following morning, and their admiration of his invention, was only the start of a proud day for Isaac. At Isaac's invitation, John Hilmes[59] arrived with his family about noon. Both John and his wife Mary Jane were immigrants, he having come from Germany and she from England. For a time they settled in Missouri where four children were born, but two more had been born since their move to Kansas. Their buggy contained a giggling, curious swarm of six children, ranging in ages from ten to the baby, still in her mother's arms. Despite their energy, they were well-behaved and Isaac enjoyed having them running around his farm, "a nice social time generally, little folks camping and having a 'country' time."[60] The family's journey from St. John had taken them through Ohio and Richland townships before they reached Albano, and they had seen several family farms—the Smith, Carnahan, Tanner, Willcox, Baker, Campbell, and others. However, it was Isaac's farm that was praised by the editor.

Hilmes devoted most of a column in the June 5 *County Capital* to describing the 320 acres entirely surrounded by trees, with individual fields of thirty and forty acres, each tract enclosed with its own surrounding tree rows. He described the wheat, corn, oats, potatoes, and other vegetables as looking "elegant and prosperous." Probably the most pleasure Isaac found in reading the article was Hilmes's mention of his invention, writing:

> One of the great attractions at this place is a new corn cultivator, of Isaac's own invention, which finishes four rows of corn, going one way, or eight rows in a single round. As Isaac expresses it, it is an implement that will revolutionize the system of corn cultivation in this country. It contains eight shovels, two to a row, easily managed, a child can handle it, and three horses can pull it easily. It is an implement which will enable a farmer to cultivate more than double the usual amount of corn in less time.

Despite Isaac's protestations that he wasn't much of a cook, Hilmes described the dinner that he served their family as "rich and delicious, and spoke volumes in favor of our bachelor friend's culinary qualification." Isaac could not have received a more favorable review if he had hired a publicist to write a promotion for his cultivator and his farm.[61]

A few days after the cultivator's debut, Will Campbell came to Isaac's for dinner. The three-horse cultivator got such an enthusiastic response from Will that the two friends discussed breaking more sod and acquiring more land to begin farming "on the bonanza plan." They agreed that this was the best way to compete with "large land thieves and managers." Isaac found hope in what Will shared about the St. Louis convention, but his personal confidence now rested largely on his cultivator, which he believed could change farming forever. Many people besides Hilmes were complimenting Isaac on his crops, some saying that his fields were among the best looking in the area. Charles Shattuc had rented ground from Isaac again and was breaking out more sod. Times were too hard to consider himself prosperous, but Isaac could describe his farm that way. His agricultural experiments had paid off. If the politico-economic structure of the nation could be brought into an equitable balance to give laborer-producers the respect and rewards they deserved, he believed the future could be bright.

Sometimes he wished his parents could see his farm, but his father was deceased and his mother too far away. More and more he seemed forgotten by his family. By June 10 he had reached the last line of the 480th page of the journal he had begun in 1870. Next time he was in town, he wondered, should he buy a blank ledger to continue recording his thoughts, or should he admit to himself that it was really a waste of his time—that no one would ever read what he had written? He could record his agricultural experiments, debts, and payments in a cheap notebook, and maybe that was all he really needed to use.

Isaac had been forced to accept that his siblings Henry and Ettie had their own lives and families, and the sibling bond he thought would last forever had been weakened by distance and time. Perhaps his father might have been proud of him. Although he had not founded a town named after himself, the work he was doing in the Farmers' Alliance might change his community, and in concert with others, maybe even the whole country. If he was able to secure a patent for his three-horse cultivator, perhaps he could call it the I. B. Werner Cultivator. Maybe his life was important in some small way, even if his family would never know. The final entry in the journal in which Isaac had recorded his life on the Kansas prairie read, "Mail matter these days coming in slim quantities as it seems."[62]

Success for the Populist movement on the national stage required the support of its local Alliance base, and community leaders like Isaac and Will faced the challenge of overcoming old party loyalties among members. Because the Kansas Farmers' Alliance and Knights of Labor had nominated only local and state candidates, without any national candidates in 1890, members had not entirely abandoned their old parties. With the formation of a national party, however, Kansas voters were being asked to vote a straight Progressive ticket. That made it harder to avoid confrontations based on old party rivalries, which had apparently led to a fist fight between two members[63] at an Alliance picnic held in Brown's Grove. The People's Party would need the votes of former members of both old parties, including the participants in that fight. If they could not keep their tempers under control at a social event, would they join in supporting national Populist candidates chosen by the new party?

As if Mother Nature were mirroring the unsettled political disposition of the farmers, the heaviest windstorm anyone had ever seen in that part of Stafford County was unleashed, the whirling destruction delivered in the darkness during torrential rain.[64] Hay and fodder stacks were scattered, and houses and barns were twisted on their foundations, including the homes and farms of some of Isaac's friends. Fortunately, there were no injuries or fatalities reported from the storm.

Despite the dry spring, the wheat crop that year was a good one, and a Republican neighbor opined in the *County Capital*: "I believe God is on the side of the Republican party in Kansas. I believe God has given us our beautiful wheat crop, in order that we may down the anarchists. I believe God has so organized things that we will get a good price, so that we will be able to shut up those calamity howlers."[65] It was a perfect example of why Isaac so often took issue, not with God, but with those who presumed to speak for Him.

If it wasn't politics or religion, there was always something else to divide people, it seemed. An interesting legal question had arisen that dated back several years to the time that citizens of St. John decided to build a courthouse and donate it to the county. The building was nearly completed by private, voluntary subscriptions, but in the 1887 legislative session, a bill was passed to bond the city for the expense and reimburse 80 percent of the money private citizens had contributed to build the courthouse. Subsequently, a legal opinion held that bonding a community for private enterprise was illegal. That raised the issue of whether taxes assessed to pay the reimbursement bonds should be paid. Some thought that because the bonds were illegal they should be repudiated, sparing citizens from the need to pay those taxes. Others thought that because the citizens of St. John had received the benefit of a courthouse, the balance owed on the bonds should be honored, whether or not there was a legal obligation. Still others reasoned that the bonds should be paid to avoid a default that could hinder or bar St. John's ability to sell its bonds in the future because of a bad rating. The editor of the *County Capital* sided with those who favored payment for ethical reasons, writing: "Let us pay the bonds not from motives of policy, but from motives of honesty."[66]

Another issue important to farmers that Republicans had failed to wholeheartedly support was regulation of railroads. Populists advocated regulation or government ownership to control abusive tariffs, so the railroads struck back, once they realized that the political power of the People's Party was actually capable of posing a threat. A political club of railroad employees distributed circulars advising fellow employees to vote the Republican ticket. In responding to the railroad's actions, Isaac's friend Will Campbell used his official title as a state representative, and replied:

> The railroads of Kansas have been robbing the people ever since their advent in the state.[67] The people have demanded a fair adjustment of

> freight rates; the Republican Party has joined the railroads in their fight against the people. How any businessman or farmer can support this gang of boodle hunters and robbers is something that I cannot understand. . . . Choose this day whom you will serve. The railroad corporation or your own and our neighbors' interest.[68]

U.S. senator Peffer also expressed concern about the bonded indebtedness created in earlier years when Kansans were hungry for railroads:

> In 1888, in Kansas there was 1 mile of railroad for every 9 1/3rd square miles of railroad, and 5 ½ miles of track for every 1,000 persons. For this the people had paid in debt and taxes, yet private holders kept the completed lines, which had cost them little or nothing. The roads were built by public mortgages, boosted along by gifts and bonuses, national, state, city, township, and village, even by individuals and farmers' clubs.[69]

The generosity from the government and individuals had resulted by 1890, according to Peffer, "in railroad bonds guaranteed by all local political units total[ing] $50,000,000; by the state $75,000,000 . . . far more than the roads were worth to build."[70]

WHILE POLITICS HAD BEEN a distraction, investigation of the attempted burglary of the county treasurer's vault had continued into autumn. Treasurer Landes's attempt to reconstruct the stolen financial records was about $4,000 short, which Landes insisted was a matter of accounting errors rather than missing money. The county commissioners had allowed him until the first of December to find the errors, but on November 9, Landes reported finding the office safe blown open yet again, the amount of smoke indicating that the explosion had nearly caused a fire. Landes told his clerk that nothing was missing, and he urged the clerk, as well as county attorney O. C. Jennings and Sheriff McWilliams, to keep quiet, theorizing that the burglars might be apprehended if they returned again to finish the job. Further, news of a second attempt would certainly upset citizens. Landes's suggestion was honored for several days, until Commissioner Estes came into town and learned of it. He demanded that two night watchmen be hired and that the other commissioners be notified immediately of what had happened.[71]

One night, with the watchmen on duty, the treasurer's office window was found unlocked, although the clerk specifically remembered locking it at the end of the day. What was most telling was the fact that this time gunpowder was found inside the safe, with a fuse running from the interior of the safe to the window. The guards had foiled an attempted explosion large enough to have seriously damaged the entire courthouse and harmed anyone inside. At the subsequent commissioners' hearing, Landes alleged that the previous theft had taken between $7,000 and $8,000, despite his earlier claim that nothing had been taken. The hearing concluded with Landes tendering his resignation. He pledged to replace the missing amount from his own property so that his bondsmen would not suffer. The commissioners retained respected businessmen, Joseph Hamlin Tudor[72] and Henry Rohr, to assist the county clerk in examining the books, and the result was a finding that Landes was short on his accounts in the amount of $15,120.73. Landes was arrested and charged with embezzlement. It was a sad ending to 1891 for Stafford County, and the likelihood that the money was stolen by a trusted public official made the whole affair even worse.[73]

For Isaac, the close of 1891 brought a painful personal sadness. As his health had declined, he had grown quite attached to a particular cat. He had always been fond of his cats, but this one was special. When he discovered one morning that someone had abused his special pet, Isaac was determined to find the person who had done such a hateful and senseless thing to his gentle animal. He had gone from house to house in the neighborhood, asking if anyone could identify the culprit. Everyone denied any knowledge, although Isaac believed someone must have known. He was hurt by the indifference of his neighbors and helpless to correct the cruelties to his poor cat. It had made for a sad Christmas.[74] Adding to his sorrow, a mocking aside appeared in the Albano column of the newspaper, published for everyone to read. The reporter, hiding behind the *nom de plume* of "Ajax," had written, "Col. Werner is girding on his armor. He claims someone has transmogrified his pet feline."[75]

CHAPTER 9

1892

There had been a shift in Isaac Werner's life, a subtle transition in priorities resulting from the combination of age, health, and experience that redirects the lives of all men. Yet the cruelty to his cat and the public mockery of his efforts to confront the culprit marked a definable moment when Isaac saw his life differently. His feelings toward the community changed.[1] He must have wondered whether he had been privately ridiculed for other things—trying to start the County Reform Club that never got past its first meeting, lecturing at Alliance meetings to members who only came to gossip with their neighbors, and keeping daily journals from the time he was a boy, a virtual story of his life that no one would find interesting enough to read. He was, after all, just one poor farmer trying to make a living off the land with enough extra to pay off the mortgages. Perhaps it was time to lay down his pen for good and take hold of the plow. Writing for the newspaper no longer seemed important. He needed to use what healthy years remained to make the best of his farm before he lost it to the bankers.

Disillusionment and disloyalty seemed to infect others in the community.[2] Once, Isaac had been surprised to see other Stafford County farmers waiting in line to sell their grain in Pratt, but that was becoming commonplace, their loyalty to St. John grain dealers diminished by what people saw as unfair treatment. Whispered criticisms between disgruntled farmers about prices and cheating with the scales were now openly discussed. The St. John merchants also suffered when farmers took their grain business to Pratt and stayed to do other shopping. Isaac had been the recipient of trust shown him by St. John merchants who had extended him credit beyond what was good business judgment, and he felt sympathy for those merchants now.

The death of one former merchant brought particular sadness to St. John. Henry Rohr's death after a brief illness meant the loss of one of the town's most respected men. Born in Germany, he immigrated to Wisconsin in 1856, and served with the 5th Wisconsin Infantry Regiment during the Civil War. He arrived in St. John in 1879, shortly after Isaac's arrival, and built one of the town's first brick buildings for his mercantile business. Later, he had chosen to raise livestock, and as a stockman Rohr had developed one of the finest farms in the county by the time of his death at age fifty-four. Regard for his integrity was apparent from the county commissioners' selection of Rohr as one of the auditors in the courthouse robbery.

The courthouse robbery had upset the entire county, with money stolen from the county school fund and someone they knew personally charged with the crime. Now, more county money was being spent on trials. At E. H. Landes's first trial, the *voir dire* questioning of the jury panel had resulted in so many men dismissed for cause that too few were left to decide the case. It was nearly impossible to find twelve jurors in Stafford County who were not either related to or friendly with one or more of the prospective witnesses, attorneys, or the defendant, or who could swear that they had never discussed or heard discussed the alleged shortage in the county treasury. An improper jury instruction resulted in a mistrial after the second attempt to get a conviction. On February 19, the frustrated editor of the *County Capital* described the law as "a regular game of hide and seek."

Schools had shortened their terms to save expenses, and the commissioners had settled with Landes's bondsmen for $4,000, plus half of the costs of the suit, hardly a pittance of the amount stolen and the related costs of the investigation and prosecution. A notice offering a "$500 Reward . . . for the capture and conviction of the person or persons who attempted to burglarize the County Treasurer's safe" seemed to confirm the rumors that others were suspected of being involved.[3]

Political animosity seemed more apparent as well. When William Brown, the Pratt County Alliance lecturer, spoke to a local group, he took a particularly harsh tone toward the Republicans. Since the People's Party had formed, political criticism was less constrained, with none of the moderation the nonpartisan Alliance had imposed.

For many in the community, however, the formation of a national People's Party offered hope. Isaac's friend Will Campbell had the honor of being selected as a delegate to February's St. Louis conference at the Exposition Music Hall. The altered tone of the conference was expressed in a new banner: "We Do Not Ask for Sympathy or Pity. We Ask for Justice." The meeting was called to order by Ben Terrell, whom Isaac had heard speak in Pratt. Terrell's role was temporary, needed only until the credentials committee could determine those persons properly authorized to participate in the conference. Eight organizations[4] were immediately recognized, but eventually delegates were seated from twenty-one different groups.

While the credentials committee worked, several speakers addressed the seated delegates, including Ignatius Donnelly and Kansans Mary Elizabeth Lease and Jerry Simpson. The speaker who gained the most respectful attention, however, was Col. Leonidas Lafayette Polk.[5] His parents had been successful North Carolina farmers and slave owners whose property was divided equally among their three sons. A Confederate soldier and officer who fought at Gettysburg, Polk had been educated at Davidson College and was elected to the North Carolina House in 1864 at the young age of twenty-three. After the war, he had come home, restored his farm, and started a weekly newspaper, the *Ansonian.* Polk soon became known for advocating agricultural diversification and education, and as a result, he was appointed the first North Carolina commissioner of agriculture in 1877. Three years later he resigned from his agency in disgust about the lack of legislative support from the Democratic majority, and began working as a reporter for the *Raleigh News.*

Polk's involvement in various Progressive farm organizations included joining the National Farmers' Alliance and Industrial Union[6] when it formed in 1887, and he was its president at the time of the St. Louis conference. Isaac knew him as the founder of the *Progressive Farmer*, to which he subscribed and for which he had written articles. Editorials published in the *Progressive Farmer* had been influential in the creation of the North Carolina College of Agricultural and Mechanic Arts under the Morrill Act."[7] Colonel Polk seemed uniquely able to win votes in both the south and the north.[8]

Although Isaac had not heard Colonel Polk speak, the southern leader had drawn huge crowds as he toured Kansas in the summer of 1890 in the company of Ben Clover of the Kansas Alliance. He had warmed up the crowds by describing the inequities of the present system: "Powerful and promising as this young great republic is, yet its power and glory cannot

Leonidas Lafayette Polk, a Confederate officer who had, through his work with the southern Alliance and speaking in the north, gained respect among Populists in both the north and the south. Courtesy Wikimedia Commons.

survive the degradation of the American farmer. . . . Never, perhaps in the history of the world has industrial and economic thought been more intensely engaged. . . [the result being] to place agriculture so far in the rear in the race of material progress."[9] Having identified the ills they confronted, Polk emphasized the absolute necessity of farmers across the nation joining forces to overpower the political influence of the wealthy:

> During the year I have visited twenty-four (24) states, and everywhere I found a zealous interest and a harmonious spirit. . . Confronted by common danger—afflicted with a common evil—impelled by a common hope, the people of Kansas and Virginia, of Pennsylvania and Texas, of Michigan and South Carolina, make common cause in a common interest. . . the evils which oppress the agricultural interest of the country, are national in their character, and that they cannot be corrected by sectional effort or sectional remedies.[10]

By way of diversion, Donnelly was selected to write the preamble to the platform, which turned out to be longer than the platform itself. He borrowed from the Populist Manifesto issued by the Kansas Central Committee in 1891 and from the convention call itself, embellishing both with his own eloquent flourishes. When Donnelly read the preamble to the full convention delegates, the cheering left them still on their feet when the actual platform was read. The enthusiasm for the preamble created such a distraction that the opposition to parts of the platform was overwhelmed.[11] The convention was adjourned, and the preplanned meeting held for the sole purpose of specifying a nominating convention was conducted by Gen. James Weaver. The bifurcated strategy established at the Cincinnati convention had succeeded.[12]

Managing the delegates charged with approving the People's Party platform on a national scale required political acumen. Southern delegates[13] made it clear that they would walk out if any program in the platform threatened white unity.

BACK IN STAFFORD COUNTY the courthouse scandal had expanded to include new culprits. The headline in the *County Capital* identified Isaac's old but deeply flawed friend, Ben Webber, as among those involved in the courthouse burglary.[14] The article began by acknowledging that there had always been a suspicion that "the robbery was not the work of one man" and continued by praising the efforts of county attorney Jennings, which led to the arrests. The article reflected the emotions of the community, first describing the resulting hardship on taxpayers, "who by reason of such payment suffered for necessaries, conveniences and comforts at home, in the family circle. The crime is monstrous and deserves no leniency nor mercy. The only question is, who are the guilty ones." The article also recognized the community's tendency toward concessions or mercy: "Most of the parties charged have loving families at home, mother, father, wife and children. . . . Who is there that will not be moved by such representations?" However, the article concluded:

> The satanic depredations were conceived and executed at the risk of human lives. . . . [T]he education of the children of our county was taken, no doubt for lewd and immoral purposes, the terms of several of our schools in the county have been shortened by reason of the theft, hence children deprived of their just right. The shortage will have to be replaced, which . . . will grind still more an already oppressed people.[15]

Isaac knew that Ben was a rascal, prone to getting into scrapes, but he likely found it hard to believe that his friend would do anything to risk lives or steal money meant for schoolchildren. Ben did enjoy gambling, and Isaac's difficulty getting payment for Mrs. Bentley's corn indicated Ben had been short of cash. Even so, it was difficult to believe Ben was involved in a murderous scheme.

Another troubling article of a different sort appeared in that week's paper. The Methodists were telling their members across the state, of which they claimed eighty thousand, not to support any party that refused to come out squarely in support of Prohibition. Although Isaac was sympathetic to Prohibition, he disapproved of religious meddling in politics, and Methodists putting Prohibition above Populist goals would jeopardize the success of the very party that was working for downtrodden members of their own churches. The names of nine Albano men had recently appeared on the final notice for unredeemed taxes on land, most in amounts owed of almost one hundred dollars. It seemed unlikely that Isaac's neighbors would find the money to save their farms, as loans had nearly dried up. Populists were trying to help men like these, and using Prohibition to pull votes from Populists seemed counterproductive to Isaac.

OMAHA HAD BEEN CHOSEN as the site for the national People's Party nominating convention, and when the nomination process began on July 4th, Donnelly's words from the preamble had particular resonance: "[O]n the anniversary of the birthday of the nation, and filled with the spirit of the grand general and chieftain who established our independence, we seek to restore the government of the Republic to the hands of the *plain people*, with which class it originated."[16]

The People's Party had suffered a severe loss since its meeting in St. Louis. Polk, their presumptive nominee for president, had died unexpectedly at the age of fifty-five. His death on June 11, 1892, while in Washington, DC, destroyed the hope of unifying Populist voters from both north and south with the nomination of a former rebel soldier, trusted and respected by most of the party's members, without regard to regionalism. No other man was so capable of bridging the old differences.

In his place, James Weaver was nominated. In 1880 Weaver had run as the presidential candidate of the Greenback Party, and most of his three hundred thousand-plus votes had come from the Great Plains and the rural West, where he continued to be widely respected. However, he needed far more votes, drawn from throughout the nation, to avoid political failure a second time, and he was unlikely to get many from the south. Even the selection of a Confederate officer who had lost a leg in battle as his vice presidential candidate could not compensate for the loss of Leonidas L. Polk at the top of the ticket. The vice presidential nominee, James G. Field, was fairly new to the Farmers' Alliance of Virginia and little known to most Alliance members. Struggling small farmers mired in debt, whether northern or southern, would find little in common with Field, who was engaged in large-scale farming.

Nearly three decades after the Civil War, wounds were not healed, as the preamble's call for unity made clear:

> We declare that this Republic can only endure as a free government while built upon the love of the whole people for each other and for the nation; that it cannot be pinned together by bayonets; that the civil war is over, and that every passion and resentment which grew out of it must die with it, and that we must be in fact, as we are in name, one united brotherhood of free men.[17]

The Republicans had long "waved the bloodied shirt" while southern Democrats revered the old south. Polk might have overcome those traditional loyalties to attract voters from both sides of the Mason-Dixon Line, with other People's Party candidates riding on his coattails. His death had ended that possibility.

The nominating convention drew a sharp line between working-class Americans and the wealthy, not only in the preamble's reference to restoring the government to the hands of plain people but also by reference to conflicts between the wealthy class and workers. Specifically stated were (1) sympathetic support for the Knights of Labor's struggle in Rochester, New York;[18] (2) condemnation of "the recent invasion of the Territory of Wyoming by the hired assassins of plutocracy, assisted by Federal officers," and (3) ending the use of private armies, such as "the Pinkerton system, as a menace to our liberties." Each was representative of abuses by powerful men using political connections and extreme wealth beyond mere political manipulation and economic overreach.[19]

The use of hired mercenaries in the Johnson County War in Wyoming during the previous April was particularly egregious to farmers and small ranchers from the western region of the country. John Hilmes had made that clear in a front page column of the September 4 *County Capital*, declaring, "No other land under the sun which pretends to treat the laboring classes fairly and justly has any such system of purchasable armed forces, and the United States has less need of them than any country."[20] The owners of large ranches had organized the Wyoming Stock Growers Association, often referred to by the initials WSGA, and its members were some of Wyoming's wealthiest and most socially important men. From their exclusive and opulent Cheyenne Club, they exerted a powerful political influence.

As the use of public land for grazing changed with the increase of small ranchers, disputes arose. When the small ranchers decided to stand up for themselves with regard to ownership of unbranded calves during open range spring roundups, the WSGA hired a private army to eliminate anyone whom they chose to identify as a threat to their authority.

Deputy U.S. marshals from Texas and veterans of the Idaho range wars were recruited for the WSGA army, but equally important was employing the assistance of acting Wyoming governor, Amos W. Barber. Despite article 14, section 1, of the Wyoming State Constitution, which prohibited any detective agency or armed body from being brought into the state to suppress a domestic dispute, Barber ordered the commander of the Wyoming National Guard to instruct all company commanders not to assemble local guardsmen without direct orders from the state commander. With this order, military interference from local militia was excluded from the WSGA's private war. It looked like the WSGA was about to get rid of their competition once and for all.

However, Sheriff William G. "Red" Angus of Johnson County, Wyoming, raised a posse of about two hundred men to confront the mercenaries and surrounded the hired guns and the cattlemen at the RA Ranch on Crazy Woman Creek. Using their political connections, the WSGA got the governor to telegraph Wyoming's U.S. senators, who in turn got Republican president Benjamin Harrison to authorize the Sixth Cavalry from Fort McKinney to rescue the mercenaries and the WSGA members riding with them. For a time, they remained prisoners of the military, but eventually they were transferred to civilian authorities. Their civilian "imprisonment" was a joke, for they lived as free men and even carried weapons. The strategy of the defense was simply to delay the prosecution, for Wyoming law prohibited counties from going into debt to pay for trials. The strategy succeeded. Having run out of county funds, the prosecutor was compelled to enter a motion for *nolle prosquei,* meaning that the prosecution could not proceed. The case concluded without a trial, and although there was no acquittal of the defendants, neither could they ever again be arrested for the murders they committed.[21]

The Wyoming case was only one of the examples of outrageous abuse of influence and power that the People's Party's "Expression of Sentiments" condemned. While the nominating convention was taking place, another use of a hired army by wealthy men was underway, in this case Pinkerton agents hired by steel magnate Andrew Carnegie to break a strike at

Pittsburgh's Homestead Steel Works. Although Carnegie managed to be elsewhere at the time, his strategy to end the strike was put in action by his chief of operations, Henry Clay Frick, and their lawyer, Philander C. Knox. Correspondence between the men made it clear that Carnegie approved every step of what came to be known as the Homestead strike.[22]

The Homestead union workers were very well organized, employing an almost military discipline. They even saw to such details as asking tavern owners to limit excessive drinking so that intoxication would not interfere with their disciplined worker blockade. Management wanted the public to believe they were attempting to negotiate fairly with the laborers, but in fact, everything that Frick did evidenced the desire to break not just the strike but the union as well. Installation of high fences topped with barbed wire, sniper towers, searchlights, and high-pressure water cannons did not suggest an environment of willingness on the part of management to enter into collective bargaining in good faith. The inevitable result was a stalemate in the negotiations and a lockout.[23]

In April, again well before the negotiations and the lockout, Frick had contracted with the Pinkerton National Detective Agency to provide three hundred mercenaries for plant security, and he had barges refurbished to bring them to the plant on the river side. When the barges containing the hired army arrived, a spokesman for the workers urged the Pinkertons to avoid any bloodshed and leave, even offering to take a committee through the plant to show that nothing was being harmed. However, he also issued a warning to the Pinkertons: "But in the name of God and humanity, don't attempt to land! Don't attempt to enter these works by force!"[24]

The appeal to the Pinkertons was ignored. It was uncertain which side fired the first shots, but the end result was that during a ten-minute firefight, nearly an equal number were killed and wounded on both sides. Initially the workers had widespread public sympathy, but when the Pinkertons surrendered under a white flag, the discipline that the workers had exhibited up to that moment broke, and unarmed Pinkerton men were abused. By dishonoring their pledge of safe passage for the surrendering Pinkertons, the workers lost public sympathy, and ultimately their cause. The workers' fight to exercise their rights against the unyielding Frick had resulted in the Pinkerton army losing the battle but Carnegie and Frick winning the war against the workers, exactly as they had set out to do. Carnegie had broken the union.

In 1890 the *County Capital* had published a story about the railroad using Pinkertons to suppress strikes and intimidate striking laborers, calling it a disgrace. The article stated, "Our laws are just and all men can live under

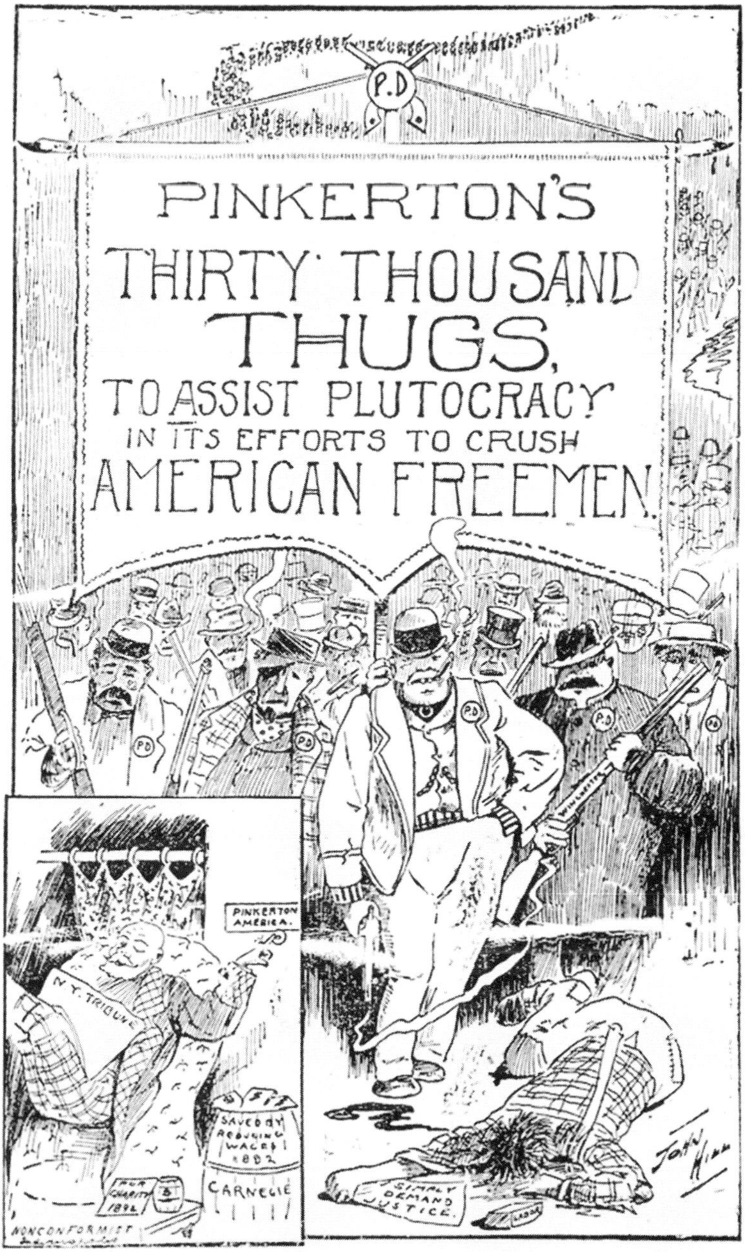

CARNEGIE: I simply press the button—Pinkerton does the rest.

Populists showed their empathy for the workers during the Homestead lockout, as is seen in this political cartoon as Carnegie summons the Pinkerton detectives with the press of a button. *County Capital*, August 12, 1892.

them and receive protection, without the assistance of hired thugs and assassins to enforce them." It condemned the railroad for bringing in "Robert Pinkerton, a man who holds no commission from the state or nation to recruit or arm men for military duty."[25] The *County Capital* also covered the Homestead strike. A political cartoon was published showing an army of thugs marching under a banner reading "Pinkerton's Thirty Thousand Thugs to Assist Plutocracy in its efforts to crush American Freedom," with an insert of Carnegie pressing a button to call the Pinkertons. Political cartoons had become a very effective way to communicate Populist positions.[26] As a subscriber to the *County Capital,* Isaac would have paid particular attention to the Pittsburgh lockout, since those events were happening near his childhood home.

THE WORK ENVIRONMENT of farmers like Isaac and the workers in the Pennsylvania steel mills could not have been more different, yet the problems they were confronting shared similarities—problems for which farmers and laborers had come together in the People's Party to form a voting bloc large enough to defeat the political power of the wealthy.[27] At the end of the nineteenth century, most Americans linked their love of liberty to individual freedom. For the working man or woman, that freedom had more to do with job security and dignity in their home, goals that required only a modest level of material acquisitions. For the wealthy men and women of the Gilded Age, that freedom meant having the liberty to expand their businesses toward monumental success, a quest that had led to an ever-growing disparity in wealth and power between laborers and those for whom they labored. The American dream of individual equality among all citizens had become a parody of the original intent. The struggles by individual farmers and industrial workers, when viewed on the national stage, illuminated the question of whether it was ever possible for all citizens of a representative system of government to maintain a balance in which wealth and power did not overwhelm the liberty and dignity of those living more humble lives.

Farmers demonized Wall Street, monopolies, and railroads, without necessarily considering their broader issues. However, the question could have been phrased: must Americans ever subordinate their individual liberty in order to serve the public needs of the whole society? Did the fact that railroad investors knew that farmers were dependent on their trains to get products to distant markets alter their liberty to extract higher shipping rates to increase the return on their investment? Because existing steel workers could be replaced by others willing to work longer hours in unsafe conditions and for less pay, should Carnegie and Frick enjoy the unfettered freedom to refuse to negotiate in good faith? Isaac may not have seen how all of these conflicts erupting across the nation were related to his own private struggle to save his farm, but resolving those questions was what linked farmers in Kansas, small ranchers in Wyoming, and the workers at the Homestead Mill.[28]

Ironically, Isaac actually shared a philosophical link with Carnegie. Implementing improvements in the means of production was admired by many for serving the common good and aiding the progress of civilization. Whether the innovations increased productivity and profits for the wealthy at the cost of lost jobs for workers was not regarded as a moral issue. Rather, in a time of rapid technological changes, when machines were replacing the labor of men, the acceptance of these changes were defined as simply by-products of the greater morality of improvement."[29] As an inventor, Isaac believed that his innovation to increase productivity and profits with the manufacturing of his three-horse cultivator would benefit all farmers. He seemed not to have considered that farming on the "bonanza plan," as he and Will Campbell had discussed, might displace smaller farmers. What Isaac saw was the means for his economic survival through patenting and marketing his invention, with the greater common good to agriculture resulting from improved production. His perception fit well with the morality of improvement that Carnegie used to justify the technological innovations employed in his steel mills.

If there were a lesson the farmers in Stafford County could take from the news they read of the Homestead lockout, it was that workers could not expect to succeed against wealth and power with violence. The best hope of farmers and laborers was to confront power with their ballots, electing politicians willing to preserve the balance of individual liberty for all Americans. Isaac and his neighbors in Stafford County were beginning to believe that was possible.

TWO OF ISAAC'S NEIGHBORS brought opposing political philosophies into sharp focus. Will Campbell had been convinced to run for the office of state representative again. His opponent on the Republican ticket was his neighbor, David Carnahan. Both were respected men in their community, having most things in common except their points of view politically.

As for capturing the office of president of the United States, farmers were less confident, and some were saying that it would be a waste of their vote to cast their ballot for Weaver. That opinion was stated so often that the *County Capital* used the question for its headline: "Is a Vote for Weaver a

Vote Thrown Away?" In answering the question, the editor gave his reasons to the contrary:

> This is a great year to vote for principle. . . . The currency and corporation monopolies of this country have a grip upon both the republican and democratic parties. . . . To a reformer there can be no significance in the success of either of the old parties. They both stand for special privileges of a few and against the interests of the many. They work together whenever there is any danger that a new party will unhorse them both. . . . The November election is not a horse race nor game of chance. It is the duty of every citizen to vote his convictions. We are upon the eve of a revival of principle, honor and equal justice.[30]

By mid-September people were beginning to believe the People's Party could prevail, as reflected in the headline, "The Hay-Seeds Actually Think They are Strictly in it."[31] The People's Rally of Stafford County on September 15 surpassed the most enthusiastic expectations, with 242 carriages and wagons in the procession around the courthouse and many more unhitched throughout the town, with the crowd estimated between 4,000 and 5,000 people. The main speaker was the Hon. Jerry Simpson, congressman from the 7th congressional district, who held the audience spellbound for two hours. Affectionately known as "Sockless Jerry," a moniker distinguishing him from wealthy politicians who wore silk stockings, Jeremiah Simpson's entry into politics was his selection as the town marshal of Medicine Lodge, Kansas, after a prairie blizzard killed his cattle herd and forced him to leave ranching. His involvement in politics, like that of most farmers and small ranchers, resulted from a search for economic solutions, first as a Greenbacker, then with the Union Labor Party, and eventually his election to the U.S. House of Representatives as a Populist. Farmers and ranchers trusted him because he was one of their own.[32]

In Stafford County, politics had even crept into the adjudication of the accused courthouse burglars. The stalled prosecution for theft of the county funds was finally resumed with the transfer of county treasurer Landes's trial to Lyons in Rice County. The trial of Ben Webber had been moved to Hutchinson in Reno County, both on motions for change of venue filed by the defendants' attorneys. When illness, conflicting schedules, and a mistrial further postponed both trials until at least December, the editor of the *Stafford Republican* seized the political opportunity to unfairly blame county attorney O. C. Jennings, who was opposing the Republican candidate in

HON. JERRY SIMPSON,
People's Congressman-elect, Seventh Kansas District.

Jerry Simpson, Populist, U.S. congressman for the 7th Kansas District. *County Capital,* February 5, 1891.

the upcoming election, although Jennings had argued in opposition to any further delays.

Although the trial postponements may have influenced some of the ballots cast for Stafford County attorney, they could not influence the election date itself. Isaac and other Populists would have analyzed the results closely when they were published in the *County Capital.* Weaver received only twenty-two electoral votes, nationally insignificant, but it was the first time a third-party candidate had received over a million votes. The People's Party elected five U.S. senators, ten U.S. representatives, three state governors, and about fifteen hundred state and county officials in its first year as a national party. In Stafford County, the People's Party claimed the majority in every race on the ballot. Campbell was elected state representative, defeating Carnahan by 355 votes countywide, although the voting in Albano Township ended in a tie of thirty-six votes for each man. Hilmes won his race for probate judge by 380 votes. Jennings was re-elected county attorney by a smaller margin than other races, his race undoubtedly having been tightened by disappointment with his inability to dispose of the courthouse prosecutions more expediently. The People's Party had gained majorities in the mid- to-high three-hundred vote range in every race except the county attorney's position.

Candidates for the U.S. Senate were chosen at that time by the vote of state legislators rather than directly by registered voters, and when there was a vacancy for the office of Kansas U.S. senator, the name of Mary Elizabeth Lease was frequently proposed, although women still lacked the right to vote in state and national elections.[33] In some ways, Kansas had been ahead of other states with regard to women's rights. The state constitution had granted women the right to acquire and possess property, as well as an equal right to custody of their children, unusual for that time. The first legislature had given women the right to vote in school elections. In 1867, the legislature had submitted to Kansas voters, (which of course meant male voters), an amendment to enfranchise white women, but the amendment had been defeated. However, the attempt made Kansas the first state to consider women's suffrage. In 1887 women's suffrage was achieved for city offices and by 1892 there were several Kansas towns with women mayors.[34]

ISAAC WOULD HAVE BEEN particularly saddened when St. John attorney John Guernsey died at the age of forty-one. Isaac's admiration dated back to Guernsey's defense of the fledging Farmers' Alliance when the group chose to merge their 1889 Fourth of July celebration with that of the Union Labor Party. After repeated attacks on that decision by the Stafford newspaper, Guernsey had defended both the Alliance and Mrs. Lease's patriotic speech. Isaac admired his calm and reasoned defense of the decision, and he felt an additional connection because both of them had come from Pennsylvania. Guernsey had earned his living there as a bookkeeper before coming to Kansas and studying law in Lyons. In Stafford he had set up his legal practice and also edited the *Stafford Democrat,* but by the time Isaac met him, Guernsey had moved his legal practice to the county seat of St. John. Now, his widow Sarah was left alone to care for their two sons.

The death of Guernsey would have been only the first of the tragedies that saddened Isaac that holiday season. He would never forget December 26, 1892. It was Monday evening about twenty minutes before five o'clock when a group of men were loafing at Winner's Drug Store, as men tended to do around the holidays. Among those gathered were some of the accused robbers, out on bail, including Ben Webber, Bill Glasscock, and Ed Landes. Ben and Bill had gone behind the prescription case for a private conversation, but Dr. W. J. Winner asked them to come away. They inquired whether he would mind if they continued their discussion in the drugstore warehouse, and Winner had no objection.

Perhaps fifteen minutes later, Milt Thomas, who was among the men congregated in the drugstore, went out to answer a call of nature. As he went through the warehouse, he noticed Ben and Bill. Bill later described what had happened, saying Thomas had greeted them with, "Hello boys. I didn't know you were there," apparently planning to continue on his way.

Instead, Ben said, "Thomas, you are trying to swear me into the penitentiary," drawing his revolver at the same time and pointing it at Thomas's face. The firing mechanism of Ben's revolver snapped so the bullet did not fire, but reacting to having been drawn upon, Thomas pulled his revolver and fired, and when Ben tried to take the gun, Thomas fired again.

Bill had dropped to his knees to crawl away from the shooting, but his was the eyewitness account of what had happened. When Thomas had finally wrenched himself free, he continued firing at Ben, and when the firing stopped, Thomas came out of the warehouse and walked through the drugstore, going immediately to the courthouse to surrender to the sheriff. The other men found Ben in a death struggle, gasping for breath, and while some carried Ben to the undertaker's establishment, another went for the doctor.[35] Dr. Hoaglin determined there were four wounds, three of which were almost certainly fatal, the fourth probably having been caused by one of the fatal trajectories. There was nothing Dr. Hoaglin could do.[36]

The inquest commenced the next morning, and the verdict of the coroner's jury was that "B. A. Webber came to his death on the 26th day of December, 1892, from pistol shot wounds from a 45 caliber Colt pistol in the hands of Milton Thomas. We further find according to the evidence that there was no felonious intent."[37]

Isaac could not know what Ben was thinking when he drew on Thomas. Nor did Isaac know what connection Thomas, a hardware salesman in St. John, might have had with the legal proceedings, nor why Ben would have thought drawing on Thomas would improve his legal situation. Had someone bought alcohol from the druggist that afternoon, which might offer some explanation for Ben's stupidly unexplainable act? Except for the success of the elections, it seemed 1892 had ended even worse than it had begun.

CHAPTER 10

1893

Isaac Werner was not yet fifty years old, but his declining health and the deaths of several friends made him feel older than his years. The victories of the People's Party in the 1892 November elections gave reason for hope but also forced the recognition of gradual changes in America since the Civil War.

As a boy in Pennsylvania, Isaac had grown up in a community of farmers whose ancestors had arrived into a wilderness of forests and swamps, from which they had carved out farms, acre by acre. By the time Isaac was born it was an agricultural valley of undulating fields, rows of crops growing in graceful curves along the gentle hillsides. Although Isaac's father platted Wernersville on his land in 1855, and some of the neighborhood houses had small businesses, like a tavern or a cabinetmaker's shop, it largely remained a community of separate farms whose center was the church. The arrival of the railroad, with "Wernersville" emblazoned on the depot, signaled a shift in the community, but Isaac left soon after.

The Civil War impacted the agrarian character of America, but because Isaac had gone west, he had not witnessed the industrial transformations of other regions. Of course, he had seen the arrival of the railroad in Wernersville shortly before he left, and the railroad had come to Rossville while he was the proprietor of the drugstore. Later, the railroad had benefitted his milling partnership, but a few years after its arrival he had relocated to

"Republican Idea of Finance" contrasted the financial management of farmers and businessmen. *County Capital,* August 28, 1896.

Kansas. There, his only mode of transportation for several years had been on foot, and the nearest sizeable towns had been miles away. The treeless prairie with its wide-open skies made it easy to ignore the industrial growth and increasing populations elsewhere.

American settlers had come to carve farms out of rocky New England and plantations in the humid South. In Isaac's time, pioneers like himself had carried that dream further west. Such an agrarian history made it seem that farmers would always be the foundation upon which the nation was built—upon which the nation depended.

Yet, the very thing that Isaac had seen as farmers' salvation, the ability for one farmer to cultivate more ground, meant that fewer farmers were needed. Extreme wealth had shifted from the prosperous landowners to the urban manufacturing giants, railroad magnates, and other monopolists, whose wealth was built on the efforts of laborers who barely participated economically. The devastation of the Civil War had altered the livelihood of both plantation and nonplantation farms, changing the lives of not only homesteaders on the prairie like Isaac but also farmers in the South.[1]

Farmers' decisions to join with the Union Labor Party had been a partial recognition that rural and urban laborers had more in common than

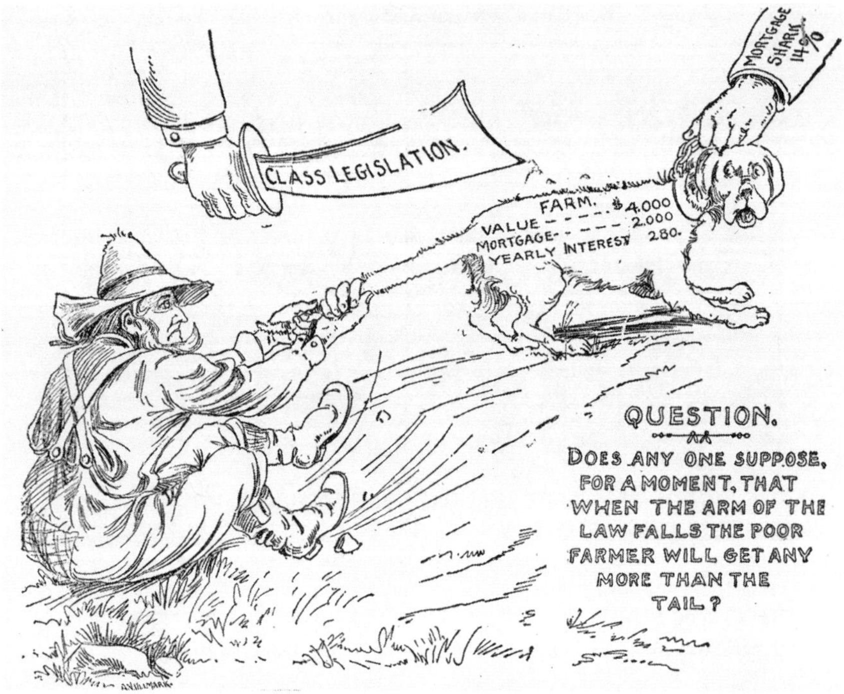

"Class Legislation" showed how unfair legislation left farmers with little but "the tail end of the dog." *County Capital*, February 23, 1894.

previously recognized. The ideal of a Jeffersonian Democracy built around farmers as the most valuable citizens and the truest Republicans had become obsolete. Perhaps, if the coalition of farmers and laborers could build on the success of the 1892 elections, the political power of the wealthy could be countered, but the agrarian life of Isaac's youth, and of generations before him who had created this nation, had forever changed.

Although Isaac's social life had decreased as his health declined, he would not have wanted to miss the surprise party for his friend Will Campbell. The recent political contest between close neighbors Campbell and David Carnahan had caused hard feelings in the community, but with the race won by Campbell, an occasion was planned in January to help sooth those feelings. When a few of Campbell's closest neighbors dropped by, their visits seemed no more than a friendly coincidence, serendipitous that they had all chosen the same evening to come. But as more neighbors began to fill Campbell's house to overflowing, and ladies began bringing out boxes and baskets and buckets of food, the organized occasion became obvious. Campbell was completely surprised and particularly enjoyed seeing neighbors who had fought him at the polls among his well-wishers.[2]

It was exciting to have a Populist governor in Topeka, and hearing Lorenzo D. Lewelling declare the People's Party themes in his inaugural address convinced farmers that they had a champion to confront the wealthy. Lewelling concluded his address by saying, "The government is not a failure. This is a generation which has come to rescue it."[3]

Despite Lewelling's hopes, his administration was not off to a smooth start.[4] Although the People's Party controlled the Kansas Senate, the Kansas House was in turmoil. Fifty-eight People's Party members had been elected, but sixty-five Republicans claimed seats, along with two Democrats. The People's Party believed that eighteen of the seats claimed by the Republicans were obtained through fraud, and the night of the governor's inauguration, the People's Party representatives adopted a resolution: "We are here by the voice of the people and we will disperse only at the point of the bayonet."[5]

In an attempt to resolve the dispute, what was termed a Committee of Fifteen," was formed to examine the evidence and devise a plan for resolving the disputed seats. The group consisted of five members from each of the three political parties, and Will Campbell was a member. Not unexpectedly, the Republicans immediately challenged the committee's power. Isaac's friend Will was now caught up in the controversy instead of settling down to the business he had been elected to do.

A letter from Mary Elizabeth Lease praising Campbell for his efforts on the Committee of Fifteen was published in the *County Capital,* and another week's paper included an interview of Campbell in which he described having used "all his influence and persuasive power with the republicans to bring the matter to an honorable and just settlement," adding that "republicans refused all, and would accept nothing but a clear back down, regardless of justice and honor."[6]

In the midst of the political turmoil, Isaac received news that his mother had passed away and was buried in Abilene, Kansas, where his sister Ettie and her family lived. It must have grieved Isaac to think of his parents laid to their final rest so far apart, preferring that his mother could have rested beside her husband William in the shaded cemetery on the hill just north of the old Hain's Church. Rebecca, as his mother was known, had been born and lived all of her life in the same general area of Pennsylvania, until moving to Kansas with Ettie's family.[7] Now, hers was the solitary grave in a plot far from her husband's burial place.[8]

The news from the state capital did not improve, and as a member of the House, Campbell had first-hand knowledge of the so-called Legislative War, which began from the moment the session was called to order on January 10. The People's Party challenged the fraudulent certifications of eighteen Republican members and seated their own candidates, proceeding to choose John M. Dunsmore as their Speaker on the grounds that they were the legitimate majority party. The Republicans ignored the challenges to the eighteen certifications and chose George Douglas as their speaker.[9]

If the disputed eighteen certifications had been awarded to the fifty-eight People's Party electees, their total representatives would have been seventy-six, and having removed the challenged Republicans, their certified representatives would have been reduced to forty-seven. Unlike the few Republicans who had been willing to listen to the evidence of fraud that had been collected, far more began shouting "Revolution!" and saying the Committee of Fifteen had no legal authority to nullify the voters' choices, despite evidence of significant vote tampering in those communities challenged by the People's Party representatives. Consequently, both sides held their positions and sent messages to Governor Lewelling and to the state senate that they were ready to do the state's business.

When the People's Party was recognized by both the governor and the state senate, the Republicans refused to accept those decisions. For thirty-one days the parties alternated use of the chamber, conducting business independently, but on February 14 the Republicans declared that if the Populists did not join them on the twenty-first, their seats would be declared vacant. Relying on the authority of having received legitimate recognition, the People's Party entered the chambers and locked the Republicans out. The Republicans responded by smashing the chamber doors, evicting the People's Party members, and issuing a call for outsiders to join in holding the chamber, at least some of whom were issued arms.[10]

Governor Lewelling went to the chambers and pleaded with the Republicans to vacate and allow the courts to resolve the matter, but they refused. At that point, Lewelling issued an executive order to Col. J. W. F. Hughes, the militia commander, to clear the hall. The colonel, a Republican, refused the order and was relieved of his command. A new commander was appointed, and with the militia stationed outside the capital, continued violence threatened. Although they realized that their concession foretold a predictable outcome, the People's Party nevertheless agreed to let the Kansas Supreme Court determine the matter. With a Republican majority on the court, the ruling in favor of the Republicans was handed down on February 28, with only eleven legislative days remaining. The session ended with few of the People's Party goals achieved.[11]

Colonel Hughes was court-martialed. His trial lasted twenty-four days, and he was found guilty, stripped of his rank, and dishonorably discharged. The Supreme Court's ruling in favor of the Republicans was not controlling in the court-martial, since it was undisputed that as an officer he had refused a direct order from his superior. The court-martial found that it was a lawful order, and Hughes's political sympathies should not have mattered. There were those, however, who regarded Colonel Hughes as a hero, arguing that his refusal may have avoided bloodshed. How people regarded his punishment generally depended on their political loyalties.[12]

THE SUBJECT THAT occupied most local conversations back in Stafford County was news of the arrests of a hog-stealing ring. The Harrison and Ross hog business had been missing hogs from their corral for some time, and although they thought they knew who was doing the stealing, they needed proof. It was the thieves themselves who brought about their capture by soliciting an employee as an accomplice. The man told them he needed to think it over, but instead he helped the sheriff set a trap by pretending to participate in the theft in order to learn when it would happen. On a dark night, the sheriff's posse was waiting for the thieves. The newspaper headline announcing the capture of the accused thieves read: "Behind the Bars!"[13]

The townspeople were furious, especially since some of the arrested men were out of jail under bond for their appearance in the courthouse burglary case. On the same front page headlining the capture of the hog thieves was the quarterly county commissioners' report, which included many bills related to the expenses of the courthouse burglary. Whether or not these hard economic facts were connected to the shift in community attitudes, the newspaper reported:

> When the burglary cases were first started quite a number of our citizens were inclined to show sympathy to the prisoners . . . and as a consequence, the cases have dragged from one term of the court to another, until the expenses of prosecution have reached thousands of dollars, and still no conviction nor acquittal. Our good people now

are free in expressing their dissatisfaction and are disgusted with such unreasonably slow procedure.[14]

The Landes case in Lyons finally went to the jury, which found Ed Landes guilty of embezzling $13,000 of the county's funds. He was sentenced to four years of hard labor at the state prison.[15] The eventual prosecution of the men arrested for stealing hogs progressed more rapidly than had the courthouse burglary trials. After having been held in the Hutchinson Jail pending trial, the accused were brought back to St. John,[16] where they were found guilty and sentenced to the Leavenworth Penitentiary.[17]

THE DROUGHT AND PRAIRIE FIRES had been difficult for farmers, but especially so for timber claimants like Isaac. A wildfire sweeping across a wheat field might destroy a year's crop, but a fire moving down tree rows could destroy many years of planting, watering, weeding, and pruning in only minutes. It was for that reason that Isaac had maintained the fireguards so religiously and cultivated his tree groves regularly. Even so, he had lost trees to a prairie fire, as had his neighbors, and drought had also taken its toll. Congress finally acknowledged those difficulties, first amending the law to allow a timber claimant to prove up by paying for the number of insufficient trees, and later allowing claimants to show efforts during the mandated eight years, even if insufficient trees had survived. It was a recognition by lawmakers that hard work for the whole time could not always produce enough trees.

Isaac had long thought another action by the legislature was needed, when at last a law to prohibit poaching native birds off of another person's land was finally passed. Isaac's neighbors would no longer be legally able to kill Isaac's half-tamed birds, so long as the birds stayed on his property. The protection had come too late for some native birds, as overhunting had nearly wiped them out, but it would limit the slaughter of those remaining.

TIMES HAD BEEN HARD in Kansas for several years, but the Panic of 1893 brought an economic depression that spread across the entire nation. Railroads had overbuilt, running lines to places that could not possibly produce sufficient freight or passenger travel to support the expense of building the lines or operating the trains that ran on them. Banks that loaned money for these ventures failed, and investors lost the money put into railroad stock. If there was a single moment to be identified as the beginning of the economic collapse, it may have been the bankruptcy of the Philadelphia & Reading Railroad, the company for which Isaac's brother-in-law, William E. Good, managed the Southwark Foundry & Machine Company in Philadelphia.[18]

Another contributing cause to the Panic of 1893 involved silver. In 1873 silver was demonetized,[19] and in an effort to compromise with the demand for a return to bimetallism, the Sherman Silver Purchase Act of 1890 increased the amount of silver the government was required to purchase each month, while maintaining the gold standard. Predictably, silver mines began producing more silver, and the market was driven down, forcing the U.S. Treasury to buy the required amount at about double its market value. Because treasury notes could be redeemed for either silver or gold, investors redeeming their notes for gold depleted the government's gold reserves. The bankruptcy of the Philadelphia & Reading Railroad happened just ten days before President Grover Cleveland's second inauguration,[20] and once in office, he immediately urged Congress to repeal the Sherman Silver Purchase Act to protect gold reserves. The Panic of 1893 resulted in the country's worst depression.

Groups connected with agriculture especially suffered. Foreign markets for crops dried up. Farmers were both unable to pay their debts and lacked cash to buy goods and services, so merchants in their communities suffered with them, as did manufacturers of farm equipment. Naturally, suppliers of the raw materials used by the manufacturers were impacted. Although banks could foreclose on farm mortgages, there were few buyers for the land or the equipment given as security, and even fewer investors willing to buy mortgages. Banks were left with mortgages they could not liquidate and customers with no cash to deposit. Depositors apprehensive about their banks' solvency made runs on banks, causing many to fail. The hard times that had begun for farmers in the mid- to late 1880s only deepened as the depression spread.

In contrast, the World's Fair: Columbian Exposition, commonly called the Chicago World's Fair, celebrated the growing stature of the young nation and its achievements. By the time the fair closed on October 30, 1893, nearly twenty-six million people had visited. With so little good news to publish, the *County Capital* covered the marvels of the fair throughout the six months it was open to the public. Isaac was left to content himself with reading about the exhibits intended to showcase America's emergence among other leading nations, for his declining health made travel impossible, even if he had felt financially able to attend.[21]

THE FAIR WAS not the only thing to attract international attention in Chicago during the summer of 1893. Controversy had surrounded the famous Haymarket Square confrontation between police and laborers since the night it happened in 1886. Four of the defendants had been hanged and a fifth had committed suicide, but three of the defendants remained in prison. Seven years after the Haymarket Square bombing, a petition for clemency was filed on their behalf with Illinois's governor.

John P. Altgeld was the first foreign-born citizen to be elected governor of Illinois, the first Chicagoan ever elected, and the first Democrat to have been elected since 1856 in a state that had been strongly Republican since Lincoln. Altgeld had served as a county prosecutor in Missouri and as a Cook County superior court judge in Chicago before becoming governor, so he was a man who knew the law, as well as the politics of Chicago. Prominent men, including lawyers, judges, bankers, and merchants, remained appalled by the legal abuses involved in the prosecution of the Haymarket defendants, and they joined in seeking executive clemency for the imprisoned men. Governor Altgeld decided to consider the case, but he began his published decision saying: "If the defendants had a fair trial . . . there ought to be no executive interference. . . . The soil of America is not adapted for the growth of anarchy." For those seeking mercy, the words from the governor must have conveyed that clemency was hopeless. However, Altgeld's decision was a detailed analysis of the trial record and sworn testimony excluded from evidence, showing legal abuses that included the improper manner of selecting the jurors, the inadequacy of the proof, the indiscriminate arresting of persons in the square, the evidence of police brutality that wasn't introduced, the testimony compelled by police threats, the political pressure applied by the mayor and city's corporate counsel, and the "malicious ferocity" exhibited by the trial judge toward the defendants during the trial and in publications and speeches made since the trial. Page by page, the former county prosecutor and superior court judge who was now governor laid bare the corruption in the Haymarket case. Altgeld granted an absolute pardon to Samuel Fielden, Oscar Neebe, and Michael Schwab on June 26, 1893.[22]

As would be expected, Governor Altgeld's actions in such a controversial case, and the manner in which his legal brief in granting the pardon placed blame squarely on influential people, earned him powerful enemies. Many in the press called him an "anarchist" and a "socialist," and his middle initial, which stood for the name Peter, was frequently used to mock the governor as John "Pardon" Altgeld.[23]

Years before, the *St. John News* had criticized John Askew for speaking in support of the defendants, calling Askew "an ignorant blatherskite." Now, Governor Altgeld had documented the deadly miscarriage of justice against the accused men.

Isaac's friend Mary Elizabeth Lease had been appointed by Governor Lewelling to serve on the state board of charities, but the unorthodox statements that made her a popular speaker had not been moderated in her new role, and she was asked to resign. Lease was not one to go quietly, and her damning statements against fusion, and against the governor, hurt the fragile coalition of the People's Party. She was not universally admired, despite Isaac's positive opinion. As one historian wrote, "Even those happiest with fusion would have been delighted to be rid of 'agrarian and paternal schemes of cranks like Mrs. Lease and her crazy followers.'"[24]

A look back to 1892 reveals the roots of a major disagreement within the People's Party. That year, a joint meeting in Kansas City of representatives from the Kansas Democratic and the People's Parties had been held to cooperate in naming the same candidates in upcoming elections in order to defeat Republican candidates. They decided that "the candidates of the two parties will be nominated at separate conventions, the Democrats on a Democratic platform and the People's Party on a reform platform, the object being to avoid endorsement by either party of the other's principles," while supporting the same candidates. With regard to state-wide races, they agreed "Democrats are to be given the candidates for Chief Justice of the Supreme Court and Congressman at Large. The rest of the State ticket is to be given to the People's Party."[25] Later, many Populists felt that the People's Party might have won the offices they ceded to the Democrats with their own candidates. Further, many believed that once in office the two old parties cooperated to defeat the political goals of the People's Party.

Disagreement about cooperating to fuse votes marked the beginning of a fatal split in the People's Party, which, it should be remembered, was from the beginning a complicated coalition. The difficulty of whether the People's Party should be content as a regional third party, at least for a while, or whether the party was ready to aspire to being a national power contributed to the disagreements.

Once the euphoria of the 1892 election successes had begun to wear off and the business of looking toward the 1893 elections began, these philosophical divisions began to fester. Fusionists (who wanted cooperation through fusion) and mid-roaders (who believed the temporary cooperation with either party only led to ineffectiveness after the election) fussed and picked at each other, and dissention infected the party like an untreated wound.

Unlike the complete success the People's Party had enjoyed in gaining county offices in the 1892 election, the local results in the 1893 election, without any fusion involved, were split. The People's Party won four offices, the Republicans also won four, and the Democrats gained none. Had a portion of the votes cast for Democratic candidates been cast for the People's Party candidates instead, the margins of Republican victories could have been easily overcome.[26] Those who favored fusion pointed to the 1893 results as proof of their position.

THE UNRELENTING HARD TIMES had reduced many Americans to such a degree of want that a population of tramps wandered the country in search of jobs, surviving on handouts. The police often treated these tramps harshly. Kansas governor Lewelling issued an appeal to the boards of police commissioners throughout the state:

> In this country, the monopoly of labor saving machinery and its devotion to selfish instead of social use, have rendered more and more human beings superfluous, until we have a standing army of the unemployed, numbering even into the most prosperous times not less than one million able bodied men; yet, until recently it was the prevailing notion, . . . that whoever, being able bodied and willing to work, can always find work to do, and Section 571 of the general statutes of 1889 is a disgraceful reminder how savage—even in Kansas our treatment has been of the most unhappy of our human brothers.
>
> . . . [T]housands of men, guilty of no crime but poverty, intent upon no crime but that of seeking employment, have languished in the city prisons of Kansas, or performed unrequited toil on "rock piles" as municipal slaves. . . . The victims have been the poor and humble, for whom police courts are courts of last resort—they cannot give bond and appeal.
>
> . . . To be found in a city "without visible means of support, or some legitimate business" is the involuntary condition of some millions at this moment, and [for which] we proceed to punish them . . .
>
> . . . The "rock pile" and the "bull pen" have only been used in degrading the friendless and poor, and as relics of the departed auction block era, should cease to disgrace the cities of Kansas.

> [. . .]
>
> It is confidently expected that their own regard for constitutional liberty and their human impulses will induce police commissioners to carry out the spirit as well as the letter of the foregoing suggestions.[27]

The response in Republican newspapers to the governor's call was immediate, referring to his appeal as an invitation to bums, tramps, thugs, and wharf-rats to come to Kansas, calling his words "another semi-socialistic manifesto" and the governor himself "a cowardly repulsive demagogue."[28]

Things seemed so divided and complicated to resolve, that many did not know where to turn for relief or solutions. Isaac had always maintained hope in the Farmers' Alliance making a difference through education and cooperation. The political movement of the People's Party had caused some of his neighbors to put their faith in the power of the ballot alone to change things. The potential economic benefits of the subtreasury plan had been shoved aside, and goals of the Farmers' Alliance neglected, as farmers relied on those they elected to confront Wall Street for them. Now, infighting between fusionists and mid-roaders was further weakening the unity of farmers.

As Isaac felt his strength draining away day by day, it seemed that his own suffering was a reflection of the suffering of the nation, continuing to lose strength with no one able to find a remedy.

CHAPTER 11

1894

Throughout his life, Isaac Werner had accommodated life's situations with a positive determination to make things better—for himself and for his community. Now those accommodations were harder, for they involved a letting go. His plans were simpler now, and dreams were for younger men.

Accommodating his aging body and its mysterious maladies was more difficult than the other transitions of his life. He was fifty years old and had never abused his body with liquor or tobacco, and while he was an indifferent cook unless he had guests, he believed his diet had been adequate, tending toward eating what was in season. With his chickens providing both eggs and meat, his diet was better than what many of his poor neighbors had to eat. As a druggist he had learned a bit about diagnosing symptoms and providing relief, if not cures, but he had no explanation for his illnesses, and recently the strength in his arms and legs had become alarmingly weak.[1]

In his small community, neighbors paid close attention to each other, sometimes helping when it was needed but other times intruding into personal matters. A sad scandal in a nearby township had been gossiped about for months but became an open secret when a young woman used a newly enacted law to file charges against a young male neighbor alleging "seduction under promise to marry." The jury had found the man guilty; however, after the matter was decided but before the judge had passed sentence, it was discovered that one of the jurors had made a run in the strip and had filed on a claim, intending to return to the strip in the spring.[2] Belatedly, the question of whether he was only temporarily residing in Stafford County was brought to the attention of the judge, who took the matter under advisement, raising the possibility that the poor young woman might have to face the humiliation of a new trial.[3]

While the judge pondered the matter of a new trial, *County Capital* editor John Hilmes chose to publish the closing argument given by the state's attorney.

> This is the first test made of the law in this county . . . [a law enacted] for the benefit of society, to restrain the young men and protect the young women who have not yet been debauched and ruined by the libertine. . . . It is not half as important that this defendant be punished as that the precedent [be] made for enforcing the law. . . . But if on the other hand notice is given that the guilty need not fear, seductions will multiply and the once pure and innocent girls who have been ruined will menace and disgrace society and reproach and shame justice. Enforce this law . . . and this class of cases will disappear from the dockets of our courts, and a promise of marriage will mean something and the young woman who places her affections and bestows her love on a young man will be secure, for true men don't attempt the ruin of those they love and intend to wed.[4]

Some thought it should have remained a private matter of little consequence (an odd argument, since a pregnancy had resulted from the seduction). From its beginnings the Populist movement among farmers had placed emphasis on personal character. The Alliance principles had specifically avoided partisan politics, stressing instead "to develop a better state mentally, morally, socially, and financially," and declaring as its cardinal doctrine "purity of thought and life." Criminalizing seduction under promise to marry, rather than imposing a civil duty of child support, reflected the continuing attitudes toward moral accountability.[5]

The judge ruled that the juror who had staked a claim in the territory was unqualified to serve on the jury, but at the conclusion of the new trial a second set of jurors reached the same guilty verdict. The young seducer was sentenced to eighteen months hard labor at Lansing Prison.

An even more disturbing event involved Isaac's former neighbor, Jacob (Jake) Baker, for whom he had acted as agent. Isaac disapproved of Jake's seeming unwillingness to settle down to plain hard work and protecting his claim. Horse racing had been a distraction, and Isaac suspected Jake had lost more money putting up his entry fees in challenge races than he ever won. Eventually Jake had married and had a little girl, settling in Naron Township to the south of Isaac. The death of Jake's wife had been a hard blow, and he had sent his daughter to live with his wife's family. His reputation in the Naron community was that of an honest, hard-working farmer, and it appeared that the faults Isaac had found in his friend had been overcome.

Therefore, the front-page headline on February 23 in the *County Capital* was a shock: "Jacob Baker Murdered." A man in McLellan Township in Pratt County had found a wagon and harness out on the prairie while he was herding cattle. Too busy to look further, the man had told his wife about the discovery but had returned to work. She waited until her children came from school and took them with her to investigate. It was one of the children who discovered Jake's body, concealed in the tall prairie grass about three hundred yards from the wagon. The woman found identifying papers in his coat pocket, and a pocket notebook had been rifled and left under his body.

When her husband came home for supper, she described their discovery, and he went to Cullison to telegraph the Pratt County coroner. Dr. J. B. Gray came the next morning, summoned a jury and witnesses, and conducted an inquest at the site. It was determined that a ball had been fired into the back of Jake's head, exiting just below one eye, and probably killing him almost instantly.

Following leads supplied by neighbors, Sheriff Williamson arrested Green Roberts and Elsworth Hacker, who almost immediately made their confessions, although their versions of what happened differed. They agreed that Jake confronted Roberts at the Hacker home about some horses Roberts had bought but for which he had neither paid nor given security. Jake stayed overnight at the Hacker's' home, and the next morning Jake, Roberts, and Hacker went to look for the horses in the sand hills.

The two confessions were consistent to this point, but about the shooting itself, their stories diverged. Roberts admitted that the shot to the back of Jake's head had been fired by him, but only because when the previous day's quarrel had resumed, Jake had drawn a knife, and both he and Hacker had drawn their guns and fired in self-defense. Roberts claimed that the shot under Jake's eye, described as an exit wound by the coroner, was instead an entry wound fired by Hacker.

Hacker's description was quite different. He described sitting next to Jake, with Roberts behind both of them. He said that after Roberts shot Jake, he feared for his own life and let Roberts take over, without ever firing his own gun. He claimed that Roberts had thrown Jake's body out of the wagon and had rifled through Jake's pocketbook, presumably looking for any record of the disputed horse sale. Then, they had removed the harness and turned the horses loose to avoid suspicion if the team were to have pulled the empty wagon home. Hacker finished his confession by telling how Roberts had thrown his revolver into the Hackers' well. Hacker believed there was nothing he could have done to help Jake, and he said he acted as he did out of fear that Roberts would shoot him as well.

Jailed in separate cells, both men adhered to their stories. This presented the court with a legal dilemma, as a defendant could not be found guilty in the first degree for a murder to which he had confessed. For that reason, Judge Bashore allowed Roberts to plead guilty to murder in the second degree, for which his sentence was hard labor in the state penitentiary for the remainder of his life. Then, relying on Roberts's confession, the jury found Hacker guilty of murder in the first degree, for which the penalty was hanging. Upon receiving his sentence, Hacker thanked the jailors for their kind treatment but softly spoke these words to the judge and jury: "You are sending the wrong man over the road. I didn't kill Baker."[6]

Isaac prided himself on his studies of logic and the law, and as he read the newspaper accounts of the case closely he could not have helped wondering why the jury had ignored the coroner's determination that the wound under Jake's eye was an exit wound. If so, Jake was killed by Roberts's single shot.[7] Isaac could only hope that Jake had died quickly, unaware of his companions' murderous intent but for a momentary flash of pain as he died.

The political animosity between Isaac's neighbors, Will Campbell and David Carnahan, had flared again. Having taken offense to a comment he wrongly attributed to Campbell, Carnahan had written in the *St. John News* that "the leaders of the pops [Populists] have done all they could to destroy the patriotism of the people toward their country."

As before, the quarrel between the two neighbors played out in the newspapers. Campbell replied to the disparagement of Populists' patriotism by attacking the Republicans' reputation for seeking votes by "waving the bloodied shirt," a term referring to the sacrifices of Union soldiers. As a Union veteran, Campbell took Carnahan's words personally:

> I am awfully tired of such charges, when they come from a man who was afraid to fight for his country when he had an opportunity. Mr. Carnahan was a native of Pennsylvania, [but] did he join the army to help repel Lee's invasion of '63? Not much. . . . He stayed at a distance and let other men from another state defend his native state. . . . [I]t makes me awfully tired in these piping times of peace to hear men who never gave a day's service or a drop of blood to the nation eternally howling about patriotism. . . . If a man wants office he generally begins to tell the dear people . . . how ready he is to sacrifice himself on the altar of his country; but my observation, in the sixties the times that tried men's souls taught me that that class of men never spilled much gore when they had such a grand opportunity. Howling patriots never do much fighting in times of national peril. It is the quiet man that does the fighting[.][8]

During the Civil War, there had been an active organization of draft resisters and southern sympathizers in Pennsylvania, particularly in Isaac's community.[9] Isaac's former schoolteacher had waited more than two decades to publish a novel about the Civil War resisters. The close resemblance of his fictional town to Wernersville, as well as what readers saw as thinly veiled descriptions of actual Wernersville residents during the 1860s, led them to believe that the author had fictionalized only about a third of his novel, two-thirds easily identifiable as specific people and events. Although Isaac never wrote about his family's attitudes about the Civil War, it is certain that he did not serve the Union, although many younger boys did, including some of his Werner cousins. However, Isaac's journal contained several critical entries about former Union soldiers in his community who continued to vote Republican, despite that party's neglect and mistreatment of Union veterans. He would have agreed with Campbell's response to Carnahan.

As Isaac's health worsened, G. G. John began calling on him daily and built an invalid chair for Isaac, similar to the one Isaac had built for Frank Curtis years before. Doc Dix called on Isaac when he was in the community, offering what medical relief he could. However, without the daily attendance of G. G. John, Isaac could not have remained in his home.[10] G. G. John was nearly two decades younger than Isaac, having come to Kansas from Virginia. He and his family lived on Persis Vosburgh's old place just to the west of Isaac's timber claim, a handy walk to Isaac's house. The younger man was quite a scholar and enjoyed browsing among Isaac's books and discussing philosophy.[11]

Attendance at the Farmers' Alliance meetings had declined after the 1892 elections, but on a rainy day in May an unexpectedly large crowd gathered at a joint Alliance meeting in St. John to hear three speakers.[12] When the rain worsened, a resolution in support of the Coxey movement was quickly passed before adjourning.

The Populist movement had built momentum from its beginning through rallies and parades, and it was natural that when unemployed men wanted to bring attention to their plight they would stage mass demonstrations. The Coxey movement was not the only such group to attempt a march to bring attention to their desperation, but with what came to be known as "Coxey's Army," led by Jacob Coxey, was the most successful in gaining nationwide publicity, although not the government remedy they sought.

Born in Pennsylvania, Coxey began his working life as a laborer, but near the age of thirty he settled in Ohio, where he did very well. Although his wealth increased, he retained a genuine concern for the working classes, which influenced his political affiliations, first as a Democrat, then as a Greenbacker, and eventually as a member of the People's Party.

Coxey devised a plan for a march of working men to Washington, DC, with the goal of having the federal government put unemployed men to work improving roads and building public works. Essential to the plan was issuance by the government of treasury notes to be placed in a fund known as the "general county road fund system of the United States." Unemployed men would be paid $1.50 per eight-hour day from this fund for their labor, and the secretary of war would oversee the construction of a national road system. The men making the march in support of Coxey's idea constituted a "living petition" to Congress.

Coxey left Massillon, Ohio, with one hundred men, picking up more marchers along the way until about six thousand men had joined the march.[13] Concern about so many men entering Washington, DC, resulted in the issuance of a notice by the office of the commissioners of the District of Columbia, expressing sympathy for their cause but warning that "the laws in force in the District of Columbia are adequate for every emergency and will be rigidly enforced." Coxey heeded the notice by arriving at the Capitol with only a small portion of the men he had led. He was immediately arrested for walking on the grass and was not allowed to read his speech on the steps of the Capitol as he had wished; however, a congressman sympathetic to the cause got the speech entered into the Congressional Record, and newspapers, including the *County Capital,* published it widely. Despite

GROVER AND HIS FRIENDS.

"Keep Off the Grass," distinguished between the welcome given by the federal government to the wealthy and to foreign dignitaries as opposed to the Coxey Army marchers who had come to plead for assistance and were arrested for stepping off the sidewalk. *County Capital*, October 19, 1894.

the government's fears of Coxey's Army, the marchers disbursed peaceably, and Coxey succeeded in gaining enormous publicity about the severity of suffering by workers throughout the nation.[14] A book about the march written by Kansas newspaperman Henry Vincent spread the message further, but the road construction work project was not implemented.[15]

The punishment Coxey received for walking on the grass was more of a scolding. The judge called Coxey "a dreamer," and sentenced him and two other men to twenty days imprisonment for displaying a banner on the Capitol grounds, with a fine of five dollars for trespassing. Coxey's speech included these words:

> The constitution of the United States guarantees to all citizens the right to peacefully assemble and petition for redress of grievances. . . . We chose this place of assemblage because it is the property of the people. . . . Upon these steps where we stand has been spread a carpet for

> the royal feet of a foreign princess . . . [and] lobbyists of trusts and corporations have passed unchallenged on their way to committee rooms, to which we the representatives of the toiling wealth producers, have been denied.
>
> We stand here to-day on behalf of millions of toilers whose petitions have been buried in committee rooms, whose prayers have been unresponded to, and whose opportunities for honest, remunerative, protective labor have been taken from them by unjust legislation. . . . We come to remind congress of the declaration of a United States senator, that for a quarter of a century the rich have been growing richer, the poor poorer, and that by the close of the present century the middle class will have disappeared, as the struggle for existence becomes fierce and relentless.
>
> . . . our march of over 500 miles through difficulties and distress, a march unstained by even the slightest act which would bring the blush of shame to any, [shows] that we are law abiding citizens, and as such our actions speak louder than words. We are here to petition for legislation which will furnish employment for every man able and willing to work. . . . We are here to tell our representatives, who hold their seats, by the grace of our ballots, that the struggle for existence has become far too fierce and relentless. We come and throw up our defenseless hands and say, "help or we and our loved ones must perish."[16]

Workers across the nation were finding ways to make their struggles known. Peaceful appeals to reason did not always succeed, and one such failure by workers attempting to negotiate with management had put Illinois governor John P. Altgeld back in the national news. George Pullman's famous sleeper and luxury railroad cars were manufactured in Pullman, Illinois, near Chicago, at a plant that included a model town, with homes, parks, shops, and a library. The Panic of 1893 had reduced the Pullman Palace Car Company revenues, and Pullman had responded to the economic downturn by cutting workers' wages. What he had not done, however, was lower the rent workers paid for their company-owned houses. Because workers were pressured, and in some cases required, to live in these houses, for which the rent was higher than comparable houses in the area, the workers selected a committee to meet with Pullman to request a rent adjustment consistent with the pay cuts. He not only refused, but he fired three of the committee members who had met with him. A strike followed.

The political cartoon "Railroad Slaughter" was intended to show railroad workers that they too had reason to join the Populist movement. *County Capital*, October 12, 1892.

When American Railway Union members joined the strike and refused to handle Pullman cars, a special federal attorney was appointed. Richard Olney, general counsel for the Chicago, Milwaukee, and St. Paul Railway was chosen, and the selection of a railroad lawyer in a position of government authority exacerbated the situation. When President Cleveland sent federal troops, things grew even worse.

On July 5th Governor Altgeld sent his protest against the use of U.S. troops to the president:

> Dear Sir: I am advised that you have ordered Federal troops to go into service in the State of Illinois. Surely the facts have not been correctly presented to you in this case. . . . So far as I have been advised the local officials have been able to handle the situation. But if any assistance were needed, the State stood ready to furnish 100 men for every man required. . . . Notwithstanding these facts, the Federal Government

> has been applied to by men who had political and selfish motives for wanting to ignore the State government. . . . To absolutely ignore a local government in matters of this kind . . . not only insults the people of the State by imputing to them an inability to govern themselves or unwillingness to enforce the law, but is in violation of a basic principle of our institutions. . . . As governor of the State of Illinois, I protest against this, and ask the immediate withdrawal of the Federal troops from active duty in this State.[17]

The governor's protest was ignored, and what had been an essentially peaceful strike erupted into mayhem when the troops arrived. President Cleveland's decision to send in federal troops was the first time soldiers fired on and killed American citizens against the wishes of the executive of a state. Lives were lost, property was destroyed, and the rents for workers' homes in the company town were not reduced. In a gesture that seemed more scurrilous than genuine, President Cleveland and Congress rushed legislation through in six days following the end of the strike to establish Labor Day as a federal holiday.[18]

Once again, a religious denomination was taking a position on political matters. Much as Methodists had intervened by telling their members not to vote for any party that did not support Prohibition, Kansas Congregationalist ministers were now taking a political position by criticizing the nation's indifference to the suffering caused by existing social conditions. Rev. George D. Herron, a professor of Applied Christianity at Iowa State University, specifically advocated what he called Christian socialism, stressing that with a quarter of America's citizens "face-to-face with absolute want, and the wealth of the land controlled by the mighty few" it was time for the government to act.[19] Although the People's Party may not have been directly endorsed, their goals were certainly more aligned with the Congregationalists' call for political action.

Although Isaac was dealing with his own poor health and no longer played an active role as a community activist, he would have been concerned by rumors that his old political friend, Mary Elizabeth Lease, was suffering problems with her heart. However, her private secretary released news that it was inflammatory rheumatism, adding that "Mrs. Lease was improving rapidly and continuing to write, using her left hand."

As Isaac had predicted, women's rights remained a forceful political issue, and editor Hilmes published his support for women's suffrage, although he acknowledged that no one in the community with whom he had spoken favored it. Hilmes challenged: "Are those (our mothers and wives) we entrust with the nurture and raising and to a large extent educating the future voters not entitled to vote. . . . It is said that we should not . . . [add] the additional burden on the mothers by expecting them to vote. Well, if they don't see fit, they need not go, but let us extend to them the right that they may go if they so desire."[20]

During their convention Republicans chose to ignore women's suffrage in their platform rather than confronting divisions within the party, and initially the Populists tried to do the same. The majority report of the People's Party Resolutions Committee omitted women's suffrage, but those who believed there should be such a plank filed a minority report.[21] The divisive issue of women's suffrage was fought on the convention floor, and although statements were limited to five minutes, the heated debate raged all morning, concluding with one final speaker from each side.

Annie LaPorte Diggs, a Populist writer and lecturer, as well as a poet, temperance advocate, suffrage advocate, and for one year the leader of a Unitarian church in Lawrence, Kansas, spoke for a suffrage plank: "If you take a noble, manly and courageous stand, as I am sure you will, then every cowardly Republican candidate will be forced to go upon the rostrum and plead the record of his party in its defense." Peter Elder was a banker, the president of a railroad, a newspaperman, and as a former Republican had been lieutenant governor of Kansas and had served in the Kansas House of Representatives where he was elected Speaker, and in 1890 had served in the House again and was elected Speaker again, this time on the Alliance ticket. Although he had been an abolitionist, he had long been outspoken against women's suffrage and concluded the argument for his side of the issue: "In the name of the great Jehovah and the Continental Congress, we have been struggling for fifteen years against Republicanism. Don't, for God's sake, ladies, don't drag us down this time so we cannot whip them. You will not gain anything." The convention voted in favor of the women.[22]

As is often typical during election years, rumoring was rampant, and the *County Capital* published the rumors about the State Bank of St. John that were circulating, alleging that debtors were told that if they wished an extension or a loan they needed to support Republican candidates.

G. G. JOHN CONTINUED through the summer to make his daily visits, allowing Isaac to remain in his own home for as long as possible; however, Isaac's mobility had deteriorated so severely that he was no longer able to manage the chair G. G. John had built for him and had to be carried. G. G. John became Isaac's link to news about the community, sharing information about local events like the harvest picnic held at Neelands Grove. The crowd was estimated at twelve hundred and people of all political persuasions were present. Will Campbell had been the chairman of the meeting, and the orators were William Fisher Brown of Pratt County and A. A. Doerr of Pawnee County. Although it was not strictly a People's Party rally, the tone tended in that direction.

Neelands Grove was also the site for two reunions, planned for consecutive days—a reunion of early settlers to the area and a reunion of old soldiers. Isaac would have enjoyed gathering with other early settlers to remember the unbroken prairie they had courageously tamed with fields and pastures, schools, and towns. Many of the same men were represented in both reunions. Aaron Beck, who had never fully recovered from the stroke he suffered, was among nearly eighty veterans attending the reunion, along with Campbell, George Henn, and several of Isaac's prairie friends that had worn the Union blue.[23] Through G. G. John, Isaac learned of those events as well.

Not even his friend Doc Dix had an explanation for Isaac's decline, but at last everyone agreed that his symptoms had become too grave for him to manage in his own home. On September 11, George Hall and W. P. Holbrook brought a wagon to transport Isaac and some of his belongings to the Hall residence on the Rattlesnake Creek to begin receiving round-the-clock care.[24, 25] George and his wife Theresa had four children, and although their hired hand Holbrook had agreed to stay with Isaac during the night, it was quickly apparent that the invalid care Isaac needed was not possible for Theresa to assume in addition to her family's needs. They began talking with other neighbors about moving Isaac.

George and Nancy Henn were Isaac's neighbors just to the north of his timber claim, and perhaps Nancy had not forgotten Isaac's kindnesses to her son Frank years ago when death had threatened. It would be crowded to make room for Isaac, but the Henns agreed.[26]

The political news from the 1894 elections was disappointing. The Republicans had swept nearly all the local races, although by generally narrow margins. Hilmes had been defeated for probate judge by H. C. Hockensmith. The People's Party had given the old parties enough of a scare in 1892 that the Democrats joined the Republicans in 1894 to defeat the People's Party. Among the good news was Campbell's return to the state House, along with candidates in Stafford, Pratt, Pawnee, and Edwards counties, whose voters had elected all People's Party candidates to the state legislature.[27]

The women's suffrage amendment failed to pass, but the support for the amendment in Stafford County was higher than expected: 830 Stafford County men having voted yea, but 729 having voted against women receiving the vote.[28] Apparently, Hilmes's informal survey of support for women's suffrage had encountered men unwilling to publicly declare their views but willing to vote in favor of women getting the vote.

As Isaac lay helpless in another man's house, these words from his beloved Shakespeare may have come him: "Since brass, nor stone, nor earth, nor boundless sea, / But sad mortality o'er-sways their power, . . . O fearful meditation! . . . what strong hand can hold his swift foot back?"[29]

CHAPTER 12

1895

The adoption of the People's Party goals into the old parties' platforms caused some to believe that the need for the Farmers' Alliance and its support of the People's Party had faded. John Hilmes warned: "True, the influence of the Alliance principles are felt even among the old parties, but let us slack up in our work . . . and in a short time the politicians will rule and dominate this country worse than ever."[1]

The political activity of recent years had not overcome hard times, and some men were driven to desperate acts. Four inept robbers attempted to hold up a train traveling from Hutchinson to Kinsley one wintery night. From their seats passengers could hear the clanging of blows to the safe in the express car, and they suspected robbing the passengers might be next. They hid their valuables, making sure to leave enough in pockets and purses to satisfy the robbers that they were handing over all that they possessed. Having failed to access the contents of the safe, the robbers entered the passenger compartment, and making a great show of despair at having to relinquish their valuables, passengers gave up the money and objects they had retained for exactly that purpose. Altogether, the amateurish robbers got about $200, but the passengers and railroad employees were unharmed.

Even those doing well sometimes experienced the despair prevalent in their communities. There seemed to be no explanation for the suicide of farmer Otto Ihl, but the will and instructions for his funeral that were found after his death indicated thoughtful preparations.

These were dark days for Isaac Werner. Although he still had many friends living in the community, it is unknown whether visitors were welcomed once he was in the care of the Henns. Perhaps it was difficult for friends to see his severe decline, or, as too often happens when friends are ill, good intentions are neglected in the rush of other responsibilities. As the end grew near for Isaac, Nancy Henn summoned Dr. W. R. Willcox,[2] but there was little that could be done. When death finally came it was no surprise. The notice of his passing was published in the *County Capital:* "DIED—At the residence of George Henn in Albano township, last Thursday evening, Mr. I. B. Werner, aged about 48 [sic] years. Deceased was a single man and had been sick for about two years. For the last six months or more, he made his home with George Henn, being unable to take care for himself."[3]

The death notice seemed inadequate for such an accomplished man who had held many offices and served his community faithfully, but no obituary was published in the *County Capital* in the following days. The obituary his family published in the *Reading (PA) Eagle* mentioned his carpentry skills and his farm, "which he converted into a fine property." It also included that "for nine months he was almost helpless."[4] How difficult it must have been for Isaac, a man of such dignity and independence, to be reduced in his final months to reliance on others for even his most personal needs. The sad details of his final year were probably not the way this proud and self-sufficient man would have wanted to be remembered.[5] So much better it would have been for his obituary to have shared his literary accomplishments and the offices he had held in his community.

When probate Judge Hockensmith learned of the death, he immediately appointed Willcox to administer the estate, and the affidavit of death and letters of administration were executed the following day.[6] With the death notice having been published, Willcox was concerned about thefts of property and quickly appointed three neighbors to inventory and appraise Isaac's estate in preparation for a sale. By the fifth of April, the appraisers had finished their task, and the life's work of Isaac Beckley Werner had been reduced to a few columns of impersonal itemization on a handful of inventory pages.

Willcox benefitted from Isaac's careful financial records. During the years of his declining health, Isaac had managed to pay off his bank notes, and there were no outstanding mortgages on homestead or personal property.[7] His only indebtedness was a small loan of thirty dollars owed Doc Dix. The legal status of the timber claim had always been confusing to his neighbors, who had watched Isaac plant every tree on the place and keep the trees growing and healthy through droughts and prairie fires. Yet, it was his twin brother Henry who received the patent from the U.S. government. Once Willcox had satisfied himself that the timber claim was not part of Isaac's estate, the matter was no longer his concern.[8] The estimated value placed on Isaacs's personal property by the three appraisers was $531.38, and combined with five notes totaling $600 owed to Isaac by some of his neighbors, it seemed that Isaac's assets would be more than adequate to cover the expenses of his burial and the administration of his estate, even excluding the value of his homestead.

Caring for a patient in Isaac's condition was an onerous responsibility requiring "round-the-clock" attention, so it was not surprising that George Henn inquired about the proper way to make a claim against the estate. What was surprising was the amount of the claim submitted by the Henns. Isaac had been in their care for exactly six months, for which they claimed a fee for boarding of ten dollars a month, $2.50 a day for nursing care, and $2.50 per night for nursing care, comprising a total claim of $960 for the six months Isaac had stayed in their home. George wasted no time in presenting his claim and asking for a draw against what he believed he was owed. The many uncompensated kindnesses Isaac had done for them, including the extraordinary efforts taken during their son Frank's life-threatening illness, seem to have been ignored by the Henns. Willcox gave George a ten-dollar draw, deferring consideration of the balance to await the liquidation of Isaac's property and the approval of the probate judge before any other amount of his claim could be paid.

Because wheat stored in the bin on Isaac's homestead made such an easy target for a thief, Willcox quickly found a buyer and hired a neighbor to haul the wheat to town. The date of the estate sale was set for April 26, and H. S. Kephart was engaged as auctioneer. Isaac's surviving heirs were his twin brother Henry, his sister Henrietta, and the four children of his deceased sister Emma, none of whom expressed an interest in his personal property. The carefully selected collections of books, photograph cards, stereoscopic views, and furnishings of Isaac's home were all put into the estate sale, none going to nieces and nephews as a remembrance of an uncle they had never been fortunate enough to meet.[9]

It was spring, and farmers were busy, but Isaac's sale drew a crowd. There were about a hundred men[10] clustered in groups around those items in which they had particular interest, sizing up who might be likely to bid against them and trying not to reveal their own acquisitiveness. There seemed to be a particular group that was most interested in Isaac's books, taking pains not to show their interest as they searched through the stacks and boxes. Willcox set aside certain volumes to be auctioned separately, among those being Milton's *Poetical Works*; *Recollections of Bryon*; John Stuart Mills's *System of Logic*; Herodotus's *The Histories*; James Boswell's *Life of Johnson*; Plutarch's *Lives of the Noble Greeks & Romans* and *Moralia*; Friedrich Schiller's *Complete Works*; Johann Wolfgang von Goethe's *Gedichet*; the tragedies of Aeschylus; and several volumes of Shakespeare. Sold in groups were multiple volumes of art, law, history, topography, drawing, bookkeeping, languages, literature, encyclopedias and dictionaries, handbooks about foreign cities, legends and myths, and many more. The doctor watched closely to keep would-be bidders from trying to rearrange the contents or hide a desired book in a box of lesser titles.[11]

As is typical of such sales, some of the people were there out of curiosity, others simply for the idea of a neighborhood gathering. A few had come because of particular items they wanted, others there to take advantage of a bargain if something sold cheaply. Isaac was known for taking good care of his property and for knowing quality, so serious bidders had come to buy. Unfortunately, in such hard times not every bidder had cash. Notes were acceptable, although such bidders were required to secure a cosigner because of their limited means to pay. Several pairs of men cosigned for each other, suggesting that the cosigner was probably no more likely to be able to pay than the bidder himself, and if one defaulted, the other would likely do the same. However, a sale in such hard times without a provision for credit would have had few buyers.

Auctioneer H. S. Kephart knew how to keep the bidding active, sometimes pulling bids out of people as much for the entertainment he provided as for the item on the bidding block. His middle name was Speaker, given to him by his parents, as he liked to tell people, because they wanted him to grow up to be a public orator. For a time he did his speaking from the pulpit of the United Brethren Church, but more people knew him for his auctioneering talents than as a preacher. As a Union soldier, he had been shot in the knee and had used a cane since then, and during an auction his cane was often flourished as a theatrical prop to draw bids. After conducting too many auctions in which the property was little more than junk, Isaac's belongings must have inspired Kephart to perform with all his skills.[12]

Two of the four men with outstanding notes owed to Isaac were bidding at the sale and giving notes for what they purchased. That made it seem even less likely that those notes would ever be paid. One of the men had given Isaac two mules and two ponies as security for his note. Willcox had taken the mules and one of the ponies in partial satisfaction of the debt (the other pony having died), and now the man had shown up at the sale to buy back the same mules at a bargain price. Although that seemed unfair, if there was no one to outbid the man, his bid was apparently the top of the market in the community.

David Carnahan was there with his son, buying Isaac's tools. Carnahan had worked on construction jobs with Isaac and knew the high quality of Isaac's carpentry tools and how professionally Isaac had used and cared for them. He seemed especially determined to buy Isaac's chisels. Even Isaac's clothing sold well. Apparently Charles Hainline wore the same size shoe, because he bought Isaac's fine boots and every pair of shoes that came up for sale. Several of the men who had worked for Isaac digging potatoes, planting corn, and breaking sod bought tools and equipment they had used doing those jobs.[13] Bidders for the dishes had their instructions from the ladies watching at a distance.

But the bidding for the books was the most active. Isaac would have liked that. William Fisher Brown was one of the most aggressive bidders, buying specific titles rather than boxes of books.[14] Doc Dix also acquired several titles. When it was time to sell the horses, everyone recalled the good care Isaac had given them. He did not always approve of the way his neighbors worked their animals, and he would never have wanted them to go where they might be ill-treated, but that day the horses were sold to whomever got the last bid.[15]

Some of Isaac's property was purchased ahead of time at private sales, not necessarily the way to realize the best price, although $143.93 had been raised, the largest amount coming from the wheat and from purchases by the Henns, which were credited against what they claimed for Isaac's care.

At the end of the day, the public estate sale had raised $562.54, some of which had been credited to claims against the estate, with $482.74 purchased with notes that might not be fully paid. The role of Willcox was about to change to bookkeeper and bill collector, but at least Isaac had been buried properly, his family had been notified, and the assets had been held safely until they were sold.

The day of the sale, Otto Ihl's suicide was the main topic of conversation, apart from talk about Isaac and his property. The peculiarity of Ihl's disinterment the week after his burial in the Hudson Cemetery where he had specifically asked to be buried caused gossip. His body had been transported elsewhere, presumably where one of his siblings wished him to be buried. It also caused gossip that Ihl left his land to his sister who lived in Germany. The executor of Ihl's estate was concerned that the law passed by the Kansas legislature in 1891 prohibiting the foreign ownership of land made it impossible to transfer title to his sister as Ihl had wished. The executor had traveled to New York to consult with Ihl's brother about the matter. The brother, who had a large and successful business in that city, was insistent that he wanted Ihl's wishes honored, so they consulted an attorney in New York and were advised that an 1847 treaty between the United States and Bavaria superseded the Kansas law. Ihl's sister received title to the farm in Stafford County as Ihl had directed.[16]

With the stored grain sold and the estate sale held, Willcox turned to collecting the notes owed to the estate and paying claims. There were immediate court costs and fees to the appraisers, the auctioneer, and the clerk at the sale, along with the expenses of the burial and the lawyers' retainer. Other than the large claim submitted by Henn, significant expenses seemed unlikely.[17]

Therefore, when a claim for photographic "views of I. B. Werner's place" was presented by Seth Blake for $246.75, Willcox was suspicious. Why would a man step forward with such a large claim after Isaac's death without any accounting of what Isaac may have been owed in return for serving as Blakes's assistant and delivering the glass plate negatives and picking up the developed pictures from studios in St. John and Pratt?[18] Furthermore, neighbors recalled that some of the photographs taken at Isaac's farm had been merely tests and experiments by Blake.

Willcox had been relieved to find Isaac's records in much better order than what he had anticipated, but the unexpectedly large claim from George Henn and the unexpected claim from Blake, together with so many notes from the estate sale remaining to be collected made it clear that his responsibilities were far from over. Isaac deserved that the accumulated labor of a lifetime be properly accounted for, and that responsibility now rested on his shoulders as the administrator of the estate.

Epilogue: After Isaac Werner, 1895–1898

1895

It was ironic that not long after Isaac Werner's death the widow of Judge Arnold Krekel, nominated to the federal bench as one of the last acts of President Lincoln, appeared in St. John to deliver a three-day lecture series on a freethinker's view of religion and death. The judge had been a leading freethinker lecturer and his widow, Mattie Parry Krekel, continued the lecturing the two of them had done before the judge's death.

Isaac had not been a freethinker, but he had disapproved of ministers who criticized farmers' united efforts to improve their situation and ministers he found lacking in knowledge of the Bible or boring in their preaching of God's word. Many of his neighbors found courage during the hard times of the late 1800s in church, and a freethinker lecturing in St. John caused quite an uproar. John Hilmes summarized his views on the center front page of the following week's *County Capital:* "As we understood her," Hilmes wrote, "her God is and consists in the sublimness [*sic*] of nature. . . . Her proposition is that, matter is indestructible, and hence the component part of our bodies can never be destroyed, and . . . when what we call death ensues, the parts that constitute our bodies, will be utilized in other living forms."[1] The idea that there was no reunion with loved ones awaiting in heaven seemed a cruel punishment to Hilmes, in a world where hard times took the lives of so many innocent children, young wives and mothers, and men struggling to tame the prairie. Hilmes rebutted Krekel's ideas, concluding: "If we believed that the short space of time we are permitted to remain in this world, was all of human life, to us it would well nigh seem a consummate failure."[2]

The leading secularist or freethinker of that time was Robert Ingersoll,[3] known as "The Great Agnostic." The huge popularity of this Civil War veteran, lawyer, popular orator, and lecturer led many to believe that he could have been president had he been a Christian. However, his ideas as a freethinker made others despise him.

If there were those in St. John who considered themselves freethinkers, they apparently kept their views to themselves. Although there was a strong freethinker movement in America at that time, it was a minority of the population and a reason for disapproval in most communities.

Isaac's closest friend Will Campbell had reason to hope that faith offered a reunion in heaven, for only a few days after Isaac's death, Will's wife died from complications of childbirth. He was left with four young children in his care, one of whom was his baby daughter. As with many infants of that time whose mothers did not survive their birth, Will's baby daughter survived her mother only a few months. His sadness, and the new responsibilities of raising his children alone, ended the elective political ambitions of this man, whose name had been put forward as both a potential U.S. senator and as Kansas governor.

As September arrived, the local political meetings began. The Kansas Republican committee on resolutions[4] led with the traditional waving of the bloodied shirt, appealing to veterans with a promise that "their widows and orphans will be liberally cared for," despite a contrary record from Washington. They taunted the Populists, resolving: "We congratulate the state of Kansas on her redemption from populist greed, avarice, plunder and mis-rule and we have full and explicit confidence in the republican party in leading our grand old commonwealth back to the exalted position she occupied among her sister states before the populist party cast disgrace and shame upon her fair name and fame."

The day after these resolutions were published, the People's Party Convention was held in St. John, and not surprisingly, their platform had an answer for the Republicans, relying on some of their own Populist themes:

> We have witnessed for more than a quarter of a century the struggles of the two great political parties for power and plunder, while grievous wrongs have been inflicted upon a suffering people. . . . [W]e seek to restore the government of the republic to the hands of "the plain people" with whose class it originated. . . . We declare that this republic can only endure as a free government while built upon a love of the whole people for each other and for the nation[.][5]

In the midst of the annual autumn political hubbub, the death notice of one of the early Populist lecturers appeared under the headline "Reform Loses a Champion." Sarah E. V. Emery, author of *The Seven Financial Conspiracies,* whom Isaac had traveled to Pratt to hear and whose book had influenced so many Populists, died at the age of fifty-seven at her home in Lansing, Michigan.

On Election Day, the People's Party fared reasonably well locally, electing the county clerk, register of deeds, treasurer, and coroner. However, Republicans won the offices of state supreme court justice, and the county sheriff, surveyor, and commissioner.

DR. WILLCOX HAD GONE about the business of handling Isaac's estate during the months following the sale, collecting on some of the notes given at the sale and receiving a few more claims against the estate. G. G. John had submitted a claim for a few things he had done for Isaac—making trips for him, working on the invalid chair, working on a well, wintering one of Isaac's horses, and checking on Isaac daily as his health failed. G. G. John had carefully reduced his claim by the amount of some grain he had bought from Isaac on credit, but even before reducing the amount, he only claimed thirty-four dollars. It was a very reasonable claim, especially in light of his having provided what he called "personal attendance" over a period of five months, claiming only ten dollars for that. Everything on the claim was modest for the work done, quite a contrast in comparison to what the Henns expected.[6]

As the new year neared Willcox continued his rounds collecting notes given at the estate sale, perhaps surprised by how often neighbors mentioned Isaac's helpfulness when they had a contract to write or a question about the best potato varieties to plant or when they needed help drawing plans for a new shed or calculating a lumber order. Some of them may have regretted having failed to tell Isaac how they had appreciated all that he did.

The economy had not improved. When the Bank of Seward went into voluntary liquidation, they notified depositors to call for their money. As for the board members' investment, however, they had learned "that farming was not the only business that did not pay dividends."[7]

The death of a young man whose parents had once lived north of St. John reflected the hardship of finding work in such hard times. He was riding the rails, having lost his job in the smelters when they closed in Pueblo, Colorado, but feeling fortunate to have found a job in Argentine, Kansas, where his brother worked.[8] Attempting to jump from a moving train, he fell under the wheels, severing both legs beneath the knees, and injuring his face and head. Unfortunately, he, like others with no more than subsistence wages, had lacked any savings with which to buy a ticket, and riding the rails to Argentine for his new job had cost his life.

Although farmers' lives were not entirely wretched, even an evening's amusement could bring ugliness. When the Bond Brothers' traveling circus came to St. John, among the entertainments were gambling stands, and the April 24 *County Capital* reported: "St. John was full of suckers confident they could cope with expert gamblers, toughs, ruffians and cut-throats in tackling the 'blind tiger.'"[9] The fleecing of foolish adults was not a criminal offense, but when some of the showmen lured underaged boys, law enforcement stepped in to arrest the professional gamblers. The first man arrested offered to reimburse the money taken from the boys, so lawmen entered one of the show cars with the prisoner to get the money. Unfortunately, outraged townspeople ignored the sheriff's instructions and burst into the car, facilitating the prisoner's escape. In the melee with circus toughs armed with clubs and other bludgeons, officers and townsmen were severely injured. Locals walking from the depot to the location of the show's encampment had also been robbed of valuables and revolvers during the evening. The militia from Newton that County Attorney O. C. Jennings asked the governor to send arrived too late to help.

The town was abuzz with talk about the circus, and although most of it was directed at the dishonesty and violence of the circus showmen, Hilmes reminded his readers of things they preferred to ignore. Specifically, young boys had been "used by the gamblers as cappers, to allure others into the game . . . get[ting] their neighbors and friends into trouble." In addition, citizens themselves could have shunned the gambling booths and avoided trouble, and had locals not ignored the sheriff's order by bursting into the show car, the prisoner would not have escaped, and the melee that erupted "only after . . . citizens on the outside proceeded to burst in the door" need not have occurred.[10]

One of the proudest political achievements by the Populists had been the Kansas legislature's passage of what became known as "the famous redemption law of Kansas." It was intended to provide relief for borrowers whose mortgages either lacked a redemption clause or had only a brief period in which to pay delinquencies and reclaim their property following foreclosure. The law applied not only to new mortgages but also retroactively to mortgages signed before the law was passed. Judge Horton, who had served on the Kansas Supreme Court at the time of the law's passage, had ruled that the redemptive law was only effective as to mortgages executed after the passage of the law. However, when he was replaced on the Kansas Supreme Court by Populist Judge Martin, the case was reconsidered and the law's right of redemption was fully reinstated.

The case was then appealed to the United States Supreme Court,[11] and the court held that the portion of the law that imposed or extended the redemption period "cannot constitutionally apply to a sale under a mortgage executed before its passage." The opinion added, "We of course have nothing to do with fairness or policy of such enactments . . . but [the Kansas law is] a substantial impairment of the rights . . . as expressed in the contract."[12] Much as the struggling farmers needed relief, the Populist legislators could not override the agreements made by the farmers at the time they negotiated their loans. The ruling impacted over $200 million of mortgage foreclosures in Kansas.[13]

Summer brought the political activity of a presidential election year. The Republican National Convention met first in St. Louis on June 19 to select William McKinley of Ohio as their presidential candidate. A month later, the Democrats met in Chicago to choose William Jennings Bryan of Nebraska as their candidate, with Arthur Sewall chosen as Bryan's running mate. Both party conventions battled over the gold standard versus bimetallism, and both parties splintered over the issue. The Republican decision to support the gold standard did little harm to their party, but the division over the Democratic platform's support for free silver would prove to be far more significant.

With times so hard in Stafford County, the local Populist county convention delegates showed the party's solidarity with the hardships of taxpayers

William Jennings Bryan, presidential nominee of the Democrats, the People's Party, and the Middle-of-the-Roaders. From William J. Bryan, *The First Battle, a Story of the Campaign of 1896* (Chicago: W. B. Conkey, 1896).

in their community by resolving that "officers should receive no greater compensation for their service than the people who employ and are taxed to pay them." Appropriate salary reductions for each county office were included, along with the provision that "all candidates to-day nominated shall be pledged to support this measure."[14] The delegates also sent a telegraph to the chairman of the Kansas delegation at the national People's Party Convention, urging Kansas delegates to support the nomination of Democrat William Jennings Bryan for president on the Populist ticket.

During the Stafford County Convention, there was no question that the mid-roaders had lost favor, and the fusionists were in control. The willingness to focus on silver had put aside the specific goals of previous platforms, which ignored the very issues that had excited crowds at rallies and had drawn members to the People's Party. It was a big political gamble.

When the Populists met in St. Louis a few days later, the stage had been set to nominate Bryan, but not every delegate was ready to fall in line, nor in fact was Bryan, who initially asked that his name be withdrawn. One problem concerned Bryan's running mate. Democrats had chosen a wealthy New England industrialist, director of the Maine Central Railroad and president of a bank, believing his credentials would attract New England voters and balance their ticket. The Populists wanted Congressman Thomas E. Watson of Georgia instead, believing the well-known Populist for vice president would balance the Populist Party ticket.

The complication of nominating the same presidential candidate but two different vice presidential nominees was complicated even further by the split within the Populists. Ballots were needed for the Democratic ticket, and two different ballots were also needed for the Populists—one for the People's Party and another for the middle-of-the-roaders.

After hours of complicated strategy and compromise, the Democrat ticket remained Bryan and Sewall, but the People's Party unanimously chose Bryan and Watson.[15] Fusion had brought about the nomination of William Jennings Bryan by both the Democrats and the Populists, and Bryan had accepted the Populist nomination after all, but there remained the problem of what to do about two vice presidential nominees. An agreement was reached and Kansas was the linchpin in case of a tie: If Arthur Sewall received even one more electoral vote from all states except Kansas, then Kansas would cast its ten electoral votes for Sewall. Otherwise, all ten of the electoral votes of Kansas would be cast for Watson. However, disagreements between fusionists and Mid-roaders remained.

As for state elections, the Democrats agreed to endorse all of the Populist nominees for state offices. Convention business moved on to selecting the nominee for governor. There were three contenders, including former governor Lewelling, but newcomer John W. Leedy won the day. He had settled in Coffey County, Kansas, in 1881 as a farmer, and his first political office was his election in 1892 as a state senator. His credentials lacked both a college education and a military career, but in the senate he had voted consistently for Populist principles and had fought hard for reduced railroad rates, and that had been enough to win Leedy the nomination.

From William Jennings Bryan's appearance in New York City at Madison Square Garden on August 13, 1896, with Arthur Sewall by his side, it was clear that Watson would be ignored, and Bryan's campaign would be a confrontation between the Republican platform upholding the gold standard and his own platform supporting free silver, a battle for the votes of the common man, leaving the wealthy minority to the Republicans.

Bryan's famous *Cross of Gold Speech* and oratorical skills had won him the nomination and had established the theme of his campaign:

> There are two ideas of government. There are those who believe that if you just legislate to make the well-to-do prosperous, that their prosperity will leak through on those below. The Democratic idea has been that if you legislate to make the masses prosperous their prosperity will find its way up and through every class that rests upon it. . . . If

> they [Republicans] dare to come out in the open field and defend the gold standard as a good thing, we shall fight them to the uttermost, having behind us the producing masses of the nation and the world. Having behind us the commercial interests and the laboring interests and all the toiling masses, we shall answer their demands for a gold standard by saying to them, you shall not press down upon the brow of labor this crown of thorns. You shall not crucify mankind upon a cross of gold.[16]

Bryan's energy seemed boundless. At the age of thirty-six (only one year past the minimum age for a presidential candidate), he tirelessly traveled by train as no other candidate had ever done, speaking to millions during three months of campaigning. On the other hand, McKinley sat on his own front porch giving speeches, using the huge Republican war chest to buy train tickets to bring thousands upon thousands of potential voters to his front lawn in Ohio to listen.

The railroad companies saw the fusion of Democrats and Populists as a growing threat to their interests and declined to allow Populist-Democratic candidates for state offices in Kansas to ride the trains on free passes. For many of the Populist candidates, whose personal finances were limited and who received little financial assistance from their party, those railroad passes had been essential. The effect, obviously intended by the railroads, was to cripple the travel of many Populist candidates.

When at last the campaigning was finished and the votes had been cast, the fusion to put a free silver president in the White House had failed. There were many reasons to cause disappointed Populists to think "*If only.*" If only some limit had existed to curb the disparity in campaign spending in which Republicans outspent Democrats by about sixteen to one; if only the old Bourbon Democrats who opposed free silver had not abandoned Bryan to form the National Democratic Party; if only Populists had felt better about Sewall; if only Bryan could have moderated his campaign with issues other than free coinage of silver. In fact, however, McKinley received 51 percent of the popular vote and Bryan received 47 percent—not the landslide the Republicans liked to pretend. Fusion had not brought about free coinage of silver, but it had transformed the old Democratic party of President Cleveland that upheld free trade, hard money, and minimalist government to one more aligned with issues backed by the Populists—empathy for the struggles of the common man.

Just as the donkey is the Democratic political symbol and the elephant is the Republican political symbol, the rooster was the political symbol for the People's Party. *County Capital*, November 6, 1896.

Despite Bryan's loss, the front page of the *County Capital* was covered with crowing roosters, the Populist symbol crowing about their victories in state and local offices. With the advantage of Democratic support of their candidates, the entire Populist county ticket had been elected, Leedy had been elected governor, and both the state senate and house now had Populist majorities.

WILLCOX CONTINUED administering Isaac's estate, and if he saw the *County Capital* article describing a local young man's wages of thirty-eight cents a day, he must have reflected on George Henn's claim against Isaac's estate. The care of an invalid was deserving of reasonable compensation, but the greed of Henn, when Isaac's health made him the most vulnerable, must have disgusted his executor.

George Hall had delayed until the end of August 1896 to submit his claim for the twelve days the Hall family had cared for Isaac, which might have indicated a reluctance to seek payment for helping his friend. If he knew what Henn had claimed for providing the same care, Hall's own financial situation may have overcome his reluctance. However, Hall's claim for daily care was less than Henn's, and he sought no fee for boarding.[17]

During 1896, Willcox had collected some of the notes and had advanced the Henns about $700 toward their claim. Nearly all of the other expenses had to do with the costs of administering the estate, including Willcox's own fee of $111. If he had not needed to spend so much time chasing people down for what they owed the estate, his fee might have been less.[18]

1897

After declining elected political office, Will Campbell had agreed to serve on the Kansas Railroad Commission in Topeka. Isaac's death, followed so quickly by the death of Will's wife Eliza, had severed both of his strongest links to the old community, except for his children who remained there. He had recently remarried and lived with his new wife, Orpha, in Richland Township, with his youngest son William. His two adolescent boys had chosen to stay in the old community, looked after by their older siblings who lived nearby. He must have wondered whether Eliza would have approved of the decisions he had made for their family.

His positions on free silver through fusion had put him in opposition to men he respected,[19] as well as having broken with Texas Populists. The perceived economic benefits of bimetallism and the nomination of Bryan, as well as a belief that the old Farmers' Alliance goals of the old Omaha Platform could be temporarily deferred without jeopardizing the future strength of the People's Party, had been the justification for his actions, foreseeing the eventual return to those old goals once bimetallism was established.[20] As J. B. C. Cook had argued when he spoke at the Mass Convention in St. John on July 11: "[L]et us lay other minor questions on the shelf for the present."[21]

The Farmers' Alliance in Texas, where the Populist movement was born, had been built on educating its members, which Isaac had always advocated. Their goals were long-term, based on reforming the existing structure that favored the power of bankers, trusts, railroads, and corporations. Texan Charles Macune's subtreasury plan involving federal warehouses and certificates of deposit would have changed the nation's monetary system and reduced the power of banks by giving farmers direct control over the marketing of their produce. The Omaha Platform represented a long-term commitment to gradual changes that would have improved the economic lives of farmers and other working-class men and women, not just the possible short-term benefits of a single election cycle.

The focus on silver and the decision to support Democrat Bryan as well as making backroom deals with Republicans that betrayed their own candidate, Watson, splintered the People's Party. Watson, who had been instrumental in founding the Georgia Populist Party in 1892 and was probably the best known and most popular Populist in the south, had no use for Democrats. In the 1892 elections in Georgia, Watson had faced extraordinary political fraud and intimidation employed against him by the Democrats, which had been repeated in 1894. Those experiences reinforced his animosity toward all Democrats.

Watson's name had been put forward at the convention in St. Louis without seeking his permission, but he accepted what his party had done and campaigned for the Bryan-Watson ticket, even after the Democrats refused to drop Sewall from their ticket. The disrespect for Watson occurred even in Kansas, where Watson had strong support from mid-roaders. A banner reading "Bryan & Sewall" hung over the Populist state headquarters, showing the fusionist support for the Democratic ticket, despite the Kansas ticket of Bryan & Watson. Ballots in Pratt County, near Isaac's homestead, included three different options for voters favoring Bryan. The ballots read: Democratic: Bryan & Sewell, People's Party: Bryan & Watson, and Middle-Of-The-Road-Populist, Bryan & Watson.[22] Nothing could have made the split between fusionists and mid-roaders more obvious than those three ballots. Watson never recovered from that betrayal, and in the following years the early values he had championed as a Populist were discarded, replaced by prejudices he had fought against in the past.

The younger Populist leadership in 1896 had arrived at the People's Party late, with new priorities, lacking appropriate appreciation and respect for the early leadership of Texas. Others, like Will Campbell, set aside old priorities and alliances to side with the fusionists, believing it was a necessary but temporary strategy. Some even described the stubborn adherence to old goals by the middle-of-the road populists in harsher terms: "[as]anything but moderate; supposed to indicate 'nonfusion,' the term more closely represented the gutter than the middle of the road."[23]

Kansas Alliance old-timers, like those who cheered Watson when he reminded them that he had "extended the hand of fellowship to your Simpsons, your Peffers . . . [and] stood by your men in Congress when others failed,"[24] gave him their votes,[25] but fusionists, willing to sacrifice the long-term for the election of a silver president (even if he was a Democrat), had led the People's Party away from its roots.

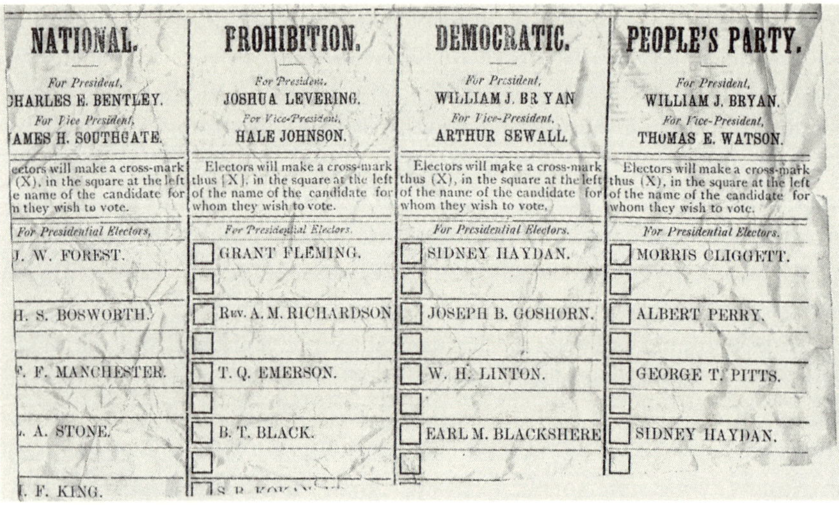

NATIONAL.

For President,
[C]HARLES E. BENTLEY.
For Vice President,
[J]AMES H. SOUTHGATE.

[El]ectors will make a cross-mark (X), in the square at the left [of th]e name of the candidate for [whom] they wish to vote.

For Presidential Electors,

J. W. FOREST.
H. S. BOSWORTH.
F. F. MANCHESTER.
. A. STONE.
. F. KING.

PROHIBITION.

For President,
JOSHUA LEVERING.
For Vice-President,
HALE JOHNSON.

Electors will make a cross-mark thus [X], in the square at the left of the name of the candidate for whom they wish to vote.

For Presidential Electors.

GRANT FLEMING.
REV. A. M. RICHARDSON
T. Q. EMERSON.
B. T. BLACK.

DEMOCRATIC.

For President,
WILLIAM J. BRYAN
For Vice-President,
ARTHUR SEWALL.

Electors will make a cross-mark thus (X), in the square at the left of the name of the candidate for whom they wish to vote.

For Presidential Electors.

SIDNEY HAYDAN.
JOSEPH B. GOSHORN.
W. H. LINTON.
EARL M. BLACKSHERE

PEOPLE'S PARTY.

For President,
WILLIAM J. BRYAN.
For Vice-President,
THOMAS E. WATSON.

Electors will make a cross-mark thus (X), in the square at the left of the name of the candidate for whom they wish to vote.

For Presidential Electors.

MORRIS CLIGGETT.
ALBERT PERRY.
GEORGE T. PITTS.
SIDNEY HAYDAN.

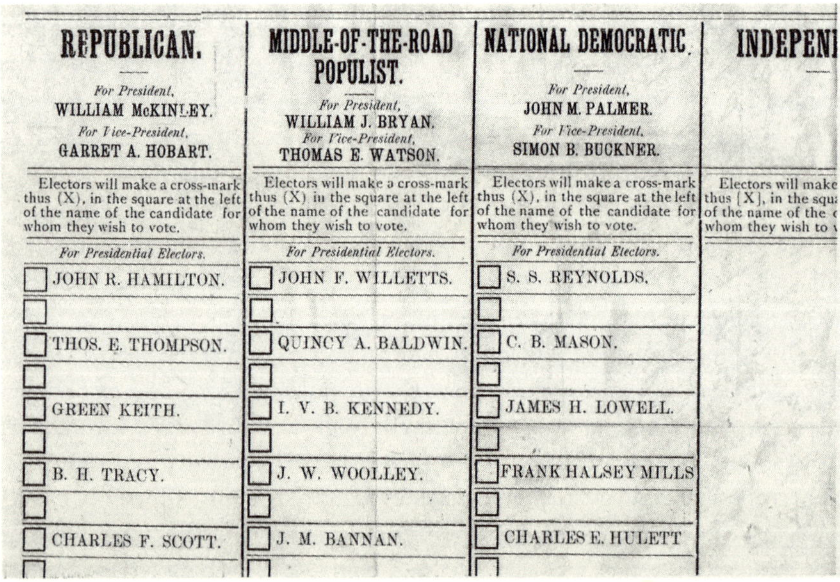

REPUBLICAN.

For President,
WILLIAM McKINLEY.
For Vice-President,
GARRET A. HOBART.

Electors will make a cross-mark thus (X), in the square at the left of the name of the candidate for whom they wish to vote.

For Presidential Electors.

JOHN R. HAMILTON.
THOS. E. THOMPSON.
GREEN KEITH.
B. H. TRACY.
CHARLES F. SCOTT.

MIDDLE-OF-THE-ROAD POPULIST.

For President,
WILLIAM J. BRYAN.
For Vice-President,
THOMAS E. WATSON.

Electors will make a cross-mark thus (X) in the square at the left of the name of the candidate for whom they wish to vote.

For Presidential Electors.

JOHN F. WILLETTS.
QUINCY A. BALDWIN.
I. V. B. KENNEDY.
J. W. WOOLLEY.
J. M. BANNAN.

NATIONAL DEMOCRATIC.

For President,
JOHN M. PALMER.
For Vice-President,
SIMON B. BUCKNER.

Electors will make a cross-mark thus (X), in the square at the left of the name of the candidate for whom they wish to vote.

For Presidential Electors.

S. S. REYNOLDS.
C. B. MASON.
JAMES H. LOWELL.
FRANK HALSEY MILLS
CHARLES E. HULETT

INDEPEN[DENT]

Electors will make thus [X], in the squ[are] of the name of the whom they wish to

Unused ballots from the 1896 presidential election. Upper image contains both the Democratic Bryan and Sewell ticket and the People's Party Bryan and Watson ticket, and lower image shows the Middle-of-the-Road Bryan and Watson ticket. Courtesy of Peoples Bank, Pratt, Kansas; author's collection.

William S. Morgan, the Texan whose book, *The History of the Wheel* had impressed Isaac, had been adamantly opposed to the focus on silver. In fact, Texas leaders had been so unhappy with Bryan's nomination by their party that they had considered supporting McKinley. The schism over nominating Bryan threatened the future of the People's Party.

THERE WERE SOME REASONS for farmers to find hope after the 1896 elections. Wheat prices had been slightly higher in the autumn of 1897, as well as fairer values being paid for cattle, sheep, and hogs. Making these slight improvements even more beneficial was the lowering of interest rates, and local farmers were managing to reduce their debts.

George H. Burr, the president of the Commercial Bank, had succeeded in bringing capitalists from the East Coast to St. John, traveling in a private car from Chicago. Carriages had taken these potential investors and local leaders to Garth's Ranch to observe his cattle operation. The possibility of an injection of eastern capital into the central Kansas cattle business was encouraging.[26] In fact, both domestic and foreign-owned cattle syndicates had existed in Kansas for several years, and Burr's promotion did not seem unfamiliar.[27]

Despite the disappointing loss of their presidential candidate, the People's Party did hold the majorities in Topeka. Disappointments over the failure to reduce legal maximums on interest and pass a railroad bill tended to eclipse other reform successes—regulation of stockyards, health and safety for miners, regulation of banks, forbidding blacklisting of workers by employers, a department for the inspection and weighing of grain, and a school-textbook commission. Trusts, which the Populists had railed against for years, were also defined and restricted. The legislative session could not be regarded as a failure.

The timber claim Isaac had planted and nurtured had been divided and sold, forty acres in the southeast corner going to Fay Vosburgh and the remaining 120 acres going to Isaac's former caregiver, G. G. John. Isaac had been friends with the Vosburghs nearly as long as he had been on his claim, and G. G. John had been very good to him, so perhaps he would have been pleased that his brother Henry had sold to those two men.

Many of Isaac's old neighbors had given up on farming, and some of them might have been among the men wandering from place to place looking for work. Although there were reasons for optimism, not everyone had succeeded in making a good life for their family in Kansas.

1898

In 1898, talk of a war with Spain brought an uneasy mood to the country. People in Isaac's old community depended on republished stories from large newspapers like Randolph Hearst's *New York Journal* and Joseph Pulitzer's *New York World,* printed in the local papers. The accounts contained sensational reports of the mistreatment of the Cubans by the Spanish. When the battleship *USS Maine* was sunk in Havana harbor by an explosion that the U.S. Naval Court of Inquiry wrongly ascribed to a mine, the United States issued an ultimatum to the Spanish government to leave Cuba. Spain rejected the ultimatum, and the later determination that the sinking of the battleship had been caused by an exploding boiler onboard rather than a Spanish mine came too late to change the course of war with Spain.[28]

Wars require men and money. President McKinley called for volunteers and proposed bonds to raise funds. Expressing the Populist attitudes of his constituents, Nebraska senator William V. Allen objected:

> "The people desire to pay as they go. . . . They do not want this government at the end of the war indebted one dollar more than it is at the present time." Allen accused speculators of using the wave of patriotism "to foist upon the people a perpetual national debt. . . . There is not one of that power, sir, who would not see this government sunk to the bottom of the ocean if he could make a fortune by it. . . . The government is to them simply a carcass upon which they are to feed and fatten."[29]

War financing only deepened the Populist distrust for Wall Street and the war speculators.

Many unemployed men who continued to wander in search of work were willing to sign on as soldiers, less concerned about the reason for the Spanish-American War than the need for regular meals and a paycheck. If putting on a uniform and taking orders provided something to eat and a little money, they would do it. In truth, many of them were so worn down they weren't fit for duty, and for those who became soldiers, unless the national economy improved, they could not expect civilian jobs waiting for them when they came home.

Sympathy for the Cubans and the need for employment may have motivated some of the calls for war, but also significant was the American belief in Manifest Destiny that had fueled the surge westward across the continent. Now, the same belief was being urged as justification for looking beyond the continental boundaries of the United States. In his 1890 book, *The Influence of Sea Power upon History, 1660–1783*, Captain Alfred T. Mahan wrote, "Whether they will or no, Americans must now begin to look outward. The growing production of the country demands it." Expansionist policies also played a role in taking America to war.[30]

Not all of the volunteer soldiers for the Spanish-American War were unemployed laborers eager for a paycheck without any particular feelings about the war itself. Having resigned as Assistant Secretary of the Navy, Theodore Roosevelt received congressional authorization to raise three cavalry regiments, and he drew recruits from colleges like Harvard, Yale, and Princeton, and from elite clubs like Boston's Somerset and New York's Knickerbocker, for no better reason than, as he said, "the same impulse that once sent the Vikings over the sea." Although Roosevelt did profess that the "war would be as righteous as it would be to the honor and the interests of the nation," there was no denying that many joined what came to be known as the Rough Riders because they were looking for an adventure.[31]

The call to war was part of the political climate, and the Populist platform included criticism of speculators seeking financial gain from war.[32] Free and unlimited coinage of both gold and silver at the ratio of sixteen to one and issuance of legal tender notes rather than interest-bearing bonds were urged, as they had been in 1896. However, the 1898 Kansas State Platform returned to the original emphasis on laws to benefit people in their everyday lives, with the addition of more social ideas aimed directly at assisting citizens. The front page of the June 24, 1898 *County Capital* declared "A Ringing Platform" and included a separate heading for the "Revenue Law," describing new taxes to raise revenue for the war and opposing bond issues, long seen by Populists as an investment ruse benefitting only the wealthy.

Instead of bonds, new war revenue laws were passed to tax the following:

- Tobacco, cigars, and malt liquors
- Banks and brokers
- Theaters, museums, circuses, billiard tables, and bowling alleys
- Telephone and telegraph messages
- Patent medicines

- Stamps on documents such as deeds, certificates of deposit, and other legal documents.

As for the Populist platform, more public social issues were included than had been in the past:

- Fire and life insurance provided by the state of Kansas at cost
- Extension of the textbook law to include all textbooks and school supplies
- County clerks' offices to serve as free public employment agencies
- Reasonable attorneys' fees recoverable in a suit to recover wages, and wages given a prior lien to all attachments and mortgages in cases of assignment or insolvency
- Revision of mining laws for greater safety and greater penalties for operators who disobey

The soldiers were not forgotten:

- A twenty dollar per month pay increase to volunteer soldiers
- Service pensions for all survivors of the Union armies of the Civil War

Making government work better and more equitably for all Kansans were included:

- A court of elected railway commissioners to fix rates and compel business reports from the railway companies
- Bureau of labor and industrial statistics an independent state department
- Output of the penitentiary mine for the needs of state institutions rather than at the mercy of combinations of private corporations
- Opposition to the issuance of bonds
- Abolition of the metropolitan police system

Finally, the Republicans were denunciated for following the dictates of foreign bondholders and for specific voting patterns:

- Against an income tax
- Against a 1 percent tax on railroad corporations
- Against any tax on Wall Street transactions[33]

Although the platform evidenced a return to earlier goals and inclusion of more assistance and protection of individual citizens, the political clout of the Peoples' Party had been mortally wounded by the internal split of fusionists and mid-roaders in 1896. Bleeding from the wounds was slow, and political death had been forestalled, but the severity of the self-inflicted wounds was obvious from the results of the 1898 elections. The entire Republican state ticket was elected and the Stafford County races were split, the Republicans and the Populists each winning three offices.

On September 7, 1898, Dr. Willcox appeared before probate Judge Hockensmith to present the final accounting of Isaac's estate. Willcox had succeeded in collecting the outstanding loans and unpaid estate sale notes. The deferred claims from George Henn were paid, and Willcox's own final claim as administrator, the attorney's fee, and a few other claims for small amounts took most of the rest. Despite the surprising assets Isaac had accumulated at the time of his death, the total liquidated balance of his estate, not including real property, had been reduced during the administration to only $58.48.[34]

Isaac's surviving siblings divided that sum, along with receiving his homestead. They sold the farm to Jacob DeGarmo.[35] The homestead upon which Isaac had worked so hard and of which he had been so proud, the same farm John Hilmes had called one of the finest in the county, was sold without any of Isaac's family having come to stand on his pinnacle hill and look down on his life's labor.[36]

An even greater heartbreak for Isaac would have been reading the letter sent by his nephew Charles to Henry, Isaac's twin brother. Charles, now a lawyer in New York City, was the teenaged nephew to whom Isaac had sent books. More importantly, it was Charles whom Isaac had invited to spend summers at the farm, to work alongside his Uncle Isaac, getting to know one another. Those invitations had been ignored. Charles's letter to his father Henry contained a single sentence buried within other news. With no mention of his Uncle Isaac, Charles simply wrote, "Your letter reached me this morning and I was glad to know that the Kansas property is beginning to pan out."

Isaac's days of bending over plugging fifteen-inch cottonwood cuttings into the sandy loam soil until his back ached too much for sleep, his days of hoeing sunflowers and sandburs away from the seedlings until his hands bled, the effort of trading his own labor in exchange for a neighbor's horse and plow to clear fireguards to protect the cottonwoods from prairie fires, the debt he had carried to buy horses and plows to protect and maintain the tree rows himself, the pruning, the carrying water, the back-firing to turn prairie fires aside, the endless attention Isaac had given to the trees on Henry's timber claim—and all Charles understood was that the Kansas property was beginning to pan out.[37]

Or was it Isaac's homestead, which passed to Henry and his sister Ettie that Charles regarded as finally panning out? It was the Paris Green Isaac used to raise the potatoes that were regarded as the best in the community that had almost certainly caused Isaac's death. Although the obituary published by his family attributed his failing health to a stroke, the symptoms of poisoning by Paris Green offer a far more likely explanation. The combination of copper II acetate and arsenic trioxide can produce the nausea and vomiting Isaac experienced in the early stages of his decline, as well as ulceration and swelling such as Isaac developed on his hand before other symptoms. More telling is that repeated exposure to this poison can cause neuromuscular disorders that affect the nerves that control voluntary muscles such as those in arms and legs, eventually resulting in the weakening and wasting of those muscles, symptoms that rendered Isaac so helpless that his final months required that he be carried about and cared for like an infant.

Isaac was a meticulous man, and his experience as a druggist would have made him aware of the need for careful handling of chemicals; however, his methods of mixing and applying Paris Green were primitive—using a whisk to sprinkle the liquid mixture on his potato plants, squirting the liquid with a syringe, and trying to build a system in which pressure from elevating the mixture in a raised barrel to create enough pressure to spray his plants had only produced a weak, drippy mess. Even the most careful application must have resulted in blowback from the prairie winds.[38]

Although Isaac might have had some idea about the dangers of the poison, the lethal nature of Paris Green was not fully appreciated at that time. An article in the *New York Times* in 1874 described an inquest following the deaths of three people. Although canned pickles were first blamed, it was discovered that the family cook had asked her employer to purchase Paris Green to kill cockroaches, and the investigation discovered that the poison had been sprinkled around the sink, in drawers containing silverware, on shelves where dishes and cooking utensils were kept, and in clothing drawers. The professor who testified in the case urged the press to warn the public against the use of Paris Green, but no such warnings were found in the *County Capital*.[39] Unfortunately, Isaac may not have realized the severity of the risk or may have thought he was taking the proper precautions. After all, many farmers in his area were using the poison, and their means of application were equally primitive.[40]

Farming on the prairie presented many risks, from fighting prairie fires to surviving the harsh environment. Yet Isaac's skill and hard work had created a fine farm, and its value, enhanced by Isaac's labor and skill when it passed to Isaac's siblings and their descendants, was probably little understood. Charles had never met his Uncle Isaac and knew him only through whatever his father had told him. Neither father nor son could have imagined the hardships Isaac had overcome to secure the two claims. Surely the words Charles wrote were not intentionally unkind, but they showed too little respect for his uncle's achievements and sacrifices in making the Kansas claims "pan out."

On a small prairie hill at the center of Neelands Cemetery, Isaac is buried, surrounded by neighbors whose names appear in his journal. Irises planted by some unknown friend grow around the base of his simple stone, but blowing prairie sand gradually covered the iris tubers until their roots were choked, and their blooms were stilled, like the lives of the many settlers buried near Isaac's grave.

The years recorded in his journal describe the life of a homesteader, ordinary to some, perhaps, but a valuable contributor to many lives around him. Isaac's life and the arc of the Populist movement seem to have followed a parallel course—the struggles, followed by a crest of success when dreams seemed possible of coming true, then a sinking realization that perhaps the dreams had been too great to be fully achieved. Despite disappointments, Isaac and his neighbors did lay a foundation for the farmers who followed, and Populist programs that the major political parties once regarded as impossible are now taken for granted.

Summarizing the goals and achievements of the Populists, historian Scott G. McNall wrote: "The farmers' call was remarkably nonradical—for a control of monopolists and an end to corruption." However, he pointed out the contradictions of their goals: regulation and control but no bureaucracy, protection of the rights of small property holders but limiting the interests of large property holders, a government answerable and accessible to them but free from the influence of the wealthy and powerful.[41]

At least some of the leaders of the Kansas Populists lived long enough to see the acceptance of ideas they had advocated. In 1902 Annie Diggs told a reporter, "We were right and this good old world regards us in a different light as it comes to understand that many of the issues so crudely advocated were really safe and sane progressive measures."[42] In 1907 former U.S. senator Peffer said, "The country now hotly demands legislation it abused me

Isaac Beckley Werner's gravestone in the Neelands Cemetery, Stafford County, Kansas. Photo by Larry D. Fenwick.

for advocating."[43] A few months before his death in 1905, former three-term U.S. representative Jerry Simpson chided some of the Republicans who had adopted Populist positions, telling them "You are just learning now what the farmers of the state knew fourteen years ago."[44]

Paraphrasing the words of noted historian Richard Hofstadter, third parties are like bees: they bring new ideas to pollinate the two old parties, and when that task is done, they die.[45] Populist ideas remain part of the American political landscape, although the People's Party did not survive. Similarly, the Progressive ideas that overlapped Populist themes and exerted significant influence from the 1890s to the 1920s continue to be part of American politics.

In his book *The Great Revolt and Its Leaders*, Carleton Beals, the son of a Populist newspaper editor in Isaac's region, described the impact of their movement: "All we can say is, the Populists made a good fight while it lasted; they are an integral part of the history of our land; they changed the thought and the pattern of American life. We can still learn much from their methods and their ideas."[46] Isaac played his part in that fight, and the journal he kept is no longer a forgotten record of one man's life during those consequential years. Had Isaac reflected on the question in Whitman's poem, might he have asked, "Will some one when I am dead and gone write my life?" Someone has.

Acknowledgments

I found Isaac Beckley Werner's journal in February of 2010, and although there were periods of time when I laid the research and writing aside, Isaac was never completely ignored. For more than a decade, my husband supported my work, a generosity I can never repay. As one friend told him, "Fenwick, you are the only man I know whose wife is having an affair with a dead man." Thank you to Larry D. Fenwick for joining me in so many research adventures, and deferring his own plans so I could pursue mine.

Lucille M. Hall recognized the importance of preserving history and endowed a museum bearing her name in St. John, Kansas, where Isaac's journal was found. Thank you to all of those who continue to keep her dream of a museum alive—board members, donors, and volunteers. Your encouragement as I found a way to share Isaac's story has truly mattered.

Many of the documents I used in my research came from small towns—whether a local author writing a book about his or her community's past, or committees and board members whose efforts preserved local history in centennial or other commemorative books, with the assistance of donors who supported these endeavors. These sources provided information unlikely to have been available elsewhere. I owe all of them, past and present, a debt of gratitude, and especially to my mother-in-law, Irene Preston, in whose collection several of those books were found.

The Stafford County Historical and Genealogical Museum houses the old *County Capital* newspapers that were so important to my research, and Director Michael Hathaway was particularly helpful during the many days I spent turning the delicate yellowed pages to find the stories about Isaac, his neighbors, and the populist movement that fill this book.

Thank you to the Pratt County History Museum and former Director Marsha Brown, who held that position during the period I was doing research there. Marsha is like a walking history directory, and her amazing memory and thoughtfulness provided me with two treasures. When someone donated a box of old photographs to the museum months after I had spent time at the museum searching for pictures from Isaac's community, she recognized Dr. Dix among the images and scanned his photograph for my collection. After she left her position at the museum, she discovered a book signed by Isaac Werner in a library de-acquisition sale and bought it for me as a gift, along with two books from Dr. Dix's library.

The kindness of strangers met on Ancestry.com resulted in connecting with Susan Davis, great-granddaughter of Isaac's sister Ettie, and our sharing of Werner research. I also connected with Betty J. Burdan through Ancestry.com, who directed me to Isaac's obituary published in the *Reading Eagle,* after I had given up my own efforts. Strangers at the "Rossville Friends" face book page helped me discover that the lots Isaac had owned in Rossville are now part of a parking lot. Earl VanMeter, who had watched my husband and me search unsuccessfully for Ettie and Rev. Palmer's graves in Lawrence, Kansas, as he tended his wife's grave, asked for our address and offered to continue our search. When he found their flat stones, separated from one another, he sent us photographs and specific directions to their locations. Several of the images in the book came from friends and strangers, and they are all appreciated and credited with their valuable contributions.

Librarians in Kansas, Illinois, and Pennsylvania helped me search their collections, both onsite and through correspondence. Sidney Garth Dreese, Director of Archives and Special Collections at Albright College where Isaac's brother Henry's diary is preserved, worked with me to acquire a copy. The importance of librarians must not be underappreciated.

Courthouse documents were especially helpful in my research, and a particular thank you goes to those in the Deed Records, Probate Records, District Court Records, and District Clerks Office in the Stafford County Courthouse in St. John, Kansas, for taking time from their regular responsibilities to assist me.

Many hours were spent walking through cemeteries, visiting the graves of Isaac's family in Wernersville, Pennsylvania, and Abilene and Lawrence, Kansas. I found the graves of many of Isaac's friends and neighbors in small town and country cemeteries in Stafford, Edwards, and Pratt Counties, which was particularly moving for me. In country cemeteries, many, if not most, of the stones are a hundred or more years old, often carved with names whose descendants no longer live in the area. These family plots commonly include small stones bearing the names of babies and young children that did not survive to become adults. Thank you to those who continue to tend the graves of the region's courageous early settlers.

I was fortunate to visit with several descendants of people mentioned in Isaac's journal, and some of them shared their own family records with me. Unfortunately, a few of those are no longer living to read about their ancestors in my book. Those interviews enriched my research.

When my husband and I finished visiting graves in the old Hain's Churchyard, we stepped into the current church, where the office staff shared their copy of the *History of St. John's (Hain's) Reformed Church,* from which I took so much history of the Werner family and early Wernersville. They also arranged for me to meet James Werner, a descendant of Isaac's uncle, who spent several hours providing me with more Werner history and documents. Thank you to all of those in Wernersville who took time from their day to help.

In September of 2011, I imagined having the manuscript ready to submit to publishers in the coming months, and I decided to start a blog to introduce future readers to my work. Every Thursday since, I have posted that blog, which many readers have followed for years, unflagging in their certainty that the right publisher would be found. A Canadian, whose home is now in Ukraine, was among my earliest followers, and his encouragement never waned, nor did a neighbor's, whose ancestors have been family friends for five generations. Thank you Allen and Doug, and so many more readers, nearby and around the world, who continued to encourage me.

Unlike the fairly prompt placement with a publisher of my first two books, the search for a publisher for Isaac took longer. However, I must thank even those editors who did not believe my manuscript fit their publishing criteria. Some of them took the time to offer encouragement and helpful advice, which softened their rejection and stiffened my resolve to keep going.

Thank you particularly to the University Press of Kansas. Together, we found a way to make my book relevant to academic readers while retaining my determination to tell the story in a way general readers could enjoy. These editors, publicists, artists, and others working behind the scenes, who ultimately overcame the challenges of bringing out a book during a pandemic, will forever have my respect and gratitude.

I also benefitted from those scholars and others who published books, papers, and other records about the Populist Movement and events of the late 1800s. Their efforts made my discovery of a homesteaders' daily journal more than just once man's story. By adding to that prior academic research with information from a particular region in Kansas, a fuller context and unique perspective has been achieved.

It is important that I also acknowledge the many unnamed but valuable sources and supportive individuals that made this book possible. In the decade since I began, no one ever suggested that I give up, and their encouragement came online, in Christmas cards, at the grocery store, at the annual Willa Cather Conferences, at parties, and in the many places where I did my research. It made a difference.

And to those who will always make a difference, I dedicate this book ~
To my husband, Larry D. Fenwick, whose support is invincible,
and
To my father, Ralph G. Beck, who taught me to love the land, and
to my mother, Pauline Hawk Beck, who was always writing stories.

Appendix

The Author's Appreciation for Isaac Werner's Library

As I began reading Isaac Werner's 480-page journal, I quickly realized that Isaac Beckley Werner was not a typical prairie homesteader. Many people in that time and place had only minimal reading and writing skills, and settlers who were educated were not always able to bring books with them when they staked their claims.

Isaac's passion for books was apparent from the opening pages of his journal, when he was a young druggist in Rossville, Illinois. Long passages describe the books he ordered and his delight in reading them. His own words from his journal best express his feelings about the library he was accumulating: "How interesting and delightful such reading is and the daily increase in familiarity with such noble literary monuments. When I think back over all my best investments yet made, what I [have] done in good Books, I must consider the Master stroke of all. What a permanent and ever increasing value does such an investment bring as interest for capital or outlay."

He did not buy randomly but rather consulted books such as C. H. Moore's *What to Read and How to Read*, and Henry Ward Beecher's recommended "Course of Reading for Beginners," published in the *Ledger*. However, the books he selected revealed that he was anything but a beginner.

Old editions replicating some of Isaac's Library. Books on top—vertical book, *The Innocents Abroad*; thick volume, *Classical Dictionary*; two books lying on top of the dictionary, *Recent British History* and *McGuffey's New Juvenile Speaker*. Books from left—*Ivanhoe*; *Fiske's Classical Antiquities; Cuba with Pen & Ink; Cooper's Justinian; Logic, Deduction & Induction; The Culture Demanded by Modern Life*. Antique stereoscope with two stereoscope cards: Cathedral of Reims and the Eiffel Tower. [The stereoscope and cards belonged to the author's Beck great-grandparents, with whom Isaac shared his own collections of books, cards, and photographs.] Photo by Larry D. Fenwick.

As a farmer on the prairie, money was tight, and Isaac could not afford to continue buying books at the same rate he had done as a druggist. However, he did not stop. Most of the well-known books from the Populist era were part of his library.

Typical of many readers, then and today, Isaac encouraged others to read. He built a cupboard to contain books for members of the local Farmers' Alliance, to be checked out and returned, and he gifted boxes of his own books to the Alliance library cupboard. Even having given many of his books away, at the time of Isaac's death he had so many books that only a portion of them were auctioned individually. Others were placed in boxes and sold in lots.

I recognized many of the classic titles and have some of them in my own library. However, there were many titles that I did not recognize. To get a better feel for just who Isaac was, I decided to order some of the books that were unfamiliar to me, in editions as close to the years Isaac would have bought as I could find. Several of these books are mentioned in the text of this book; however, others are not specifically identified by title, having little direct relation to the Populist movement. Yet, I gained a far greater understanding of who Isaac was, and who he aspired to be, by having acquired the titles listed below.

Finally, there are three specific books deserving mention. When the Pratt City Library conducted a de-acquisition sale of books at the time of their library renovation, a friend acquired three books that she gifted to me. Two belonged to Isaac's friend Dr. Dix and were given to the library by his estate, one of which contains the signature of I. H. Dix. It is likely that Dix could have purchased these books from Isaac, perhaps at Isaac's estate sale. These two books, believed to have once belonged to Isaac are *McGuffey's New Juvenile Speaker: Containing More Than Two Hundred Exercises,* Cincinnati: Winthrop B. Smith, 1860, and David Masson, *British Philosophy: A Review, with Criticisms,* New York: D. Appleton, 1866.

The third book, however, is a beautiful green, leather-bound book titled *Among My Books,* by James Russell Lowell, published in 1870. It, too, contains the label indicating that it was a gift to the public library from the Dix collection, but on the flyleaf, in Isaac's very recognizable penmanship, is written: "I. B. Werner, Rossville, Ill., May 29th, 1870."

The specific books I obtained to get a sense of what Isaac had chosen to read are listed below, followed by the list of books he acquired during the Rossville years of 1870–1871 and the estate inventory of books he owned at the time of his death. If, as many believe, the true intellect and aspirations of a person can best be revealed by studying the book titles on the shelves of his library, then Isaac is shown by the following lists of books in his collection as a truly remarkable man:

Anthon, Charles. *Classical Dictionary, . . . Ancient Authors . . . of the Greek and Romans.* 4th ed. New York: Harper & Brothers, 1847.

Bain, Alexander. *Logic: Deductive and Inductive.* New York: American Book, 1924. First published 1870.

Cooper, Thomas. *The Institutes of Justinian with Notes.* 3rd ed. New York: John S. Voorhies, Law Bookseller and Publisher, 1852.

Cruden, Alexander. *Cruden's Complete Concordance to the Old and New Testament, (William) Youngman's Edition.* J. Dinnis Publisher, 1833. (Owned by the Stafford County Genealogical and Historical Museum; author's copy is a recent reproduction.)

Fiske, N. W. *Classical Antiquities*, 4th ed. Philadelphia: E. C. and J. Biddle, 1869.

Hazzard, Samuel. *Cuba with Pen and Pencil.* Hartford, CT: Hartford Publishing ("sold only with subscription"), 1871. Facsimile, Miami, Florida: Editorial Cube, 1989.

Scott, Sir Walter. *Ivanhoe.* London: Longmans, Green, 1913.

Shakespeare, William. The Complete Works of, edited by William George Clark and William Aldis Wright with a Copious Glossary [and] an index to familiar Passages and an index to the characters in each play, NY: The American News Company.

Twain, Mark. *Innocents Abroad,* vol. 1.1. New York: Harper & Brothers, 1869, 1879. Republished 1911.

Youmans, E. L. *Introduction to The Culture Demanded by Modern Life* (copyright 1867). New York: A. Appleton and Company, 1897.

Isaac's Library

This inventory of books in the library of Isaac Beckley Werner is compiled from two sources. First, during the years 1870–1871, he compiled lengthy descriptions of books he ordered as a druggist in Rossville, Illinois. Second, at the time of his death, an inventory of his books was made before the estate auction. During his life on the Kansas prairie, he acquired other books that are mentioned in this story of his life during the Populist movement. He also acquired Populist newspapers and other literature. To encourage adult education in his community, his journal documents the delivery of boxes of books he gave to the book cupboard he built for the schoolhouse, where the Farmer's Alliance met. Therefore, the following list is not a complete compilation of Isaac's library but rather a description of what he acquired and possessed at two specific times in his life.

Books ordered in 1870–1871 by Isaac Beckley Werner while a druggist in Rossville, Illinois:

Otto's German Summons & Scholars Diaries

Murry's books on paintings:
- Dutch and Flemish Schools, 2 vols.
- Italian Schools, 2 vols.

Cooper's Justinion "Institutes"
Broom's Legal Maxims
Clark's Concordance to Shakespeare
Hayden's Dictionary of Dates
Dore's Don Quixote
Becket's "Comic History of England"
Becket's "Comic History of Rome"
Wharton's History of English Poetry
The Early Flemish Painters, Their Lives by Crowe & Cava [illegible]
Gibbon's Roman Empire
Authors' Classical Dictionary
Allibone's Dictionary of American & British Authors
Crudence Concordance to the Bible

Magazines sent to be bound:
- Scientific American
- American Law Review
- Putnam's Magazine
- Scribner's Monthly
- Fruebrer's Literary Record
- Jane's Almanac

Blydenbury on Usury (his order interlined 'out of print')
Pomeroy's Constitutional Law
Metcalf on Contracts
Lippincott's "Biographical Dictionary"
Zall's Encyclopedia
"Wonders of Italian Art"
Biographical Dictionary
Nicholson's "Manuel of Book Binding
Rouanord's History of Medicine
Spencerian's Compendium
Liddel's History of Rome
Shaw's Manuel of Literature
Ruskin's Modern Painters
Plutarch's Lives
Hallam's Middle Ages
Mark Twain's "Innocents Abroad"
Spencerian Penmanship
Mackeldig's Civil Law
Stratton's Country House Book-keepng
C. H. Moore's "How to and what to Read"
Haines' Legal Advisor
Pitt Swevelbrenn's "Hamlet"
Wm Saterwhite's "Elements of Political Economy
Fiske's "Manual of Classical Lterature"
E. A. Abbott's Shakesperian Grammar
Swartz "Caesar's Commentaries"
Letters to Cicero
Bryant & Stratton Book-keeping
Clark's Shakespearian Concordance
White's Shakespeare
W. H.(G?) Green's Elementary Hebrew Grammar
Schiller's Eclectic Edition
Stuart's Caesar's Commentaries
Murray's Handbook of Paris
Young, Citizen's Manual
Wedgwood's Government & Law
Stuart Mills (in the *New York Tribune* of Feb. 15, 1871) "Protection in America"
Cave on Coloring
Modern Women
Schiller's Complete Works
Hein's Pictures of Trains

Blackstone's Commentaries
Howell's Venetian Life
Benjamin's Greek & Turk
Literary World, a small monthly published in Boston
Cuba with Pen & Pencil
Bastiats, Essays on Political Economy
H. C. Carey's Social Science

Inventory of Books in Isaac Werner's Estate Records

The penmanship and abbreviations used by the men hired to conduct the inventory are often difficult to interpret. To the extent possible, abbreviations are completed in brackets and names of the authors and titles of the publications are identified. The titles are listed in the order in which they appeared in the estate records.

Scrib[ners]'s Mont.
Battle of Gettysburg
Manual [of] Photography
Dictionary (Eng. & French)
Dictionary, French
Auth, of Shakes[pere]
Middle Ages
How to Educate Yourself
Introduction [to the] Study [of] Rom[an] Laws
Dictionary
Hemlo's Watch rep[air]
Guide
Surveyors Guide
Student's H[and] B[ook] Com[position]
Cave on Color
Goeth's Gedichet, 2 Vols. (Johann Wolfgang von Goethe
Green's G.
Lawry School Room
Box E Containing Books etc.
Don Quixote
12 books
8 books
27 books
Scientific American, Bound, 8 Vols.
Three Books Shakespeare "In Big Box"
Package of Books (In Box No. 6)
Thos. Med[ical] Dict[tionary]
Romeo & Juliet
Grammar of Eng[lish]
Grammar
Life & Genius of Shakespeare
Hist[ory] of Eng[lish] Lit[erature]
Life of G[eorge] Stephenson
Shades and Shadows
Middle Ages
Knowledge is Power
Zell's Encyclopedia
Lippicott's Biog. Dict[tionary]
Gibbon's Roman Emp[ire], 7 Vols. (Gibbon's Rise & Fall of the Roman Empire)
Diary & Corresp[ondence] of Pepys (The Diary & Correspondence of Samuel Pepys)
Mental & Soc[ial] Cults
Marshes Wed, Ed
Sir Joshua Reynolds
Middle Ages
Book of Life at 20
Art & Artists
Tragedies of Aeschylus
Printers Camp
Burk on Sub(stance) & Beauty
Bayard Taylor's Works
History of the U.S.
Dict. Class Quotations

Milton's Poetical Works
Dictionary, Biographies
English Poetry
Modern Painters
Gil—Blass, 3 Vols.
Princes of Art
Comp[osition] Class Lit[erature]
Recollections of Byron
Dict[ionary], Terms [of] Art
Art, Recreations
Law Lectures, 2 Vols.
Military Engineering—Civil Eng[ineering], 2 Vols.
Wealth of Nations, 2 Vols.
Schillers Complete, 2 Vols. (Jahann Christoph Friedrich Schiller)
Last Hours [of] Great Men
Hand B[ook] Legend & M[yths
Potter's Hand B[ook]
Hand Book Rome
Hand Book London
Josephus Taines Eng[lish] Lit[erature]
Beechers Life [of] Christ (Henry Ward Beecher, Life of Jesus Christ (1871)
Dictionary of Bography
Bryon's Poetical (The Poetical Works of Lord Byron)
Bible (Large)
Buchey Cookery
S. Edward Warren, Elements of Machine Construction & Drawing, 1878
Warren's Elements of Mach[inery]
Public Bus[iness]
Shakesp[eare]
Schiler
Danas Manual of Geology (James Dwight Dana)
Dictionary—Simons Com[position]
Grem's En, S.
Gram[mar] (Brown's Eng[lish])
The Com[plete] Blackstone
2 House Painting
Handbook of Adm[inestration]
Ray's H[andbook], Arith[matic]
Marriage & Home
Study of Words
Penmanship & L[?]
Writing—Precious Thoughts
Skillful House B[uilding]
What is Communism?
Cook's Voyages
Two Years Before the Mast
Familiar Quotations
Com[plete] Man[ual] of Liter[ature]
Sessonson E[ctemporaneous] Speak[ing]
Coppee's Elem. Log. (Henry Coppee, Elements of Logic (1821–1895)
Crabb's Synon. (Crabb's English Synonym's—George Crab)
Appleton's
Arabian Knights
Allibons Dic[tionary] of Authors, 2 Vols.
Encyclopedia, Drawing
Copley's [Plain & Ornamental] Alphagets, (John Singleton Copley)
War & Weather
Lat[in] Grammar
Books & Authors
Allen's Class[ics]
French Pronounc[iation]
Smith Linear
Dict[ionary], German
Com[plete] Hist[ory] Rome
Dict[ionary] German
Hist[ory] Spanish Lit[erature], 2 Vols.
Mills Logic (John Stuart Mill's, System of Logic)
Ency[lopedia] Eng[lish] Lit[erature]
Lit[erature] of Europe
Chapman's American
Popes H. Illied (Alexander Pope's The Iliad of Homer)
Webber's Bus[iness]

Univ., Hist. — Heroditus (Herodotus, The Histories)
Before Footlights
Practical Pharm[acy]
Blank Book
True & Beautiful
Life of Johnson (James Boswell, Life of Johnson)
Hand B[ook] Printing, 3 Vols.
Manuel [*sic*] Literature
Bookkeeping
Plutarch's Lives, 5 Vols. (. . . of the Noble Greeks & Romans)
Plutarch's Morals, 4 Vols. (Plutarch's Moralia)
Geometry Disc.
Evelyn, Mem[oir], His Life & Times (John Evelyn, 1620–1706, English)
Atlas, Mod[ern], Historical
Books & Reading
Thoughts About Art
Med[ical] Education
Lect[ures] On Law
Art, Its Laws etc.
Topograph, Drawing
Supplemental Plates
Warren's Con. Mach etc.
Michael Angelo etc. (Michelangelo (1475–1564), Renaissance artist)
Hand Book, Paris
Critten's Comm. Arithmetic
Forti & Stone Cut[ting]
Sale of Pattens
Day Book
Science of Govern[ment]
Studies of Shakespeare
Mech[anical] Move[ment]
Shakespearean Gramm[ar]
W. Country Homes
Shakespeare Treasury
Shakespeare's Works, 12 Vols.
Political Economy
Comp[osition] & Rhetoric
Harvey's Rhetoric
Political Economy
Woodard's Rural Art
2 Dict[ionaries]
Chase receipt book
Misscellany [*sic*]
Blank book, 2 pocket books, 3 tablets
Box with Drawing Materials
Book for Bank Bills
Envelopes, Writing Paper

It should also be remembered that Isaac had given several boxes of books to the book cupboard he built for the schoolhouse, as well as books sent to his nephew Charles Werner. Many of the books described in his journal do not appear in this inventory, and their specific disposition is unknown. Also, this estate inventory mentions boxes with unidentified titles in those boxes.

Notes

Introduction

1. *County Capital,* May 17, 1888.

The Funeral: March 1895

1. *County Capital* is published in St. John, Kansas.

2. Joanna L. Stratton, *Pioneer Women: Voices from the Kansas Frontier* (New York: Simon & Schuster, 1981), 65, 68.

3. References to Isaac's attention to the District 33 schoolhouse are found in his journal, and the neglected condition of the school is shown in a photograph from the early 1900s.

4. From Isaac's probate records it is known that his final caretakers were friends and neighbors G. G. John, George and Theresa Hall, and George and Nancy Henn.

5. Stafford County History, 1870–1990, Stafford County Historical and Genealogical Society, 1990, 15.

6. Stafford County Probate Records, Isaac B. Werner, St. John, Stafford County, Kansas.

7. I. B. Werner Probate Records.

8. Songs chosen by author were popular to that specific period.

9. Isaac's fondness for Shakespeare is clear from entries in his journal, as well as from several volumes of Shakespeare documented in his probate inventory.

10. Isaac's dissatisfaction with long-winded ministers is referenced in his journal, as is his preference to study his Bible at home using Cruden's Concordance. His library reflects his faith, but his journal also reflects his dissatisfaction with most ministers, so it seems likely he would have been well satisfied by having his friend lead the group in the Lord's Prayer.

11. Identity of Isaac's friends and neighbors and the relationships they reveal in their conversations come from references in his journal. Additional personal information about those friends and neighbors comes from interviews of their descendants and genealogy research.

12. I. B. Werner Probate Records.

13. David McCullough, *The Course of Human Events*, National Endowment for the Humanities, Jefferson Lecture in the Humanities 2003.

Chapter 1: 1884

Details of Isaac Werner's day-to-day life in this chapter come from his journal, Rossville, Illinois, years 1870–1871, 1–128, and Kansas years, beginning August 24, 1884, 129, through December 31, 1884, 141. No explanation for the lengthy interruption in Isaac's journaling is known. The details of Isaac's life are taken from his journal, and although his entries may have been made in abbreviated form, the descriptions of his activities are true to what he recorded.

1. *Journal of Isaac Werner*, Wednesday, January 22, 1871, 33–34.

2. Anna E. Arnold, *A History of Kansas* (Topeka: State of Kansas, B. P. Walker, 1931), 95–96, and Sol Miller, "The Homes of Kansas," stanza 3. The reference to "title" points to the fact that many homesteaders staked their claims by building very humble dwellings such as dugout homes, which were just as valid to establish the required residence on their claims as a fancy mansion would have been.

3. Roger L. Welch, *Sod Walls: The Story of The Nebraska Sod House* (Lincoln, Nebraska: J & L Lee, 1991), 93–94.

4. Stafford County History, 1870–1990, Stafford County Historical & Genealogical Society, 1990, 17.

5. By 1884, Isaac was living in his house, but throughout his journal he mentions locations by referring to their proximity to his first or second dugout. Isaac's dugouts are assumed as being of the types common to his area.

6. Susan Naramore Maher, *Deep Map Country: Literary Cartography of the Great Plains* (Lincoln: University of Nebraska, 2014), 82–83.

7. Joanna L. Stratton, *Pioneer Women: Voices from the Kansas Frontier* (New York: Simon & Schuster, 1981), 62. The dust jacket of Stratton's book displays the photograph of a farm woman pushing a wheelbarrow filled with buffalo chips. This photograph from the Kansas State Historical Society collection is so frequently reproduced that it is practically a Kansas icon.

8. Extensive genealogy research for Isaac's extended family; William Jacob Kershnes, *History of St. John's (Hains) Church, 1852–1916* (Reading, PA: I. M. Beaver, 1916); Charles Hain Werner, Letter to his Father Henry B. Werner, November 3, 1897; Henry Beckley Werner, Diaries, Special Archives Collections, Albright College, Reading, PA; James Werner, descendant, Interview and Shared Documents, June 2011; author's visit to Wernersville, PA.

9. *Journal of Isaac Werner*, 48.

10. *Journal*, 26.

11. *Journal*, 10. The source of this declaration is uncertain. Similar is: "O thou God of my fathers, who hast given me wisdom and might," Daniel 2:23.

12. *Journal of Isaac Werner*, 22, 35, 44.

13. *Journal*, 39.

14. *Journal*, 104.

15. Kershnes, *History of St. John's*, 266–267; Henry B. Werner wrote in the preface to *Collection of Tombstone Inscriptions, 1735–1911* about the Hain's churchyard, "No doubt in the lapse of time, when the sandstone and marble of that ancient graveyard shall have crumbled into dust, some copy of this list will give the descendants of the many different families a trace of their lineage. There is no spot that ever becomes so dear to a man as the spot where cling the memories of his childhood."

16. Ancestry.com; correspondence with Susan Davis, descendant of Henrietta "Ettie" Werner Palmer.

17. Gary R. Entz, "Zion Valley: The Mormon Origins of St. John, Kansas," *Kansas History: A Journal of the Central Plains* 24, no. 2 (Summer 2001): 98–117.

18. James R. Shortridge, *Peopling the Plains: Who Settled Where in Frontier Kansas* (Lawrence: University Press of Kansas, 1995), 76–78. Railroads were eager to sell land and attract farmers who could grow produce to be shipped on trains, and they developed marketing plans focused on certain regions. One of the states the railroad targeted with their marking was Illinois, where Isaac was living before his move to Kansas. This targeting may have influenced Isaac and some of his neighbors to claim homesteads in Kansas.

19. Ancestry.com; multiple references to Henn and Curtis family members in Isaac's journal.

20. *Journal of Isaac Werner*, 130–131.

21. Ancestry.com; multiple references to the Dix family in Isaac's journal.

22. Two full-page diagrams of Isaac's design for the thatching machine, including both the drawing of the belt to feed the prairie grass into the binder and the drawing of the mechanical thatch binder, were found inside his journal.

23. The hill remains, but current owner Fred Grunder believes its height has gradually been reduced by at least forty feet for better agricultural use.

24. Descriptions of raging grass fire based on author's own experiences of controlled and uncontrolled fires in Isaac's former community. Also see Stratton, *Pioneer Women*, 84–85.

25. Stratton, 81.

26. Stratton, 80.

27. Ancestry.com; interview of and shared documents from Don Vosburgh, great grandson of Jerome Vosburgh, autumn 2011. Early rural communities were often described by the name of the family operating the post office, and Isaac's first journal entry in 1884 referred to Vosburgh, Kansas. This conflicts with information in Stafford County History, 1870–1990, 12, which states that the Vosburgh Post Office was established September 16, 1878 (which was the year of Isaac's arrival), but was discontinued September 22, 1881. There is some confusion about the location of the community post office during the years immediately after the Vosburgh Post Office closed. There were other families

mentioned as having a post office in their homes; however, Isaac mentioned none of those until the Dix Post Office was the location for his mail delivery.

28. David M. Kearney, *Belpre, Kansas: The Story of a Small Town* (Lewis, Kansas: The Lewis Press, 1978), 8.

29. Steven Hahn, *The Roots of Southern Populism: Yeoman Farmers and The Transformation of the Georgia Upcountry, 1850–1890* (New York: Oxford University Press, 2006), 240–268. The significance of fencing disputes were minimal in Isaac's community, but Hahn documents its importance in southern communities.

30. Ancestry.com; Gereke Family History, Family History Notebook, Pratt Kansas Public Library; various references in Isaac's journal.

31. *Journal of Isaac Werner*, 135.

32. There is no record in Isaac's journal nor in the detailed estate inventory at the time of his death of his having owned a gun, although he did record killing a skunk with a hammer. His weapon in this case is unknown.

33. *Centennial Edition of the Fourth Annual Report of the State Board of Agriculture to the Legislature of the State of Kansas* (State Board of Centennial Managers, Geo. W. Martin, Public Printer, 1878), 350.

34. James Turner, "Understand the Populists," *The Journal of American History* 67, no. 2 (September 1980): 366–367. Turner stresses the importance of the "background of rank and file Populists'" previous political activity.

Chapter 2: 1885

Details of Isaac Werner's day-to-day life in this chapter come from his journal: January 1, 1885, 141, through December 31, 1885, 184.

1. Ancestry.com; multiple references to the Green family in Isaac's journal.

2. Craig Miner, *West of Wichita: Settling the High Plains of Kansas, 1865–1890* (Lawrence: University Press of Kansas, 1986), 36. The United States Land Office in Larned was established in 1874.

3. The reason for this transaction could not be verified, although at the time of transfer, Isaac may have tended his trees for the eight years required to prove up a timber claim. Perhaps the transfer was somehow related to the terms of their father's estate managed by Henry.

4. Joanna L. Stratton, *Pioneer Women: Voices from the Kansas Frontier* (New York: Simon & Schuster, 1981), 83–84.

5. Stratton, 83.

6. The Beck family genealogy records researched by the author.

7. Journal entry made April 29, 1885. Isaac stated his intention to plant fifteen hundred more cuttings that season.

8. Craig Miner, *Next Year Country: Dust to Dust in Western Kansas, 1890–1940* (Lawrence: University Press of Kansas, 2006), 60–61.

9. Family information sources cited in chapter 2. For Henrietta "Ettie" Werner Palmer, author shared genealogy research with Susan Davis, descendant of Ettie.

10. Gray, J. Rufus Gray, *Pioneer Saints & Sinners* (Pratt, KS: Pratt Rotary Club, 1968), 79–80: "It was not uncommon for a settler, after a trip to town, to return to find someone in possession of his home. . . . If the settler had not yet proved up on his Land such claim jumping frequently led to litigation in the courts, if not actual bloodshed."

11. Miner, *West of Wichita*, 138–140.

12. *Journal of Isaac Werner*, 146–147.

13. Ancestry.com; references to the Goodwin family in Isaac's journal.

14. "Depending on time and place, approximately 5 to 20 percent of homesteaders were women." National Park Service, U.S. Department of the Interior Publication, *The Homestead Act of 1862*," August 2000.

15. *Journal of Isaac Werner*, 143.

16. Ancestry.com; interview of Bob Moore, descendant.

17. Ancestry.com; numerous references to Jake Baker in Isaac's journal.

18. Ancestry.com; references to Charles Shattuc in Isaac's journal.

19. Gray, *Pioneer Saints*, 80.

20. *Journal of Isaac Werner*, 157–158, 162.

21. *Journal*, 167.

22. *Journal*, 168.

23. Workers at the school were Isaac, Jesse Green, Gus Gereke, Lewis (Lou) Clouse, and Fred Rowe. Identity of the person nicknamed Dilly is unknown.

24. Ancestry.com; numerous references to Carnahan family in Isaac's journal. David Carnahan was a prominent citizen of Stafford County, and references to him were common in both the Republican *St. John News* and the Populist *County Capital*.

25. *Journal of Isaac Werner*, 177–178.

26. *Journal*, 181.

27. Stratton, *Pioneer Women*, 61.

28. Miner, *Next Year Country*, 10. "The mirages arising when the sun baked the plains showed distant towns floating above the horizon."

29. Stratton, *Pioneer Woman*, 137–139. Isaac's journal references several dances in neighbors' homes, with Gavin's barn the location for large gatherings.

Chapter 3: 1886

Details of Isaac Werner's day-to-day life in this chapter come from his journal: January 1, 1886, 184, to December 31, 1886, 226.

1. *Journal of Isaac Werner*, 185.

2. Joanna L. Stratton, *Pioneer Women: Voices from the Kansas Frontier* (New York: Simon & Schuster, 1981), 92–93.

3. Benedict Freedman and Nancy Freedman, *Mrs. Mike: The Story of Katherine Mary Flannigan* (New York: Coward-McCann & Geoghegan, 1947).

4. Craig Miner, *West of Wichita: Settling the High Plains of Kansas, 1865–1890* (Lawrence: University Press of Kansas, 1986), 164, 219.

5. *Journal of Isaac Werner*, 185.

6. "Topeka Commonwealth," January 19, 1885, quoted in David M. Kearney, *Belpre, Kansas: The Story of a Small Town* (Lewis, KS: The Lewis Press, 1978), 18. See also J. Rufus Gray, *Pioneer Saints & Sinners* (Pratt, KS: Pratt Rotary Club, 1968), 100–102.

7. Kearney, *Belpre, Kansas,* 19. That line was built but never went past Kinsley to the Edwards-Ford County line as had been represented to investors in the 1886 bond issue.

8. Lawrence Goodwyn, *The Populist Moment: A Short History of the Agrarian Revolt in America* (New York: Oxford University Press, 1978), 70.

9. Alexander Cruden, *Cruden's Complete Concordance to the Old and New Testament*, William Youngman's edition (J. Dinnis Publisher, 1833). A thick volume used as a reference in Bible study, compiled by an Englishman but often found in the libraries of American worshipers of the 1800s.

10. *Journal of Isaac Werner*, 191.

11. *Journal*, April 4, 1886, "Eve[ning] wrote correcting to Henry for Family Record."

12. The Diaries of Henry B. Werner, Special Collections, Albright College, Reading, PA, donated by Charles Hain Werner, son of Henry and nephew of Isaac Werner. Henry did not maintain his diaries as diligently as did Isaac, and only occasionally did their conversations overlap. There were no explanations in Henry's diaries describing the details of administering their father's estate.

13. Richard White, *Railroaded: The Transcontinentals and the Making of Modern America* (New York: W. W. Norton, 2011), 236–243.

14. Kansas census 1885, Frank Gullet.

15. *Journal of Isaac Werner*, 195.

16. White, *Railroaded,* 521; Map B: Kansas Railroads, 1893.

17. *Journal of Isaac Werner*, 196.

18. Stafford County History 1870–1990, Stafford County Historical & Genealogical Society, 1990, 176.

19. In the race between the two towns, Casody was the loser. In 1884 there was a post office there, which was vacated in 1889 when the failed town merged with Macksville. They also had a newspaper, *The Casody Mirage*, from 1887 to 1889, as well as a bank, a lumberyard, a drugstore, a hotel, and a general store. Like Isaac, who wrote either "Casody" or "Cassody" in his journal, people tended to vary the spelling of the town's name. See the following sources as examples of three different spellings: Stafford County History 1870–1990, 72; Macksville, Kansas Community History, 1886–1986, 194, and its inside back cover for three different spellings. To be consistent with Isaac's spelling and the spelling of the newspaper, Casody is used.

20. Stafford County History 1870–1990, 70–72.

21. Dolly Varden is the name of a Charles Dickens character, a woman who dressed in a colorful costume, perhaps indicating the mare's colorful coat as well as Isaac's familiarity with Dickens.

22. Ancestry.com, I. Ross. Spellings of her given name include Isabell, Isabelle, and Isabele, although Isaac only wrote her given name once in his journal, referring to her elsewhere as Mrs. Ross.

23. Divorce File: In the District Court of Stafford County, Kansas: Isabell D. Ross v. Raphael Ross.

24. Stratton, *Pioneer Women,* 258. Kansas women were given the right to possess and retain property and equal custody of their children in the 1859 Wyandotte Constitution Convention before the admission of Kansas to the Union. That equal custody right would have been significant to Ross in her disputed divorce.

25. Monet's blindness, Van Gogh's neurological disorders, and Cezanne's severe diabetes have now been linked to their use of Paris Green, along with the use of mercury-based Vermillion and solvents such as turpentine.

26. J. Rufus Gray, *Pioneer Saints & Sinners* (Pratt, Kansas: Pratt Rotary Club, 1968), 52–53.

27. Lucile Asher, *The Saratoga Story* (Pratt, KS: Pratt County Historical Society, 1985), 6.

28. *Journal of Isaac Werner*, 201–202.

29. The proposed railroad line is shown on the 1888 map of Stafford County, p. 33.

30. White, *Railroaded*, 214. Local railroad lines were often built by sharpers with the intention of forcing some railroad companies to buy the lines for their own use or to buy them in order to keep a competing line from acquiring them. No confirmation was found of the line platted across Werner's land having been built.

31. *Journal of Isaac Werner*, 206.

32. Author witnessed shooting of an anvil at the 2010 Santa Fe Trail Days, Larned, Kansas, performed by family members Larry, Melody and Gary Freeman, with Darin Meier, who supplied the information describing how shooting anvils is done.

33. *Journal of Isaac Werner*, 217.

Chapter 4: 1887

Details of Isaac Werner's day-to-day life in this chapter come from his journal: January 1, 1887, 227, to December 31, 1887, 284.

1. J. Rufus Gray, *Pioneer Saints & Sinners* (Pratt, KS: Pratt Rotary Club, 1968), 144.

2. *The Casody Mirage,* December 14, 1887, reported the Casody Literary Society's "literary entertainment" and the December 17, 1887, Prattsburg's Sleepy Valley "selected readings, declamation, dialogues, and essays, interspersed with vocal and instrumental music." Another evening, Sleepy Valley heard a Union veteran describe "his life in that prison hell of the South, Andersonville."

3. *Journal of Isaac Werner*, 228.

4. *Journal*, 228–230.

5. *Journal*, 233–234.

6. *Journal*, 233.

7. O. Gene Clanton, *A Common Humanity: Kansas Populism and the Battle for Justice and Equality, 1854–1903* (Manhattan, KS: Sunflower University Press, 2004), 69.

8. *Journal of Isaac Werner*, 262.

9. The *Casody Mirage,* December 28, 1887. As new land was opened for settlement to the west, struggling homesteaders were often tempted to immigrate, their enthusiasm commonly referred to as a "fever."

10. Elizabeth Bacon Custer, *Tenting on the Plains, or General Custer in Kansas and Texas* (New York: Charles L. Webster, 1887), quoted in Nina Baym, *Women Writers of the American West, 1833–1927* (Urbana: University of Illinois Press, 2011), 40.

11. *Journal of Isaac Werner*, 271.

12. Tim Stucky, *Pratt, Kansas: A Centennial View, 1884–1984* (Pretty Prairie, KS: Prairie Publications, 1984), 2–3, 13–15.

13. Lucile Asher, *Saratoga, Kansas* (Pratt, KS: Pratt County Historical Society, 1985), 11–12.

14. Gray, *Pioneer Saints & Sinners*, 50. "The obstacle that stood in the way . . . was the legality of the county's organization by the swindlers in 1872."

15. Gray, 50–51.

16. A legislative effort to expunge Stafford County and attach them to adjacent counties had accidentally omitted giving away a few square miles. When the existence of Stafford County was reinstated, the Pratt County line changed accordingly.

17. Gray, *Pioneer Saints & Sinners*, 53.

18. Asher, *Saratoga, Kansas*, 6–8. The legislative effort to expunge Stafford County and attach townships 24 and 25, range 15, to adjacent counties occurred in 1875, and the Kansas Supreme Court had nullified the attempt in 1878.

19. Gray, *Pioneer Saints & Sinners*, 96, 104–113.

20. Asher, *Saratoga, Kansas*, 32–34; Gray, *Pioneer Saints & Sinners*, 115–116.

21. Kansas Historical Society, https://kshs.org/p/cool-things-ballot-box/10281.

22. Isaac's journal entries provide only hints about this woman's identity and their long-distance romance.

23. Doc Dix and his family did not stay in Saratoga very long. For a period just before Pratt Center gained the county seat, people believed it would go to Saratoga. During that time, Saratoga was aggressive about selling lots, and it is possible Doc bought a lot at that time. He had told Isaac his plans to move a year before actually moving, and in the meantime, Pratt may have been named as the county seat, causing him to leave Saratoga and move into Pratt.

Chapter 5: 1888

Details of Isaac Werner's day-to-day life in this chapter come from his journal: January 1, 1888, 343, through December 31, 1888, 284.

1. During 1888 there were at least twenty-three different entries in Isaac Werner's journal juggling debts owed bankers and merchants.

2. A poultice is a medication, generally spread on a cloth, and applied to the site of a sore or wound; it also refers to the act of applying the medication.

3. *Journal of Isaac Werner*, 288.

4. *Journal*, 300; *County Capital*, April 19, 1888. The officers were elected as follows: Gen. Joseph A. Cooper as president, C. G. McNeil as vice president, Joseph Coe as secretary, and Isaac Werner as treasurer. The committee of five to draw up bylaws and other rules included Isaac Werner, G. T. Selfridge, Ira Northrup, G. A. Gonder, and John Hilmes.

5. *Journal of Isaac Werner*, 291.

6. Walter T. K. Nugent, *The Tolerant Populists: Kansas Populism and Nativism* (Chicago: University of Chicago Press, 1963), 57.

7. Hogback: a ridge with a sharp summit and steeply sloping sides.

8. *Journal of Isaac Werner*, 305.

9. Scott G. McNall, *The Road to Rebellion: Class Formation and Kansas Populism, 1865–1900* (Chicago: University of Chicago Press, 1988), 208.

10. *County Capital,* p. 8, col. 4, May 17, 1888.

11. Isaac's article published in *County Capital,* front page, May 31, 1888.

12. *Journal of Isaac Werner*, 307.

13. *County Capital,* p. 1, col. 3–4, May 24, 1888; bank president: T. W. Simpson; employees: bookkeeper, E. E. Farmer; cashier, I. E. Page; teller, Will Pitzer.

14. *County Capital,* June 8, 1888.

15. Craig Miner, *West of Wichita: Settling the High Plains of Kansas, 1865–1890* (Lawrence: University Press of Kansas, 1986), 222–223.

16. David M. Kearney, *Belpre, Kansas: The Story of a Small Town* (Lewis, KS: Lewis Press, 1979), 30.

17. Kearney, *Belpre, Kansas*, 28.

18. D. S. Carnahan, Director; trustees included J. T. Armstrong, Great Bend; G. A. Gonder, St. John; G. M. Detwiler, Seward; J. H. Campbell, Stafford; Ira D. Northrup, Cleveland; and Joseph Darling, St. John.

19. Nugent, *The Tolerant Populists*, 50. In their newspaper, the Vincent brothers had called the trial of the Haymarket riot "judicial murder."

20. *County Capital*, September 13, 1888.

21. *Journal of Isaac Werner*, 329.

22. *County Capital*, October 25, 1888.

23. Isaac refers to the meeting as taking place in the "rink" but the newspaper refers to the location as "the opera house." It was common at that time for a single building to serve both purposes.

24. *County Capital*, p. 4, col. 4, November 1, 1888. In addition to Isaac's signature, the following neighbors signed: James W. Tanner, A. J. More, Mrs. Long, Lewis A. Edingfield, J. W. Long, Mrs. Millie Frack, Miss J. K. Bodenhammer, Mrs. Minnie Tobias, A. Cubbage, Mrs. A. Vandeveer, U. T. Stimatze, Mrs. L. Furguson, J. F. Stinemetze, Mrs. J. E. Frack, Mrs. N. C. Henn, James Osgood, Alexander Ervin, Abba U. Lanman, Mrs. I. P. Ross, Wm Long, Ada Frack, C. G. Gereke, J. Hacker Jackson Long, E. B. Smith, Chas B. Goodwinn, Albert A. Shoop, Noah Long, Mrs. E. More, Miss Millie Long, Mrs. E. J. Edingfield, Miss N. J. Long Lewis J. Tobias, C. C. Tobias, G. F. Vandiveer, Mrs. L. Stimatze, Joseph Furguson, Mrs. A. Stinemetze, Wm F. Frack, George Henn, Frank Curtis, Mrs. Laura Osgood, D. F. Lauman, Michael Lynch, Horace Frack, W. B. Long, Charles Frack, Mrs. Mary Gereke, Clara E. Shoup, Mary Cullison, Mrs. Long, Mrs. Stell Smith, T. E. Dennison, W. H. Cullison. Below the signatures were two specific endorsements, the first given by Elder C. A. Bowker and his wife, and the second given by L. Thomkins.

25. Trustee, W. F. Frack; treasurer, H. M. Frack; clerk, J. Fountain; constables, J. Ferguson and S. A. Eddingfield; road overseers, Gus Gereke and D. F. Lanman.

26. Lawrence Goodwyn, *Democratic Promise: The Populist Movement in America* (New York: Oxford University Press, 1976), 102.

27. Rebecca Edwards, *The Life of Mary E. Lease: People's Advocate* (Poughkeepsie, NY: Vassar College, 2000); Kathryn Price, "Mary Elizabeth Lease: Lawyer, Politician & Hellraiser," paper written for Professor Barbara Babock, Stanford Law School, 1997; Craig Miner, *Wichita: The Magic City* (Wichita, KS: Wichita-Sedgwick County Historical Museum Association, 1988), 95.

28. Quote from Emporia, Kansas, newspaper editor, William Allen White, who was presumed to refer to Elizabeth Lease as one of the "Harpies" mentioned in his famous 1896 editorial, "What's the Matter with Kansas?"

29. About fifty-four bushels; with the Bentleys having moved and their land in possession of a renter, Isaac served as their agent.

30. Miner, *West of Wichita*, 185–187. In 1889 there were nine sugar plants operating in Kansas, Miner, 227.

31. *Journal of Isaac Werner*, 340.

Chapter 6: 1889

Details of Isaac Werner's day-to-day life in this chapter come from his journal: January 1, 1887, 343, through December 31, 1887, 405.

1. *Journal of Isaac Werner*, 343 ("About 1/2 past 2 o'clock eclipse commenced."). See also Todd David Peck, "Instructions for Observing the Total Eclipse of the Sun, January 1, 1889," Amherst College Observatory.

2. *Journal of Isaac Werner*, 346.

3. *Journal*, 346.

4. Adam Smith, *An Inquiry into the Nature and Causes of the Wealth of Nations* (Adam Smith, 1776), book 1, chapter 5. Project Gutenberg (accessed January 1, 2020). http://www.gutenberg.org/files/3300/3300-h/3300-h.htm.

5. *An Inquiry into the Nature and Causes of the Wealth of Nations,* more commonly called *The Wealth of Nations*, was first published in 1776 and continues to be read today. *Progress and Poverty,* published in 1879, was a fuller development of Henry George's *Our Land Policy,* published in 1871. During his lifetime, George was one of the most famous Americans, well- known internationally. During the nineteenth century, only sales of the Bible exceeded sales of *Progress and Poverty.*

6. S. S. Hamill, *New Science of Elocution: The elements and principles of vocal expression in lessons* (Phillips & Hunt, 1886).

7. *Journal of Isaac Werner*, January 29, 1889; McNall, *The Road to Rebellion*, "Language provides a means for people to analyze their troubles . . . by the very vocabulary or ideology with which one makes sense of the world," 180–181.

8. *Journal of Isaac Werner*, February 19, 1889, 349.

9. *Journal*, February 19 and 20, 1889, 349.

10. *County Capital*, February 21, 1889.

11. S. E. V. Emery, *Seven Financial Conspiracies which have Enslaved the American People* (Robert Smith: Lansing Michigan, 1887). Fifty thousand copies were distributed during the political campaign in 1888. Emery's book "served as a movement bible on

this topic," Jeffrey Ostler, *Prairie Populism: The Fate of Agrarian Radicalism in Kansas, Nebraska, and Iowa, 1880–1892* (Lawrence: University Press of Kansas, 1993), 79.

12. Emery, *Seven Financial Conspiracies.*

13. The letter announcing the admission of Mary Elizabeth Lease to the bar arrived May 5, 1889.

14. Walter T. K. Nugent, *The Tolerant Populists: Kansas Populism and Nativism*, 2nd ed. (Chicago: University of Chicago Press, 1963), 37.

15. Apoplexy is caused by a rupture or obstruction of an artery of the brain and results in diminished or loss of sensation, motion, or consciousness.

16. *Journal of Isaac Werner,* 366, clipping glued in margin; baptismal records, William Jacob Kershnes, *St. John's (Haines) Church History, 1852–1916* (Reading, PA: I. M. Beaver, 1916), 253.

17. Ostler, *Prairie Populism*, 102–103.

18. *County Capital,* p. 1, col. 4, June 6, 1889. The initial casualty estimates were excessive; however, 2,209 were known to have died, and of those, 777 victims were never identified.

19. David McCullough, *The Johnstown Flood* (New York: Simon & Schuster, 1968).

20. John Wesley Powell, "The Lessons of Conemaugh," *North American Review*; quoted in McCullough, *The Johnstown Flood*, 263.

21. *Journal of Isaac Werner*, 369.

22. *Journal*, 345, 353, 360, 374, 389, 398.

23. The newspaper announcement of the Albano Farmers' Alliance identified it as the eleventh to be formed in Stafford County and listed names of all the officers, including I. W. Logan, doorkeeper; Frank Curtis, assistant doorkeeper; Orvill L. Glassgow, sergeant at arms; I. Steinmetz, chaplain; with Joseph Furguson, lecturer. *County Capital,* p. 4, col. 4, June 20, 1889.

24. Although not stated explicitly, apparently Baldy was the name given to Jule's roan colt. It is presumed that "Frazee" referred to Stephen, who was thirteen years younger than Isaac. Later, the two men formed a friendship, and this journal entry may have been written in anger about the injury to his young horse.

25. When the picnic was reported in the *County Capital,* the crowd was estimated at two thousand.

26. Peter H. Argersinger, "Road to a Republican Waterloo: The Farmers' Alliance and the Election of 1890 in Kansas," *Kansas History: A Journal of the Central Plains* 33, no. 4 (Winter 1967): 443–469.

27. Argersinger, "Road to a Republican Waterloo," 454.

28. *Looking Backward,* published in 1888, remains a classic, read for the philosophical and social ideas it contains.

29. The Southwark Foundry & Machine Co. produced Machinery-Steam Engines and Boilers, occupying the entire quadrangle between Washington Avenue, Federal Street, South 4th Street, and South 5th Street in South Philadelphia. Information made available at http://www.philageohistory.org by Athenaeum of Philadelphia and its partners. No more children were born to Emma.

30. Two more children were later born.

31. *Journal of Isaac Werner*, 387.

32. McNall, *The Road to Rebellion,* 186–189.

33. General Weaver's quotes are taken from his book, *A Call to Action: An Interpretation of the Great Uprising, Its Source and Causes* (Des Moines: Iowa Printing, 1892).

34. Shattuc, sometimes spelled Shattuck, was now Isaac's neighbor to the north, occupying the land once claimed by Baker.

35. *Journal of Isaac Werner*, 395.

36. Nugent, *The Tolerant Populists*, 122–123, 133.

37. Larry A. McFarlane, "Nativism or Not? Perceptions of British Investments in Kansas, 1882–1901," *Great Plains Quarterly* (1987), 236–237. Urban areas and their political representatives were more likely to favor the idea of investment capital for their regions while rural areas, led by their elected politicians and Farmers' Alliances, feared being displaced by foreign syndicates acquiring the last available land or seizing it through foreclosure of farm mortgages. Some large parcels of land were owned by foreign syndicates in the 1800s, and some foreign companies held mortgages.

38. *Journal of Isaac Werner*, 400.

39. W. Scott Morgan, *History of the Wheel and Alliance and the Impending Revolution* (Hardy, Arkansas, pub. by author, 1889).

40. *Journal of Isaac Werner*, 401.

41. John Rogers came to Kansas in 1876 and later became editor of the *Kansas Commoner* in Wichita. He moved to Washington State in 1890 and was elected in 1895 as governor.

42. *County Capital*, October 10, 1889.

43. *Journal of Isaac Werner*, 403.

44. Baby William Roy Loftiss, born October 18, 1889, died August 11, 1890.

45. *Dr. J. H. McLean's Family Almanac* (St. Louis: J. H. McLean) was an annual, pocket-sized pamphlet published with weather predictions and cycles of the moon but primarily as a vehicle for marketing patent medicines.

46. Laurence Gronlund, *The Co-operative Commonwealth in its Outlines, An Exposition of Modern Socialism* (New York: Lee and Shepherd Publishers, 1884), 7–8.

47. Ostler, *Prairie Populism*, 107.

48. *Journal of Isaac Werner*, 405.

Chapter 7: 1890

Details of Isaac Werner's day-to-day life in this chapter come from his journal: January 1, 1890, 405, through June 10, 1890, 480.

1. Exchanges had been established in other places, particularly Texas, but most struggled from inadequate operating capital.

2. *Journal of Isaac Werner*, January 20, 1890, 407.

3. *County Capital*, January 16, 1890. In an almost full column letter to the editor written by someone using the pseudonym "Farmer," the *Newton Republican* is blamed for ridiculing farmers and ignoring the influence of Republican legislators who voted tax dollars to support the sugar mills.

4. *Journal of Isaac Werner*, January 31, 1890, 408.

5. W. Scott Morgan, *History of the Wheel and Alliance and impending revolution* (Hardy, Arkansas, pub. by author; Fort Scott, Kansas: J. H. Rice & Sons, 1889), 275–282.

6. The term "span" refers to a full extent of something, so either Ben Webber was asked to hold all of the salesman's horses involved in the trade, or perhaps a matched span desired for pulling a wagon or buggy. The specific number is unknown.

7. Unknown at that time, the Bentleys would also give up on Colorado and would move on to Salt Lake City, Utah.

8. *Journal of Isaac Werner,* February 16, 410.

9. Walter T. K. Nugent, *The Tolerant Populists: Kansas Populism and Nativism*, 2nd ed. (Chicago: University of Chicago Press, 1963), 112.

10. Nugent, *The Tolerant Populists*, 79–80.

11. *Journal of Isaac Werner*, April 28, 1890, 418.

12. The Topolobampo Collection is a Special Collection at the Henry Madden Library of California State University, Fresno, California.

13. *Journal of Isaac Werner*, April 4, 1890, 415.

14. The Vincent brothers divided their responsibilities at *The American Nonconformist*: Henry was responsible for editorial policy, Leopold was the business manager, and Cuthbert did most of the public speaking as field representative.

15. Harold Piehler, "Henry Vincent: Kansas Populist and Radical-Reform Journalist," *Kansas History: A Journal of the Central Plains* 2, no. 1 (Spring 1979): 14–25; O. Gene Clanton, *A Common Humanity: Kansas Populism and the Battle for Justice and Equality, 1854–1903* (Manhattan, KS: Sunflower University Press, 2004); Lawrence Goodwyn, *The Populist Moment: A Short History of the Agrarian Revolt in America* (New York: Oxford University Press, 1978); Henry Vincent, *The Story of the Commonweal: Complete and Graphic Narrative of the Origin and Growth of the Movement* (Chicago: W. B. Conkey Company, 1894).

16. William A. Peffer, *Populism: Its Rise and Fall,* ed. and with an introduction by Peter H. Argersinger (Lawrence: University Press of Kansas, 1992), 31–32.

17. Nugent, *The Tolerant Populists*, 60–61.

18. Among the delegates were Farmers' Alliance (thirty-six), Knights of Labor (twenty-six), Farmers' Mutual Benefit Association (fourteen), Patrons of Husbandry (three), and other groups, including single-tax clubs.

19. *Journal of Isaac Werner*, June 19, 1890, 426.

20. Isaac had also enjoyed a correspondence with Ellen Greene of Illinois. After this uncertain entry, there were no more mentions of Ellen Green or Lena in his journal. Among his books was *Marriage and Home*, indicating his possible intention to marry. Perhaps Lena was the diminutive for Ellen.

21. William Fisher Brown used the pseudonym "old Bill Fisher" in his newspaper column.

22. *Journal of Isaac Werner,* July 17, 1890, 431.

23. Nugent, *The Tolerant Populists,* 112.

24. Donnelly (1831–1901) was an amateur scientist who published his theories about the mythical lost continent of Atlantis, as well as theories about a near collision of the earth with a massive comet. He had also become entangled in financial failures; yet, his organizational and literary skills placed him in some prominence within the People's Party.

25. Ignatius Loyola Donnelly [writing as Edmund Boisgilbert, MD], *Caesar's Column: A Story of the Twentieth Century* (Chicago: F. J. Schulte & Publishers, 1890), 3.

26. David M. Kearney, *Belpre, Kansas: The Story of a Small Town* (Lewis, KS: The Lewis Press, 1979), 34–35.

27. The threatened foreclosure sales did not occur for everyone listed in the newspaper, for many of the people continued to farm in these locations. In Clear Creek, William Wilson, Charles Farwell, Aaron Beck, and Holbrook and Webber; in Albano, E. D. Stambaugh, Charles Bowker, Joseph Ferguson, I. W. Stimatze, Lelia Farwell, Joseph Mayes, Frank Stimatze, William Frack, Mary Bentley, Enoch Davison, and two listings for David Carnahan.

28. *Journal of Isaac Werner*, August 23, 1890, 438.

29. Robert Smith Bader, *Prohibition in Kansas: A History* (Lawrence: University Press of Kansas, 1986), 106.

30. *Journal of Isaac Werner*, August 25, 1890, 438.

31. *County Capital*, February 13, 1890.

32. *Kansas: A Cyclopedia of State History*, vol. 3 part 1 (Chicago: Standard Publishing, 1912), 56–59.

33. *Journal of Isaac Werner*, October 25, 1890, 446.

34. Journal references to Cairo, Charles Shattuc's hired hand, and to the "colored speaker from Topeka" are the only mention of black Kansans in Isaac Werner's journal. Among the Exodusters who came to Kansas after the Civil War, a colony of former slaves came to Stafford County, settling mostly in Ohio Township, and Cairo may have been a member of this group. See Stafford County Historical and Genealogical Society pamphlet published for their "Exodusters of Stafford County" exhibit of 2011. The speaker from Topeka may have been John Lytle, who had come to Kansas with his mother and four siblings in about 1882 and was active in the Populist Party. John's daughter, Lutie, who attended Topeka schools before studying law in Nashville, Tennessee, became the first African American woman admitted to the Kansas bar.

35. *Journal of Isaac Werner*, October 25, 1890, 447.

36. S. E. V. Emery, *Seven Financial Conspiracies which have Enslaved the American People* (Lansing, MI: Robert Smith, 1894), 8. The passages quoted are taken from the Robert Smith 1894 edition. Emery first copyrighted her book in 1887. Fifty thousand copies were distributed during the political campaign in 1888.

37. The seven conspiracies identified by Emery, with the dates of their enactments, were: (1) the "Exception Clause," 1862; (2) the National Bank Act, 1863; (3) retirement of "greenbacks" as currency, starting in 1866; (4) the "Credit Strengthening Act," 1869; (5) refunding of national debt, 1870; (6) the demonetization of silver, 1873; and (7) destruction of fractional paper currency, 1875.

38. Emery, *Seven Financial Conspiracies*, 70.

39. *Pratt County Register*, November 8, 1890.

40. *County Capital*, September 4, 1890. The summaries are those of the author.

41. Kathryn Price, *Mary Elizabeth Lease: Lawyer, Politician & Hellraiser,* Paper for Professor Barbara Babcock, Women's Legal History, Stanford Law School, Fall 1997, http://wlh-wiki.law.stanford.edu/index.php/Late_Nineteenth_Century_Politics; Brooke Speer Orr, *Mary Elizabeth Lease: Gendered Discourse and Populist Party Politics in*

Gilded Age America, Kansas State Historical Society, http://www.kshs.org/publicat/history/2006winter_orr.pdf.

42. U.S. senators were not directly chosen by voters until 1913. Initially the Constitution provided for their election by state legislators, so the influence of Mary Elizabeth Lease would have been the result of helping indirectly through winning votes for the state legislators who chose the U.S. senator from Kansas.

43. *Journal of Isaac Werner*, November 4, 1890, 449.

44. *Journal*, November 21, 1890, 450–451.

45. *Journal*, December 24, 1890, 454.

Chapter 8: 1891

Details of Isaac Werner's day-to-day life in this chapter come from his journal: January 1, 1891, 455, to June 10, 1891, 480. His journal ends on June 10, 1891, and subsequent references to Isaac come from newspaper articles, references or opinions from earlier pages in the journal, or suppositions supported by what Isaac would have been likely to have believed based on earlier references. Greater use is made of the local *County Capital* newspaper.

1. *County Capital*, January 15, 1891.

2. Rebecca Edwards, *Angels in the Machinery: Gender in American Party Politics from the Civil War to the Progressive Era* (New York: Oxford University Press, 1997), 101.

3. Jeffrey Ostler, *Prairie Populism: The Fate of Agrarian Radicalism in Kansas, Nebraska, and Iowa, 1880–1892* (Lawrence: University Press of Kansas, 1993), 109.

4. Walter T. K. Nugent, *The Tolerant Populists: Kansas Populism and Nativism* (Chicago: University of Chicago Press, 1963), 135.

5. Edwards, *Angels in the Machinery*, 100.

6. Edwards, 88; R. Alton Lee and Steven Cox, *When Sunflowers Bloomed Red: Kansas and the Rise of Socialism in America* (Lincoln: University of Nebraska Press, 2020), 74–81.

7. Edwards, *Angels in the Machinery*, 137.

8. Edwards, 5.

9. The *Leader* was published between 1890 and 1894. "English Biennial Report of the Board of Directors of the Kansas Historical Society for the period November 18, 1890 and ending November 15, 1892" (bound newspapers and periodicals), 106.

10. Taken from the front page of the January 29, 1891, *County Capital* but without the phonetic spelling Isaac used in the article.

11. *Journal of Isaac Werner*, January 30, 1891, 460.

12. James Turner, "Understand the Populists," *The Journal of American History* 67, no. 2 (September 1980): 366.

13. Peter H. Argersinger, *The Limits of Agrarian Radicalism* (Lawrence: University Press of Kansas, 1995), 75–77.

14. Michael Lewis Goldberg, *An Army of Women: Gender and Politics in Gilded Age Kansas* (Baltimore: Johns Hopkins University Press, 1997), 135.

15. *Journal of Isaac Werner,* February 4, 1891, 460.

16. *County Capital,* January 29, 1891.

17. *Journal of Isaac Werner,* January 3, 1891, 460.

18. *Journal,* February 11, 1891, 461.

19. *Journal,* February 15, 1891, 462.

20. To list is to prepare or plant land in ridges or furrows, and the equipment used is called a lister or lister plow.

21. *Pratt County Times,* February 27, 1891.

22. *Journal of Isaac Werner,* 464–465, March 2–4, 1891. It is known that Aaron Nutt Beck suffered a stroke sometime in the early 1890s, although the exact date is uncertain. The references in Isaac's journal to the "Beck's Sale" (March 10, 1891) and the moving of the post office from the Beck residence (March 4, 1891) suggests that Beck's stroke was the reason for these events. The Beck family remained in the community following Beck's stroke.

23. *Journal of Isaac Werner,* March 15, 1891, 466.

24. Thirty of the fifty states had land available under the Homestead Act between the years of 1863–1986. In 1976 the act was repealed in the lower forty-eight states, but it continued in Alaska until 1986. Ultimately, ownership of over 270 million acres was conveyed by the government to private ownership. Information from "Homestead National Monument," National Park Service, U.S. Department of Interior.

25. Fees quoted in the March 19, 1891 *County Capital* were preemption: $207.50, homestead: $11.50, timber claim: $9.50.

26. Craig Miner, *Next Year Country: Dust to Dust in Western Kansas, 1890–1940* (Lawrence: University Press of Kansas, 2006), 237–238.

27. Craig Miner, *Kansas: The History of the Sunflower State, 1854–2000* (Lawrence: University Press of Kansas, 2002), 150–155. Miner's quotes are taken from *Thirty Years in Topeka: A Historical Sketch* (Topeka: Kansas Publishing House, 1886), 367–370, and he describes Giles as "an early resident and historian."

28. William Blanch, J. S. Smith, Lou Clouse, and Isaac Werner.

29. *County Capital,* January 8, 1891.

30. *County Capital,* April 2, 1891. "First, list east and west; Second, improvements to implements are needed; Third, rows should not be listed too close; Fourth, sub-soilers should leave a 'V' furrow so seeds will be sown in a straight line to facilitate cultivation; Fifth, seed should be soaked to deter pests; Sixth, the holes in the dropping plates must be adjusted to accommodate the soaked seeds; Seventh, a brush cut-off should be used to avoid damaging the seeds as they are dropped; Eighth, the drop distances must be adjusted for the various small, medium, and large stalks grown in the vicinity—from 18 to 26 inches apart for proper growing room, depending on the variety; and Ninth, weather predictions must improve to allow better choice of varieties for the projected rain fall."

31. *Journal of Isaac Werner,* February 24, 1891, 463.

32. The Halls were the author's great-grandparents, and family genealogy records provided information. The oral history about buying the train tickets to Belpre came from the Hall's granddaughter, Doris Beck Sharp.

33. Occasional newspaper references to Isaac Werner spell his last name as "Verner."

34. *Journal of Isaac Werner,* April 30, 1891, 473.

35. *Journal,* May 20, 1891, 476.

36. *Journal*, June 20, 1890, 426.

37. Edmund Shaftesbury was the pseudonym of Albert Webster Edgerly (1852–1926), a graduate of the Boston University School of Law who practiced in Boston, Kansas, and Washington, DC. In addition to the book Isaac bought, Shaftesbury wrote many others, several of which we would find offensive or foolish today; however, he did recommend eating whole grain cereals. When the Purina Mills began making a breakfast cereal similar to what Shaftesbury had described in his book, they sought and obtained his endorsement. The cereal became so popular that Purina Mills was renamed Ralston-Purina. Isaac mentioned purchasing *The 200 Year Club* book in his journal entry of June 20, 1890. Edmund Shaftesbury, *Our Existences, The Doctrine of Diversity, A Study of What We Are—Where We Are, Our Origin and Destiny,* Washington, DC: Shaftsbury College, http://archive.org/details/shaftsburyschoo100shaf.

38. *Kansas: A Cyclopedia of State History* (Chicago: Standard Publishing, 1912), 622–629.

39. Robert C. McMath, *American Populism: A Social History 1877–1898* (New York: Hill & Wang, 1993), 133.

40. Carleton Beals, *The Great Revolt and Its Leaders: The History of Popular American Uprisings in the 1890s* (New York: Abelard-Schuman, 1968), 171. Carleton Beals was the son of Leon Beals, and the author of many books in his own right.

41. Nugent, *The Tolerant Populists*, 60.

42. Argersinger, *Limits*, 39–40.

43. Mcmath, *American Populism*, 133.

44. Lawrence Goodwyn, *The Populist Moment: A Short History of the Agrarian Revolt in America* (New York: Oxford University Press, 1978), 121–123; Steven Hahn, *The Roots of Southern Populism: Yeoman Farmers and The Transformation of the Georgia Upcountry, 1850–1890* (New York: Oxford University Press, 2006), 204–205.

45. William A. Peffer, *Populism: Its Rise and Fall* (Lawrence: University Press of Kansas, 1992), 179.

46. Goodwyn, *The Populist Moment*, 90–93.

47. Argersinger, *Limits*, 86.

48. McMath, *American Populism*, 139–141, 146.

49. Argersinger, *Limits*, 132. Ignatius Loyola Donnelly of Minnesota was the author of one of the books in Isaac Werner's library, *Caesar's Column.* He warned Populists, "Let us subordinate everything to the success of the cause; but do not let us subordinate the cause to success."

50. Argersinger, *Limits*, 134, quoting Peffer: "how filthy the corruption of 'practical politics' among Reformers became"; McMath, *American Populism*, 157; Goodwyn, *The Populist Moment*, 169.

51. Charles Postel, *The Populist Vision* (New York: Oxford University Press, 2007), 153–155.

52. Goodwyn, *The Populist Moment*, 20–25. "Once a farmer had signed his first crop lien he was in bondage to his merchant as long as he failed to pay out . . . the crop lien system became for millions of Southerners, white or black, little more than slavery."

53. Hahn, *Roots*, 173–174.

54. Peter H. Argersinger, *Populism & Politics: William Alfred Peffer and the People's Party* (Lexington: University Press of Kentucky, 1974), 83–94.

55. McMath, *American Populism*, 146.

56. Miner, *Next Year Country*, 32; quoted from the *Hays City Sentinel*, July 7, 14, 1891.

57. Nugent, *The Tolerant Populists*, 104.

58. *Journal of Isaac Werner*, 477.

59. Ancestry.com for the Hilmes family and many references to his relationship with Helms in Isaac's journal.

60. *Journal of Isaac Werner*, May 31, 1891, 479.

61. Isaac mentioned in his journal that Isabel Ross had done some cooking for his visitors, so perhaps the cooking of the bachelor farmer that John Hilmes praised had received a little unmentioned help. Seth Blake also came that day to photograph the Hilmes family posing with the cultivator.

62. Although Isaac's journal ends, the author continues to use opinions expressed in the journal when they apply to subsequent circumstances in later years.

63. *County Capital*, June 5, 1891.

64. *County Capital*, July 31, 1891.

65. *County Capital*, September 8, 1891.

66. *County Capital*, September 18, 1891.

67. By the act of Congress admitting Kansas to the Union, certain public lands were established, divisible into four classes: lands owned by the general government, lands granted to higher institutions of learning, common school lands, and grants made to railroad companies. The grants to aid railroad construction were made in 1863, subject to approval of the legislature and the governor. A lawsuit resulted from railroads attempting to charge settlers for land occupied before the railroad land grants. In 1875 the United States decided in favor of the settlers' prior claims. *Kansas: A Cyclopedia of State History*, vol. 2, 1912 transcription.

68. *County Capital*, November 6, 1891.

69. Beals, *The Great Revolt*, 227.

70. Beals, 227.

71. *County Capital*, November 27, 1891.

72. Joseph Hamlin Tudor built the two-story brick Tudor building on the west side of the town square in St. John in 1910, with a full basement beneath, which now houses the Lucille M. Hall Museum, in which basement Isaac Beckley Werner's journal was found in 2010.

73. *County Capital*, November 27, 1891.

74. *County Capital*, December 25, 1891.

75. *County Capital*, December 25, 1891. Transmogrify: To change, often with absurd effect; to transform.

Chapter 9: 1892

1. Story of Isaac Werner's cat in *County Capital*, December 25, 1891, 4, col. 3.

2. James Turner, "Understanding the Populists," *The Journal of American History* 67, no. 2 (September 1980): 367. Turner elaborates on the impact of isolation and social connections for farmers.

3. *County Capital*, February 19, 1892.

4. The National Farmers' Alliance and Industrial Union, the Knights of Labor, the Patrons of Industry, the Farmers' Mutual Benefit Association, the National Citizens' Industrial Alliance, the National Citizens' Alliance, the National Farmers' Alliance, and the National Colored Alliance & Co-operative Union.

5. Leonidas L. Polk is not to be confused with controversial Confederate General Leonidas Polk (sometimes mistakenly called Leonidas K. Polk). The two men are not related.

6. Called the Southern Alliance in North Carolina.

7. Now North Carolina State University.

8. Goodwyn, Lawrence, *Democratic Promise, The Populist Movement in America* (New York: Oxford University Press, 1976), 190–191.

9. *County Capital*, December 18, 1890.

10. Stuart Noblin, Leonidas LaFayette Polk, Agrarian Crusader (Chapel Hill: University of North Carolina Press, 1949).

11. Goodwyn, *Democratic Promise*, 265–266.

12. William A. Peffer, with Introduction by Peter H. Argersinger, *Populism: Its Rise and Fall*; *County Capital* (Lawrence: University Press of Kansas, 1995); *Kansas: A Cyclopedia of State History* (Chicago: Standard Publishing, 1912) https://skyways.lib.ks.us/genweb/archives/1912/p/public_lands.html; North Carolina History Project, "Leonidas L. Polk (1837–1892)"; John D. Hicks, "The Birth of the Populist Party," *Minnesota History* 9 no. 3, September 1928; Peter H. Argersinger, "Road to a Republican Waterloo: The Farmers' Alliance and the Election of 1890 in Kansas," *Kansas Historical Quarterly* 33, no. 4 (Winter 1967): 443–469; William J. Bryan, *The First Battle: A Story of the Campaign of 1896* (Chicago: W. B. Conkey, 1896).

13. Led by L. F. Livingston of Georgia.

14. "ARRESTED—E. H. Landes, Bill Glasscock, Ben Webber, Joe Cline, and Jim Oliver—Charged with the Burglary, the taking of the County Treasurer's Books, and the County's Funds, on January 25, 1891," *County Capital*, March 25, 1892.

15. *County Capital*, March 25, 1892.

16. Gerhard Peters and John T. Woolley, *Minor/Third Party Platforms, Populist Party Platform of 1892*, Online, Presidency Project, https://www.presidency.ucsb.edu/node/273285.

17. Gerhard and Woolley, *Minor/Third Party*, 218–219.

18. Rochester was a shoe-making town, and there had been a long-running struggle between the manufacturers and the workers there.

19. Expression of Sentiments, resolutions as an addendum at the close of the 1892 platform. https://www.norton.com/college/history/archive/reader/trial/directory/1890_1914/12_ch22_04.htm.

20. *County Capital*, September 4, 1890.

21. Bill O'Neal, *The Johnson County War* (Austin, TX: Eakin Press, 2004); The Johnson County War is also known as the War on Powder Creek, and it has inspired many fictionalized versions, some adhering more closely to the facts than others, the representation of which side was in the right and which in the wrong shifting according to the fiction writers' whims. Some of the more well-known motion pictures with roots in the Johnson County War are *The Virginian, Shane,* and *Heaven's Gate.*

22. Henry Clay Frick Business Records, 1892–1987, Archives Service Center, University of Pittsburgh. For an account of the Homestead strike, see Paul Krause, *The Battle for*

Homestead, 1880–1892: Politics, Culture, and Steel (Pittsburgh: University of Pittsburgh Press, 1992).

23. Although generally called the Homestead strike, it was actually a lockout, since Frick locked the workers out of the plant the day before the old contract expired and the workers entered the plant only after the Pinkertons arrived.

24. Krause, *The Battle for Homestead*, 18; taken from Arthur G. Burgoyne, *Homestead Strike* (Pittsburgh: Rawsthorne Engraving and Printing, 1983) 58, 59; *PCG, NYH, NYS, and NYW, July 7, 1892*; and U.S. House, *Report* 2447, p. 8, 133; Myron R. Stowell, *Fort Frick: or the Siege of Homestead* (Pittsburgh: Pittsburgh Printing, 1893), 45–46.

25. *County Capital,* 1, col. 4, September 4, 1890; it was the New York Central & Hudson River Railroad.

26. Scott G. McNall, *The Road to Rebellion: Class Formation and Kansas Populism, 1865–1900* (Chicago: University of Chicago Press, 1988), 208–209.

27. While non-farmer members were among the organizations that came together to form the People's Party, the strength and enthusiasm existed primarily among farmers.

28. Chapter 1 of *The Battle for Homestead, 1880–1892* discusses the difficulties of the Gilded Age after the Civil War with reference to the steel workers as well as the "challenge the emerging inequalities of power—'vices'—that arose from unchecked accumulation" was creating in America between the extremely wealthy and the laboring classes.

29. Krause, *Battle for Homestead*, 50.

30. *County Capital*, August 5, 1892.

31. *County Capital*, September 16, 1892.

32. Walter T. K. Nugent, *The Tolerant Populists, Kansas Populism and Nativism* (Chicago: University of Chicago Press, 1963), 76–78.

33. Article 1, section 3 of the United States Constitution provides: "The Senate of the United States shall be composed of two Senators from each state, chosen by the legislature thereof for six Years" and it was not until 1913 that senators were elected by the people directly.

34. Joanna L Stratton, *Pioneer Women: Voices from the Kansas Frontier* (New York: Simon & Schuster, 1981); timeline compiled from Stratton's book at http://www.kancoll.org/voices/1997/0997sufr.htm.

35. Before towns had hospitals, the badly injured were often taken to the undertaker's establishment for treatment.

36. *County Capital*, December 30, 1892.

37. *County Capital,* December 30, 1892, 1. The members of the coroner's jury were J. H. Tudor, Jacob Ring, F. C. Shaler, W. W. Shepherd, W. M. Clemans, and J. T. Bartlett, with Bartly Smith, coroner.

Chapter 10: 1893

1. Stephen Hahn, *The Roots of Southern Populism: Yeoman Farmers and The Transformation of the Georgia Upcountry, 1850–1890* (New York: Oxford University Press, 2006), 138–139.

2. *County Capital*, January 13, 1893.

3. *County Capital*, January 18, 1893.

4. Walter T. K. Nugent, *The Tolerant Populists, Kansas Populism and Nativism* (Chicago: University of Chicago Press, 1963), 146.

5. Scott G. McNall, *The Road to Rebellion: Class Formation and Kansas Populism, 1865–1900* (Chicago: University of Chicago Press, 1988), 280–283.

6. *County Capital*, February 10, 1893.

7. Isaac Werner had written in his journal's flyleaf: "Mother was born Dec. 12th 1812 and yet living June 7th 1890—I. B. Werner." News of her death would have come from Ettie, with whom their mother lived. Ettie's family moved from Abilene after Rebecca's death, so hers remains the solitary grave on that family plot.

8. Rebecca Werner remains the solitary occupant of the plot in Abilene, Ettie and her husband having moved to Lawrence, Kansas, after her death. They chose to be buried in Oak Hill Cemetery in Lawrence.

9. McNall, *The Road to Rebellion,* 280.

10. The use by Republicans of axes to break down the chamber doors and their call for armed civilians to assist in holding the chamber was the first use of armed combatants in the so-called Legislative War.

11. Executive Order No. 2, Governor Lorenzo Lewelling, February 17, 1893, Legislature History (Coll. 614), Box 1, Folder Legislature 1893; Executive Order No. 3, Governor Lorenzo Lewelling, February 16, 1893 (Coll. 614), Box 1, Folder Legislature 1893; Macferran, "Colonel Hughes and the Legislative War," Museum of the Kansas National Guard, https://www.kshs.org/kansapedia/james-clark-hughes/19881; O. Gene Clanton, *A Common Humanity, Kansas Populism and the Battle for Justice and Equality, 1854–1903* (Manhattan, KS: Sunflower University Press, 2004).

12. The Republican governor following Lewelling recalled Colonel Hughes to the Kansas National Guard with the rank of brigadier general, and from 1905 to 1909 Hughes was adjutant general of Kansas.

13. Accused hog thieves: Sam Higgins, Dutch Landes, Ed Landes, "Slip" Bryant, and Bill Brown. *County Capital*, April 14, 1893.

14. *County Capital*, January 13, 1893; Several witness, including Editor Hilmes, were in Lyons for the trial, and separate postings, dated January 9, 10, and 11, appeared in that week's paper.

15. E. H. Landes was also charged in the hog-stealing theft, but neither the newspaper nor the district court records available mention any adjudication of that matter with reference to Landes.

16. *County Capital,* p. 1, col. 2, May 5, 1898; justice of the peace, Stafford County Kansas, State of Kansas v. E. H. Landes, William Willis, William Brown, and Samuel Higgins, Commitment Order, signed by J. B. Smith, justice of the peace, 8th of April, 1893.

17. Samuel Higgins was found guilty and sentenced to one year hard labor at Leavenworth Penitentiary in cause number 2439 on May 9, 1893, for theft of a hog, and in cause number 2440 on May 12, 1893, to 18 months following completion of his incarceration for cause number 2439 for the theft of a black hog; Lewis Bryant was sentenced to one year hard labor in cause number 2439 on May, 11, 1893, for theft of a black and white spotted hog; district court of Stafford County, Kansas, cause number 2539 and 2440. Trial records for the other defendants were not found.

18. The federal census records for 1900 show William Good and his four children no longer living in Philadelphia.

19. Demonetized: (1) To deprive of value for official payment, (2) To withdraw the status of legal tender from a coin and remove it from circulation.

20. Cleveland was the 22nd and 24th president of the United States, having won the popular vote in 1888 but not the electoral college votes. His second term followed his first term by four years.

21. J. W. Buel, *The Magic City, A Massive Portfolio of Original Photographic Views of the Great World's Fair* (St. Louis: Historical Publishing, 1894); books of popular history about the fair continue to be written, including Eric Larson, *The Devil in the White City: Murder, Magic, and Madness at the Fair that Changed America* (Crown, 2004) and Frances McNamara, *Death at the Fair* (Allium Press, 2009).

22. Text of "The Pardon of the Haymarket Prisoners," written by John P. Altgeld, signed June 26, 1893; http://law2.umkc.edu/faculty/projects/ftrials/haymarket/pardon.html.

23. Michael Magidson, "John Peter Altgeld," 1896 Vassar Projects, Rebecca Edwards, Vassar College, 1996; http://projects.vassar.edu/1896/altgeld.html.

24. Nugent, *The Tolerant Populists,* 133–134. Though Nugent places the text in quotations, he does not provide a source or endnote for their original speaker.

25. "Fusion in Kansas, The Democrats and People's Party Will Join Their Forces," *The New York Times,* June 2, 1892.

26. The People's Party won district judge with a majority of thirty-eight and no Democratic candidate, and also register, coroner, and surveyor with opposition from both Republicans and Democrats; the Republicans were victorious in balloting for county clerk, sheriff, treasurer, and commissioner.

27. L. D. Lewelling, Governor, "Executive Circular: To All Boards of Police Commissioners," December 4, 1893, published in the *County Capital,* p. 1, col. 2–3, December 15, 1893.

28. O. Gene Clanton, *A Common Humanity: Kansas Populism and the Battle for Justice and Equality, 1854–1903* (Manhattan, KS: Sunflower University Press, 2004), 204.

Chapter 11: 1894

1. These symptoms are things Isaac Werner mentioned in his journal and from information in his probate records.

2. This reference is to the Cherokee Strip Land Run on September 16, 1893.

3. District Court of Stafford County, Kansas, motion for new trial, filed the 16th day of February, 1894.

4. *County Capital*, February 23, 1894.

5. *County Capital*, February 23, 1894; see also William A. Peffer, *Populism: Its Rise & Fall* (Lawrence: University Press of Kansas, 1992), 31 for the Alliance principles.

6. *County Capital,* March 16, 1894, reprinted from the *Pratt Union*; according to a study by M. Watt Espy Jr. and John Ortiz Smykla, there were only nine executions in Kansas between 1866–1899. The 1900 federal census shows Elsworth Hacker as a prisoner in Leavenworth, Kansas, at the Kansas State Penitentiary, born April 1870 in Iowa,

age thirty and single as of June 28, 1900. At least six years after his conviction, he had not been hanged. No mention of Roberts was found. Someone named Hacker had briefly been a tenant in the homestead adjacent to Isaac's claim, but it could not be determined if that Hacker had any relationship to the Hackers involved in Jacob Baker's murder.

7. In Isaac's personal library were Alexander Bain's *Logic: Deductive & Inductive* (first published 1870, the edition most likely to have been owned by Isaac; later revised edition, American Book Company, 1924), as well as Broom's *Legal Maxims* and other books on law.

8. *County Capital*, April 6, 1894.

9. Francis Trout Hoover, *Enemies Behind in the Rear: Or, a Golden Circle Squared, A Story of Southeastern Pennsylvania in the Time of Our Civil War* (Boston: Arena Publishing, 1894).

10. Isaac's probate records indicate that G. G. John made daily visits for the five months before Isaac needed to leave his own home to receive round-the-clock care, which meant that John began coming about April 9, 1894. The probate records also mention the invalid chair. Doc Dix presented a bill for medical consultations to Isaac's estate.

11. A newspaper clipping titled "Byers Author Is Remembered" describes G. G. John as a "farmer-scholar" and the author of a book of "philosophical writing" titled *Whose Son Is This*, which a reviewer called "socialistic in theme, but scintillatingly brilliant." No date or source was saved on the clipping. Anna Marie Beck, Private Scrapbook, Stafford County Historical & Genealogy Museum, Stafford, Kansas. Interview with Milton Mason John Jr. and Joan John Moody, whose grandfather Olen Olo John was G. G. John's brother.

12. Will Campbell, Warren Foster, editor of the Hutchinson *Alliance Gazette,* and E. Beardsly of Pawnee Rock.

13. Henry Vincent, *The Story of the Commonweal, Complete and Graphic Narrative of the Origin and Growth of the Movement* (Chicago: W. B. Conkey, 1894). The author of this book was one of the Vincent brothers, publishers of *The American Conformist* that originated in Winfield, Kansas.

14. *County Capital*, "The Coxey Movement Has Proved a Great Eye-Opener," May 11, 1894, and "Coxey Got it in the Neck," May 25, 1894; "Keep Off the Grass!: Coxey's Army Invades the Nation's Capital," http://historymatters.gmu.edu/d/5364; "The Depression of 1893," http://projects.vassar.edu/1896/depression.html.

15. Henry Vincent, *The Story of the Common Weal, Complete and Graphic Narrative of the Origin and Growth of the Movement* (Chicago: W. B. Conkey), 1894.

16. *County Capital*, June 1, 1894.

17. Letter from John P. Altgeld, Governor of Illinois to the Hon. Grover Cleveland, President of the United States, Washington, DC, July 5, 1894. Northern Illinois Digital Library, *Governor Altgeld's Protests Against the Use of Federal Troops in Illinois During the Late Strike and the President's Replies.*

18. Almont Lindsey, *The Pullman Strike: The Story of a Unique Experiment and of a Great Labor Upheaval* (Chicago: University of Chicago Press, 1942).

19. *County Capital*, May 11, 1894.

20. *County Capital*, May 25, 1894.

21. Walter T. K. Nugent, *The Tolerant Populists, Kansas Populism and Nativism* (Chicago: University of Chicago Press, 1963), 159–160.

22. O. Gene Clanton, *A Common Humanity: Kansas Populism and the Battle for Justice and Equality, 1854–1903* (Manhattan, KS: Sunflower University Press, 2004), 214, 217–218.

23. *County Capital,* October 12, 1894; neighbors in attendance included Beck, Co. D, Reg. 1, Ohio; Campbell, Co. K, Reg. 26, Indiana Infantry; Henn, Co. E, Reg. 57, Michigan Infantry; A. J. Hazelton, Co. H, Reg. 20, New York Cavalry; J. A. Mayes, Co. A, Reg. 85, Illinois Infantry; C. N. Waters, Co. G, Reg. 2, Ohio Cavalry; Samuel Grunder, Co. A, Reg. 26, Ohio Infantry; A. Cubbage, Co. D, Reg. 57, Indiana Infantry; and several others.

24. Proof of Claim filed by W. P. Holbrook, In the Matter of the Estate of Isaac B. Werner, for taking care 12 nights, beginning September 11 and ending September 23, 1894, $18, subscribed & sworn, September 2, 1895; Proof of Claim filed by George Hall, In the Matter of the Estate of Isaac B. Werner, for taking care of I. B. Werner at various times from September 11, 1894 up to and including September 23, 1894, in all 12 days at $2.00 per day, subscribed & sworn, August 31, 1896. Proof of Claim, Probate Records, Stafford County, Kansas, Isaac B. Werner.

25. It is likely that Isaac took his journal with him that day and that it remained in the Hall home when he was later moved. That would explain how it came to belong to Hall's granddaughter Lucille M. Hall.

26. Proof of Claim filed by George Henn, In the Matter of the Estate of Isaac B. Werner, for board from September 23, 1894, until March 22, 1895, at $10 per month; for nursing care at $2.50 per day and $2.50 per night, a total of $60 board and $900 nursing care, subscribed & sworn, April 11, 1895.

27. *County Capital,* November 16, 1894. The Stafford County officers elected in 1894 were as follows: commissioners: H. M. Lyons, A. J. Harter, and J. W. Horn; representative, Wm. M. Campbell; probate Judge, H. C. Hockensmith; treasurer, L. B. C. Cook; county clerk, Ike S. Lewis; register of deeds, M. I. Thompson; sheriff, B. T. Dykes; coroner, D. S. Sparks; county attorney, O. C. Jennings; clerk of district court, E. J. Westgate; surveyor, W. F. Noble; and superintendent, R. Benefiel. *County Capital,* February 22, 1895.

28. *County Capital,* November 16, 1894.

29. Shakespeare, "Sonnet 65."

Chapter 12: 1895

1. *County Capital,* January 18, 1895.

2. Dr. W. R. Willcox was a country doctor, living in the Livingston community. *Stafford County History, 1870–1970.* Stafford County Historical and Genealogical Society, 1990, 122. His name is often spelled Wilcox, but when he signed probate records in handling Isaac's estate, he spelled his name with two *l*'s.

3. *County Capital,* p. 4, col. 2, March 22, 1895.

4. *Reading Eagle,* March 27, 1895; www.berks.pa-roots.com/obits/ObitsSaa-Sc.html.

5. The source for the information included in the family's Pennsylvania obituary is unknown, but it included the statement that he "had to be carried about and tended like a child."

6. In the Matter of the Estate of I. B. Werner, Probate Records of Stafford County, Kansas, Stafford County Courthouse, St. John, Kansas.

7. Stafford County Deed Records, SW/4, Section 33, Range 25, Township 14; Vol. 27, p. 305; Mortgage to St. Bank of St. John, April 7, 1892; Release Vol. 24, p. 312, and Vol. 27, p. 305, August 4, 1893. It is uncertain how Isaac paid his indebtedness and accrued assets between the time his journal ended and his death; however, possibilities are inheritance from his mother's death in 1893, favorable rental income for his land being farmed with Isaac's horses and equipment, and revenue realized in some way from his three-horse cultivator invention.

8. Stafford County Deed Records, NW/4, Section 33, Range 25, Township 14; Vol. 1, p. 148; Patent to Henry B. Werner issued April 25, 1894.

9. No correspondence between Dr. Willcox and Isaac's family was found in the probate records.

10. There were seventy-eight buyers at Isaac's sale and even more likely to have been present among the purchasers, bidding through surrogates. Others may not have been the highest bidder or came only as spectators. There were no female bidders except for Nancy Henn and a Miss Pruitt (who bought a platter), but it is almost certain that many wives accompanied their husbands, along with some of the unmarried ladies living in the community being present, given the customs of country estate auctions.

11. The probate records contain a listing of items, purchasers, and prices paid, and a partial index of his books.

12. Family history about H. S. Kephart provided by great-grandson, Steve Kephart.

13. Gus Gereke, George Hall, William Holbrook, Charles Shattuc.

14. Doc Dix donated books from his library to the Pratt Library, and in a library sale in 2014, one of the Dix books contained Isaac's signature on the flyleaf.

15. Isaac's journal contained critical references to misuse and neglect of horses by others in the community.

16. *County Capital*, April 26, 1895.

17. In the Matter of the Estate of I. B. Werner, Probate Records, Stafford County Courthouse, St. John, Kansas.

18. Blake's claim was found in the probate records, but there was an offsetting note owed Isaac by Blake that had been assumed by other parties. There was found no indication that any amount from Isaac's estate was paid to Blake.

Epilogue: After Isaac Werner, 1895–1898

1. *County Capital*, May 3, 1895.

2. *County Capital*, May 3, 1895.

3. Robert Green Ingersoll (1833–1899) was the son of a Presbyterian minister who is believed to have turned away from the church after seeing his father unjustly accused by his bigoted congregation of unministerial conduct when Ingersoll was only nine years old. Susan Jacoby, *Freethinkers: A History of American Secularism* (New York: Henry Holt, 2004). Ingersoll is included among the freethought speakers appearing before the New York Freethinkers Association, see http://spirithistory.iapsop.com, note 15.

4. Consisting of Paul R. Nagle, R. B. Gates, I. C. Hadsall, Ed O'Conner, and Frank J. Benscoter.

5. *County Capital*, May 3, 1895.

6. In the matter of the Estate of I. B. Werner . . . County Court House, Stafford County, Kansas, Probate records.

7. *County Capital*, May 6, 1896.

8. The town of Argentine is a part of Kansas City, Kansas, located in the southern part of Wyandotte County. Its roots can be traced to the forced resettlement of twenty-eight eastern Indian tribes who were removed to the undeveloped frontier west of the Missouri River in 1825 to land promised: "so long as the sun shines and water runs down hill." But, twenty-five years later, as settlers began to demand that the land be opened to them, the Indians were removed to Oklahoma.

9. *County Capital*, April 24, 1896, 1, col. 2; The term "blind tiger" generally refers to an establishment that illegally sells alcoholic beverages, particularly those of a lower-class nature. It is unclear whether Hilmes chose this term because of the extent of illegal drinking going on in connection with the gambling or if he used it in a more generic way to describe any crooked, low-class business.

10. *County Capital*, April 24, 1896, 1, col. 2.

11. George Shiras Jr. (1832–1924) who wrote the opinion, was nominated to the court by President Benjamin Harrison, a Republican. He served ten years and authored 253 majority decisions and fourteen dissents.

12. Barnitz v. Beverly 163 U.S. 118 (1896), 16 S.Ct. 1042, 41 L.Ed. 93.

13. *County Capital* reprinting article from the *Topeka State Journal*, p. 1, col. 3, May 22, 1896.

14. *County Capital*, July 24, 1886.

15. Walter T. K. Nugent, *The Tolerant Populists, Kansas Populism and Nativism* (Chicago: University of Chicago Press, 1963), 189.

16. William Jennings Bryan, "Cross of Gold" speech, Democratic National Convention, Chicago, July 9, 1896); text from History Matters, http://historymatters.gmu.edu/d/5354/ (accessed January 1, 2020). Modern politicians arguing this theory refer to "trickle-down economics."

17. In the Matter of the Estate of I. B. Werner, Probate Records, Stafford County Courthouse, George Hall claim filed August 31, 1896, for two dollars a day, Holbrook claiming $1.50 per night. There were no additional boarding fees. Had the Henns claimed those same fees, their claim against the estate would have been reduced by over $420.

18. Willcox is used in this chapter to express opinions about the estate and events in the community, although the author had no means to determine what his observations and feelings actually were beyond what is documented in the probate records.

19. Peter H. Argersinger, *Populism and Politics, William Alfred Peffer and the People's Party* (Lexington: University Press of Kentucky, 1974), 276–301; Robert C. McMath Jr., *American Populism, A Social History, 1877–1898* (New York: Hill & Wang, 1993), 201–204.

20. The goals of the Farmers' Alliance and the Omaha Platform of 1892 had expressed issues important to members, issues that drew farmers to the People's Party. The

assumption that focusing on Free Silver and nominating a Democrat for president could be done without weakening the party's base was wrong.

21. *County Capital*, July 24, 1896. Stafford County Treasurer Cook concluded his speech with these words: "Let us be more patriotic than partisan; let us lay other minor questions on the shelf for the present, and unite our forces and make one mighty pull for the American dollar and victory will perch upon our banner."

22. An 1898 ballot, found during the author's research, was discovered in Pratt, Kansas, the county seat near Isaac's homestead, containing three choices for electing Bryan: Democratic: Bryan/Swell, People's Party: Bryan/Watson, and Middle-of-the-Road: Bryan and Watson on the same presidential ballot.

23. Nugent, *The Tolerant Populists*, 157.

24. Lawrence Goodwyn, *The Populist Moment: A Short History of the Agrarian Revolt in America* (New York: Oxford University Press, 1978).

25. Tom Watson's bitterness from the mistreatment by Democrats in Georgia political races, and disappointments during the 1896 presidential race changed him. The character he had shown in winning the respect of mid-roaders in the first half of the 1890s, with words that were inclusive of all working-class Americans, narrowed after 1896. He was no longer the champion of all laborers, without regard to race or religion. His ideals morphed into something quite opposite. Where once he had called for unity, he came to denounce not only blacks but Catholics, Jews, and any ideas he found socialistic. Although his early reputation lingered among some Populists, he was no longer the same man.

26. *County Capital*, June 11, 1897. The eastern capitalists were John T. Eddy, president, and H. B. Forbes, cashier, of the National Bank of the Commonwealth, Boston; J. M. Adderman of the Industrial Trust Co., Providence, RI; G. Henry Whitcomb of the Standard Cattle Company; H. W. Stevens, cashier of First National Bank of Northampton, MA; and David Whitcomb of Worcester, MA.

27. Nugent, *The Tolerant Populists*, 118.

28. "President's Message, Principal Part Devoted to a Narrative of the War with Spain," *County Capital*, December 16, 1898. Near the closing of the year, President McKinley addressed the Senate and the House, giving a detailed summary of the Spanish-American War, including the peace negotiations, the plans for the Cuban government, and the studies underway for a Nicaragua Canal to the Atlantic and Pacific oceans concluding with the situation in China.

29. *County Capital*, "Senator Allen on Bonds. An Infamous Scheme of the Money Power," June 17, 1898.

30. Alfred T. Mahan, *The Influence of Sea Power upon History, 1660–1783* (Boston: Little, Brown, 1890); discussion of Manifest Destiny and the political schism between laborers and capitalists in Paul Krause, *Battle for Homestead, 1880–1892: Politics, Culture, and Steel* (Pittsburgh, PA: University of Pittsburgh Press, 1992), 285.

31. Theodore Roosevelt, *The Rough Riders* (Charles Scribner's Sons: New York, 1899).

32. Nugent, *The Tolerant Populists*, 208–219.

33. *County Capital*, June 24, 1898.

34. In the Matter of the Estate of I. B. Werner, Probate Records, Stafford County Courthouse, St. John, Kansas.

35. Jacob Asberry DeGarmo was born in 1856 in Illinois and married Jerusha Adeline "Addie" Pelsor in 1881. Sometime after the birth of their first child, daughter Ethel Lee, they came to Kansas. By 1898, three sons and three more daughters had been born to the couple. Kansas census records show them living in Pawnee Rock in 1895, but granddaughter Dorothy Degarmo Meisel wrote in the *Macksville, Kansas Community History 1886–1986* (Lewis, KS: The Lewis Press, 1986), 160, that the family lived in St. John before buying Isaac's homestead. She described his house as "3 rooms on 3 floors."

36. Deed Records, Stafford County Courthouse, St. John, Kansas; Henry B. Werner et al to Jacob A. Degarmo, August 10, 1898; Meriam Good et al to Jacob A. Degarmo, October 6, 1898; W. E. Good, Guardian, to Jacob A. Degarmo, November 21, 1898.

37. Letter from Charles H. Werner to his father and Isaac's twin brother, Henry B. Werner, dated Nov. 3, 1897, written on law firm letterhead: "SHEEHAN & COLLIN, 32 Nassau Street, New York, attorneys: William F. Sheehan, Charles A. Collin, Thomas L. Hughes, Charles H. Werner," addressed to Mr. Henry B. Werner, 1138 Douglass, Reading, PA.

38. Ted Genoways, *This Blessed Earth: A Year in the Life of an American Family Farm* (New York: W. W. Norton, 2018), 136–144. The importance of careful handling of chemicals by farmers remains essential today.

39. The *County Capital* did publish instructions for treating bedbugs, but no warnings about the application of Paris Green were found in that local Populist newspaper, even though there was a significant use of Parris Green throughout the region.

40. Perhaps some future scholar will research other deaths in Isaac's community during that time period to determine whether the explanation for undiagnosed illnesses and deaths of farm workers might be traced back to Paris Green.

41. Scott G. McNall, *The Road to Rebellion: Class Formation and Kansas Populism, 1865–1900* (Chicago: University of Chicago Press, 1988), 306.

42. O. Gene Clayton, *A Common Humanity: Kansas Populism and the Battle for Justice and Equality, 1854–1903* (Manhattan, KS: Sunflower University Press, 2004), 293.

43. Clayton, *A Common Humanity*, 294–295.

44. Clayton, 293.

45. Richard Hofstadter, *The Age of Reform* (New York: Vintage Books, 1955), 97: "Third parties are like bees: once they have stung, they die."

46. Carleton Beals, *The Great Revolt and Its Leaders: The History of Popular American Uprisings in the 1890s* (New York: Abelard Schulman, 1968), 347.

Bibliography

Adams, Alexander B. *Sunlight and Storm: The Great American Plains.* New York: G. P. Putnam's Sons, 1977.

Adams, Pauline and Emma S. Thornton. *A Populist Assault: Sarah E. Van De Vort Emery on American Democracy, 1862–1895*. Bowling Green, OH: Bowling Green State University Popular Press, 1982.

Altgeld, John P. "Letter to Grover Cleveland, July 5, 1894." http://lincoln.lib.niu.edu/file.php?file=jpaprotests.html.

———. "Pardon of the Haymarket Prisoners, June 26, 1893." http://law2.umkc.edu/faculty/projects/ftrials/haymarket/pardon.html.

American Nonconformist and Kansas Industrial Liberator. Winfield, Kansas: H. & L. Vincent, 1186–1891.

Argersinger, Peter H. *The Limits of Agrarian Radicalism: Western Populism and American Politics*. Lawrence: University Press of Kansas, 1995.

———. *Populism and Politics: William Alfred Peffer and the People's Party.* Lexington: University Press of Kentucky, 1974.

———."Road to a Republican Waterloo: The Farmers' Alliance and the Election of 1890 in Kansas." *Kansas Historical Quarterly* 33, no. 4 (Winter 1967): 443–469.

Arnold, Anna E. *A History of Kansas*. Topeka: State Printer, 1931.

Asher, Lucile. *The Saratoga Story.* Pratt, KS: Pratt County Historical Society, 1985.

Athenaeum of Philidelphia, *Southwark Foundary and Machine Company.* http://www.philageohistory.org.

Bader, Robert Smith. *Prohibition in Kansas: A History.* Lawrence: University Press of Kansas, 1986.

Baker, Jean H. *Sisters, The Lives of America's Suffragists.* New York: Hill and Wang, 2005.

Barnitz v. Beverly 163 U.S. 118 (1896), 16 S.Ct 1042, 41 L.Ed. 93.

Baum, L. Frank. *The Wonderful Wizard of Oz,* n.p. George M. Hill, 1900; republished Justin Knowles Publishing Group for Easton Press. Afterword by Peter Blassman, 1987.

Baym, Nina. *American Women Writers and the Work of History, 1799–1860.* New Brunswick, NJ: Rutgers University Press, 1995.

———. *Women Writers of the American West, 1833–1927.* Urbana: University of Illinois Press, 2011.

Beals, Carleton. *The Great Revolt and Its Leaders: The History of Popular American Uprisings in the 1890s.* New York: Abeland-Schuman, 1968.

Beck, Anna Marie. Personal Scrapbook, Stafford County Historic and Genealogy Museum, Stafford, Kansas.

Beck, Wilma Carr. *History of Byers, Kansas.* Self-published, 1964.

Bellamy, Edward. *Looking Backward.* Boston: Houghton, Mifflin, 1888. Signet Classics Paperback edition 2009 with Introduction by Walter James Miller, Afterword by Eliot Fintushel.

Biographical Directory of the United States Congress, Peffer, William Alfred (1831–1912). https://bioguideretro.congress.gov/Home/MemberDetails?memIndex=p000188.

Blackmar, Frank W., ed. *Kansas: A Cyclopedia of State History, Embracing Events, Institutions, Industries, Counties, Cities, Towns, Prominent Persons, Etc.* Chicago: Standard Publishing Company, 1912.

Brown, Dee. *Hear That Lonesome Whistle Blow, Railroads in the West.* New York: A Touchstone Book, Simon & Schuster, 1977.

Brown, William Fisher. *Pratt County Union.* January 31, 1890.

Brumbaugh, Daniel W. "The Lynching of My Great Aunt." http://www.geocities.com/pentagon/bunker/2555/aunt.htm?20091.

Bryan, William J. "Cross of Gold Speech." http://historymatters.gmu.edu/d/5354/.

———. *The First Battle: A Story of the Campaign of 1896,* n.p. W. B. Conkey, 1896.

Buckhout, Dave. "The Rise and Fall of Populism in the South." *The Almanack, The Inheritage Journal of History, Travel, & Lore.* http://www.inheritage.org/almanack/b_populism_01.html.

Buel, J. W. *The Magic City, A Massive Portfolio of Original Photographic Views of the Great World's Fair.* St. Louis: Historical Publishing, 1894.

Bull, Floyd R. *Reminiscence of the 1893 Legislative War, July 15, 1955.* Kansas State Historical Society, identifier DaRT ID: 210801.

Burgoyne, Arthur G. *Homestead Strike.* Pittsburgh: Rawsthorne Engraving and Printing, 1983.

Cassoday Mirage (newspaper), Cassoday, Kansas.

Centennial Edition of the Fourth Annual Report of the State Board of Agriculture to the Legislature of the State of Kansas. State Board of Centennial Managers, Geo. W. Martin, Public Printer, 1878.

Chanute Daily Tribune. "Col. J. M. Dunsmore Dead," March 13, 1922.

Chicago Chronicle, Chicago, Illinois.

Citizens United v. Federal Election Commission, 558 U.S. 310 (2010).
Clark, Justin. "The Conspirators: Eugene V. Debs, Clarence Darrow, and the ARU Trials of 1894–95." *Hoosier State Chronicles: Indiana's Digital Newspaper Program.* https://blog.newspapers.library.in.gov/the-conspirators.
Clayton, O. Gene. *A Common Humanity: Kansas Populism and the Battle for Justice and Equality, 1854–1903.* Manhattan, KS: Sunflower University Press, 2004.
———. "Intolerant Populist? The Disaffection of Mary Elizabeth Lease." *Kansas State Historical Society* 24, no. 2, 1968.
———. *Kansas Populism, Ideas and Men.* Lawrence: University Press of Kansas, 1969.
Coe, Clelland, and Helen Malin Reuber with Verl Manwarren. *No Cyclone Shall Destroy.* Ardmore, PA: Dorrance, 1981.
"Colonel Hughes and the Legislative War." Museum of the Kansas National Guard, http://kansasguardmuseum.org/legiwar.html.
Connelley, William E. *A Standard History of Kansas and Kansans,* vol. 5. Chicago: Lewis Publishing, 1919.
"Cook County Marriage Index." *County Capital.* http://ffrf.org/news/day/dayitems/item/14254-judge-arnold-krekel.
Cruden, Alexander. *Cruden's Complete Concordance to the Old and New Testament, (William) Youngman's Edition.* J. Dinnis Publisher, 1833.
Curtis, George E. "Who Sold This Wheat for $1.40?—Or An Examination of the Value of Blake's Tables." *Transactions of the Kansas Academy of Science,* vol. 12 (1889): 37–42.
Dartmouth College v. Woodward, 17 U.S. 518 (1819).
District Court of Stafford County, Kansas: Isabell D. Ross v. Rapheel Ross.
———. Deed Records, vol. 27, p. 305.
———. In the Matter of the Estate of Isaac B. Werner.
———. Motion for New Trial, Seduction Under Promise to Marry, February 1894.
Dodge City Times, Dodge City, Kansas.
Donnelly, Ignatius Loyola. *Caesar's Column.* 1st published 1890. Teddington, Middlesex, England: The Echo Library, 2007.
Edwards, Rebecca. *Angels in the Machinery: Gender in American Party Politics from the Civil War to the Progressive Era.* New York: Oxford University Press, 1997.
———. "Mary E. Lease and the Populists: A Reconsideration." *Kansas History: A Journal of the Central Plains* 35, no. 1 (Spring 2012): 26–41.
———. *New Spirits: Americans in the Gilded Age, 1865–1905.* New York: Oxford University Press, 2005.
Ellis, Joseph J. *American Dialogue, The Founders and Us.* New York: Alfred A. Knopf, 2018. See esp. chapter 2, "Equality, Now: Our Gilded Age."
Emery, S. E. V. *Seven Conspiracies which Have Enslaved the American People.* Lansing, MI: Robert Smith, 1887.
Exodusters of Stafford County, Exhibition Pamphlet. Garden City, Kansas: Stafford County Historical Museum and Genealogy Society, 2011.
Fairground Heritage. http://www.fairground-heritage.org.uk/newsite/learn/learn-sr.html.
Faulkner, Ronnie W. "North Carolina History Project: Fusion Politics." http://northcarolinahistory.org/encyclopedia/58/entry.

Fenwick, Lynda Beck. "A Documentary Treasure," November 9, 2018. https://lynfenwick.blogspot.com/2018/11/a-documentary-treasure.html.

Freedman, Benedict, and Nancy Mars Freedman. *Mrs. Mike, the Story of Katherine Mary Flannigan.* New York: Coward-McCann and Geoghegan, 1947.

Garden Web. http://gardenweb.com/forums/heirloom.

Garner, Mark. *Santa Fe Trail.* Tucson: Southwest Parks and Monuments Association, 1993.

Gayor, Annie Laurie. "Arnold Krekel." http://ffrf.org/news/day/dayitems/item/14254-judge-arnold-krekel.

Genoways, Ted. *This Blessed Earth: A Year in the Life of an American Family Farm.* New York: W. W. Norton, 2018.

George, Henry. *Progress and Poverty: An Inquiry into the Cause of Industrial Depressions and of Increase of Want with Increase of Wealth. The Remedy.* New York: D. Appleton, 1879, 10th ed. 1882.

———. *Protection or Free Trade: An Examination of the Tariff Question, with Especial Regard to the Interests of Labor.* Copyright Henry George, 1886. Republished, Robert Schalkenback Foundation, 1980.

Gereke Family History. Family History Notebook, Pratt, KS, Public Library.

Goldberg, Michael Lewis. *An Army of Women, Gender and Politics in Gilded Age Kansas.* Baltimore: Johns Hopkins University Press, 1997.

Goldner, Cheri. "The Homestead Strike." http://www.bgsu.edu/departments/acs/1890s/carneige/strike.html.

Goodwyn, Lawrence. *Democratic Promise: The Populist Movement in America.* New York: Oxford University Press, 1976.

———. *The Populist Moment: A Short History of the Agrarian Revolt in America.* New York: Oxford University Press (an abridged edition), 1978.*Grace United Methodist Church, 100th Anniversary.* Private publication, 1952.

Gray, J. Rufus. *Pioneer Saints & Sinners.* Pratt, KS: Pratt Rotary Club, 1968.

Great Bend Daily Tribune. Great Bend, Kansas.

Greeley, Horace. *What I know of Farming: A Series of Brief and Plain Expositions.* G. W. Carlton, 1871. See esp. chapter 14, Plowing—Deep or Shallow."

Grinspan, Jon. "How a Ragtag Band of Reformers Organized the First Protest March on Washington, DC," May 1, 2014. https://www.smithsonianmag.com/smithsonian-institution/how-ragtag-band-reformers-organized-first-protest-march-washington-dc-180951270/.

Gronlund, Laurence. *The Cooperative Commonwealth in its Outlines: An Exposition of Modern Socialism.* Lee and Shepherd Publishers, 1884.

Grunder, Fred. Present owner of Isaac Werner's homestead claim, Interviewed 2011.

Guisepi, R. A. "The Spanish American War." http://history-world-org/Spanish%Spanish%20America%20War.htm.

Hahn, Steven. *The Roots of Southern Populism: Yeoman Farmers and the Transformation of the Georgia Upcountry, 1850–1890.* New York: Oxford University Press, 2006.

Hamill, S. S. *New Science of Elocution: The Elements and Principles of Vocal Expression in Lessons.* Phillips and Hunt, 1886.

Havens, F. C. "Extracts from the Book of the Ralston Health Club." In *The Possibility of Living 200 Years*. n.p. The Two Hundred Company, 1896.

Heat-Moon, William Least. *PrairyErth: A Deep Map*. Boston: Houghton Mifflin, 1999.

Henry Clay Frick Business Records, 1892–1897, Archives Service Center, University of Pittsburg.

Hicks, John D. "Birth of the Populist Party." *Minnesota History* 9, no. 3 (September 1928).

Higer, Ramona Garro. Interview 2014.

History Matters. "Keep Off the Grass: Coxey's Army Invades the Nation's Capital." http://historymatters.gmu.edu/d/5364.

Hofstadter, Richard. *The Age of Reform*. New York: Vintage Books, 1955.

Holt, Marilyn Irvin. *The Orphan Trains, Placing Out in America*. Lincoln: University of Nebraska Press, 1992.

Hoover, Francis Trout. *Enemies in the Rear, or a Golden Circle Squared, A Story of Southeastern Pennsylvania in the Time of Our Civil War*. Boston: Arena Publishing, 1894. Republished by NABU (print on demand), 2011.

Horwitz, Morton, J. *The Transformation of American Law, 1870–1960*. New York: Oxford University Press, 1992.

In re Debs, Petitioner, 158 U. D. 564, 15 Supreme Court 900, May 1895.

Iowa Biographies Project. "History of Poweshiek County, Iowa, 1880, Grinnell Township." www.beforetime.net/iowagenealogy/poweshiek/HistoryOfPoweshiekCounty1880/index.html.

Jacoby, Susan. *Freethinkers: A History of American Secularism*. New York: Henry Holt, 2004.

John, Milton M., deceased, grandnephew of G. G. John. Interview 2015.

Kansapedia. "Annie Diggs." https://www.kshs.org/kansapedia/annie-diggs/12–35.

———. "Frederick Funston." https://www.kshs.org/kansapedia/frederick-funston/12060.

Kansas Historical Society. "Reminiscence of the 1893 Legislative War." Written Testimony of Floyd R. Bull. www.kansasmemory.org/item/210801.

Kansas State Board of Centennial Managers. *Centennial Edition of the 4th Annual Report of the State Board of Agriculture to the Legislature of the State of Kansas*. Topeka: George W. Martin, 1878.

Kazin, Michael. *The Populist Persuasion: An American History*. New York: Basic Books, a division of HarperCollins Publishers, 1995.

Kearney, David M. *Belpre, Kansas: The Story of a Small Town*. Lewis, KS: The Lewis Press, 1979.

Keehn, David C. *Knights of the Golden Circle: Secret Empire, Southern Secession, Civil War*. Baton Rouge: Louisiana State University Press, 2013.

Kephart, Steve, great-grandson of H. S. Kephart. Correspondence, May 2012.

Kershnes, William Jacob. *History of St. John's (Hains) Church, 1852–1916*. Reading, PA: I. M. Beaver, 1916.

Kramer, Dale. *Chicago Renaissance, The Literary Life in the Midwest, 1900–1930*. New York: Appleton-Century, 1966.

Krause, Paul. *The Battle for Homestead, 1880–1892: Politics, Culture, and Steel*. Pittsburgh: University of Pittsburgh Press, 1992.

Landau, Elaine. *The Homestead Act.* New York: Scholastic Press, 2006.

Lapore, Jill. "Eugene V. Debs and the Endurance of Socialism," *The New Yorker.* February 18 and 25, 2019. https://www.newyorker.com/magazine/2019/02/18/eugene-v-debs-and-the-endurance-of-socialism.

Lavin, Stephen J., Fred M. Shelley, and J. Clark Archer. *Atlas of the Great Plains.* Lincoln: University of Nebraska Press, 2011.

Lease, Mary Elizabeth. *The Problem of Civilization Solved.* Chicago: Laird & Lee, 1895.

Lee, R. Alton. "Anti-Fusion Election Laws in Populist Kansas." https://esirc.emporia.edu/bitstream/handle/123456789/3386/R.%20Alton%20Lee.pdf?sequence=1.

———. "The Populist Dream of a 'Wrong Way' Transcontinental." *Kansas History: A Journal of the Central Plains* 35, no. 2 (Summer 2012): 74–89.

Lee, R. Alton, and Steven Cox, *When Sunflowers Bloomed Red: Kansas and the Rise of Socialism in America* (Lincoln: University of Nebraska Press), 2020, 74–81.

Leip, David. "1896 Presidential General Election Results." *National Election Results Atlas.* https://uselectionatlas.org/RESULTS/national.php?year=1896&off=0&elect=0.

Lerner, Adrienne Wilmoth. *Spanish-American War.* http://www.encyclopedia.com/topic/Spanish-American_War.aspx.

Le Sueur, Meridel. *North Star Country.* New York: Book Find Club, 1945.

Lewelling, Lorenzo. "Executive Circular: To all Boards of Police Commissioners, December 4, 1893," *County Capital,* December 15, 1893.

———. Executive Order No. 2, Legislative History (Coll 614) Box 1, Folder Legislature 1893.

———. Executive Order No. 3, Legislative History (Coll 614) Box 1, Folder Legislature 1893.

Lindsey, Almont. *The Pullman Strike.* Chicago: University of Chicago Press, 1942.

Lloyd, Henry Demarest. *Wealth Against Commonwealth.* New York: Harper and Brothers, 1902.

Luchetti, Cathy, with Carol Olwell. *Women of the West.* New York: Three Rivers Press, 1982.

Macksville, Kansas Community History, 1886–1986. Lewis, KS: The Lewis Press, 1986.

Magidson, Michael. *John P. Altgeld, 1896.* Vassar Projects, 1996. http://projects.vassar.edu/1896/altgeld.html.

———. *Tom Watson.* http://projects.vassar.edu/1896/watson.

Mahan, Alfred T. *The Influence of Sea Power upon History, 1660–1783.* Boston: Little, Brown, 1890; Cosimo, 2007.

Maher, Susan Naramore. *Deep Map Country: Literary Cartography of the Great Plains.* Lincoln: University of Nebraska, 2014.

McCullough, David. *The Johnstown Flood.* New York: Simon & Schuster, 1968.

McFarlane, Larry A. "Nativism or Not? Perceptions of British Investments in Kansas, 1882–1901." *Great Plains Quarterly* 1987: 232–243, http://digitalcommons.unl.edu/greatplainsquarterly/353.

McGerr, Michael. *A Fierce Discontent: The Rise and Fall of the Progressive Movement in America.* New York: Oxford University Press, 2003.

McGirr, Lisa. *The War on Alcohol, Prohibition and the Rise of the American State.* New York: W. W. Norton, 2016.

McLean, J. H. *Dr. J. H. McLean's Family Almanac.* St. Louis, published annually.

McMath, Robert C. Jr. *American Populism: A Social History 1877–1898*. New York: Hill & Wang, 1993.

McNall, Scott G. *The Road to Rebellion: Class Formation and Kansas Populism, 1865–1900*. Chicago: University of Chicago Press, 1988.

Miner, Craig. *Kansas: The History of the Sunflower State, 1854–2000*. Lawrence: University Press of Kansas, 2002.

———. *Next Year Country: Dust to Dust in Western Kansas, 1890–1940*. Lawrence: University Press of Kansas, 2006.

———. *West of Wichita: Settling the High Plains of Kansas, 1865–1890*. Lawrence: University Press of Kansas, 1986.

———. *Wichita: The Magic City*. Wichita, KS: Wichita-Sedgwick County Historical Museum Association, 1988.

Moore, Bob, descendant. Interview 2014.

Morgan, W. Scott. *History of the Wheel and Alliance and Impending Revolution*. Fort Scott, Kansas: J. H. Rice and Sons, 1889.

Moyers, Bill. "This is Your Story—The Progressive Story of America. Pass It On." Speech at Take Back America Conference, Washington, DC, June 4, 2003. http://www.commondreams.org/views/2003/06/10/your-story-progressive-story-america-pass-it.

National Park Service. *The Homestead Act of 1862*. Department of Interior Publication, August 2000.

New York Times, "Fusion in Kansas, The Democrats and People's Party Will Join Their Forces," June 2, 1892. http://www.spiderbites.nytimes.com/free_1892/articles_1892_06_0000.1.html.

———. "In Dreams He Sees an Army," March 25, 1894.

———. "Killed by Paris Green, The Mysterious Poisoning of Three Persons," August 8, 1874.

———. "Saints and Kickers at War," August 12, 1883.

———. "The Sinaloa Colony, A Batch of Misrepresentations Disposed Of," February 20, 1883.

———. "The Union Labor Party, No Connection with the Henry George Movement," May 4, 1887.

———. "Wyoming Cattle War, The President & Cabinet Discuss the Situation," April 20, 1892.

Noblin, Stuart. *Leonidas LaFayette Polk: Agrarian Crusader*. Chapel Hill: University of North Carolina Press, 1949.

North American Galloway Herd Book, Agriculture and Arts Association of Ontario, Globe Printing, 1883.

Northern Illinois University Libraries Digitization Projects, "Governor Altgeld's Protests Against the Use of Federal Troops in Illinois During the Late Strikes and the President's Replies." http://lincoln.lib.niu.edu/cgi_bin/philologic/getobject/pl?c.5778:1.1incoln.

Nugent, Walter T. K. *The Tolerant Populists, Kansas Populism and Nativism*. Chicago: University of Chicago Press, 1963.

O'Connor, Sandra Day, with H. Alan Day. *Lazy B, Growing Up on a Cattle Ranch in the American Southwest*. New York: Random House, 2003.

Okrent, Daniel. *Last Call: The Rise and Fall of Prohibition*. New York: Scribner, 2010.

Olivia, Leo E. *Fort Larned: Guardian of the Santa Fe Trail.* Newton: Kansas State Historical Society, 1997.

O'Neal, Bill. *The Johnson County War.* Austin: Eakin Press, 2004.

Orr, Brooke Speer. *Mary Elizabeth Lease: Gendered Discourse and Populist Party Politics in Gilded Age America.* https://www.kshs.org/publicat/history/2006winter_orr.pdf.

Ostler, Jeffrey. *Prairie Populism: The Fate of Agrarian Radicalism in Kansas, Nebraska, and Iowa, 1880–1892.* Lawrence: University Press of Kansas, 1993.

Panorama of Progress, Pawnee County 1872–1972, A Century of Living. Larned, KS: Tiller & Toiler, 1972.

Paulsen, Gary M. *Keeping up with Research, #136, A History of Wheat Improvement at Kansas State University.* Manhattan: Kansas State University, March 2003. https://www.ksre.k-state.edu/historicpublications/pubs/SRL136.pdf.

PBS Online. "People and Events: George Pullman (1831–1897)." http://www.pbs.org/wbgh/amax/chicago/peopleevents/p-pullman.html.

PBS Online. "The Richest Man in the World: Strike at Homestead Mill." https://www.pbs.org/wgbh/americanexperience/features/carnegie-strike-homestead-mill.

Peck, Todd David. "Instructions for Observing the Total Eclipse of the Sun, January 1, 1889." Amherst, MA, Amherst College Observatory, 1889.

Peffer, William A. *Populism: Its Rise and Fall.* Edited and Introduction by Peter H. Argersinger. Lawrence: University Press of Kansas, 1992.

Pegram, Thomas R. *Battling Demon Rum: The Struggle for a Dry America, 1800–1933.* Chicago: Ivan R. Dee, 1998.

Peskin, Allan. "Were the Populists Prophets?" *Hayes Historical Journal* 9, no. 2 (Winter 1990): 5–13.

Piehler, Harold. "Henry Vincent: Kansas Populist and Radical-Reform Journalist." *Kansas History* 2, Spring 1979.

Postel, Charles. "Market Populism: Farmers and Cooperative Enterprise." *American Populism 1876–1896.* http://dig.lib.niu.edu/gildedage/populism/popessay5.html.

———. "Populist (People's) Party." http://digital.library.okstate.edu/encyclopedia/entries/P/P0013.html.

———. *The Populist Vision.* New York: Oxford University Press, 2007.

Pratt County Register. "People's Party Rally," November 8, 1890.

Pratt County Tribune Times. (Ben Terrell speech in Pratt, KS, summarized), November 29, 1889.

Press, Donald E. "Kansas Conflict, Populist Versus Railroader." *Kansas Historical Quarterly* 43, no. 3.

Price, Kathryn. "Mary Elizabeth Lease: Lawyer, Politician and Hellraiser." A paper written for Professor Barbara Bagcock, Stanford Law School, 1997. http://wlh-wiki.law.stanford.edu/index.php/LateNineteenthCenturyPolitics 24,403.

Reading Eagle, "Obituary for Isaac Beckley Werner, March 27, 1895." www.berks.pa.roots.com/obits/ObitsSaa-Sc.html.

Reed, Louis. "Railroads in Kansas." kansasheritage.org/research/rr/rrhistory.html.

Representative, The. "The Depression of 1893," August 29, 1894. http://projects.vassar.edu/1896/depression.html.

Rhoads, Jane Glotfelty. *Kansas Opera Houses, Actors & Community Events 1855–1925.* Newton, KS: Mennonite Press, 2008.

Roker, Al. *Ruthless Tide, The Heroes and Villains of the Johnstown Flood, America's Astonishing Gilded Age Disaster.* New York: HarperCollins, 2018.

Roosevelt, Theodore. *The Rough Riders.* New York: Charles Scribner's Sons, 1899.

Sandow, Robert M. *Deserter Country: Civil War Operation in the Pennsylvania Appalachians.* NY: Fordham University Press, 2009.

Santa Clara County v. Southern Pacific Railroad, 118 U.S. 394 (1886).

Schneirov, Richard. "George M. Pullman and the Sleeping Car Business." *The Pullman Strike.* http://dig.lib.niu.edu/gildedage/pullman/events.1html.

Shaftesbury, Edmund [Albert Webster Edgerly]. *The Book of Complete Membership in the Ralston Health Club.* Washington, DC: Martyn College Press Association, 1892.

———. *Our Existences, The Doctrine of Diversity: A Study of What We Are—Where We Are, Our Origin and Destiny.* Washington, DC: Shaftsbury College. http://archive.org/details/shaftsburyschoo100shaf.

Shakespeare, William. *The Complete Works of, edited by William George Clark and William Aldis Wright with a Copious Glossary [and] an index to familiar Passages and an index to the characters in each play,* New York: American News, n.d.

Shortridge, James R. *Cities of the Plains: The Evolution of Urban Kansas.* Lawrence: University Press of Kansas, 2004.

———. *Peopling the Plains: Who Settled Where in Frontier Kansas.* Lawrence: University Press of Kansas, 1995.

Smith, Adam. *The Wealth of Nations.* New York: Everyman's Library, Alfred A. Knopf, 1910 with Introduction, Bibliography, and Chronology, 1991.

Smith, Carey. "Condition of Our Country," *The Dodge City Times,* 1888.

———. "Money, Transportation, Land and Labor," *The Dodge City Times,* 1888.

Smith, Melva Towns. *Through the Eyes of William Fisher Brown aka Old Bill Fisher, 2 Vol.,* 1887–1930. Private publication, 2002.

Stafford County Deed Records. St. John, Stafford County, Kansas.

Stafford County District Court Records. St. John, Stafford County, Kansas.

Stafford County Historical and Genealogical Society, 1990. Stafford County History, 1870–1990. St. John, Stafford County, Kansas.

Stafford County Probate Records. St. John, Stafford County, Kansas.

Stowell, Myron R. *Fort Frick: or the Seige of Homestead.* Pittsburgh: Pittsburgh Printing, 1893.

Stratton, Joanna L. *Pioneer Woman: Voices from the Kansas Frontier.* New York: Simon & Schuster, 1981.

Stiller, Richard. *Queen of Populists, The Story of Mary Elizabeth Lease.* New York: Dell Publishing, 1970.

Stucky, Tim. *Pratt, Kansas: A Centennial View, 1884–1984.* Pretty Prairie, KS: Pretty Prairie Publications, 1984.

Taft, Robert. "The Pictorial History of the Old West, No. III, Henry Worall." *Kansas Historical Quarterly* 14, no. 3 (August 1946): 241–263.

Tocqueville, Alexis de. *Democracy in America.* New York: A. S. Barnes, 1851.

Topeka Populist, "Lewelling's Position. Stated in Plain Language and Emphasis." https://www.kansasmemory.org/item/210852.

Topolobampo Collection, Henry Madden Library, California State University, Fresno, CA.

Trachtenberg, Alan. *The Incorporation of America, Culture and Society in the Gilded Age*. Hill and Wang, a division of Farrar, Straus and Giroux, New York, 1982,

Tracy, A. C. *Chronicles of Pratt and Pratt County.* Pratt: KS: Pratt Commercial Club, 1911.

The Truth Seeker Annual & Freethinkers Almanac. New York, 1884.

Tucker, Luther, and John J. Thomas, eds. *Cultivator and Country Gentleman*, vol. 52, Departments of Rural and Domestic Economy, 1887.

Turner, James. "Understanding the Populists." *The Journal of American History* 67, no. 2 (September 1980): 354–373.

Twain, Mark. *Innocents Abroad*, vol. 1. New York: Harper & Brothers, 1869.

U.S. Congress, Congressional Record, Statement of Congressman Stevens, February 20, 1862.

Utley, Robert M. *Fort Larned National Historic Site, Kansas.* Tucson: Southwest Parks and Monuments Association, 1993.

Vincent, Henry. *The Story of the Commonweal: Complete and Graphic Narrative of the Origin and Growth of the Movement.* Chicago: W. B. Conkey, 1894.

Weaver, James B. *A Call to Action: An Interpretation of the Great Uprising, Its Source and Causes.* Des Moines: Iowa Printing, 1892. https://archive.org/details/TheStoryOf TheCommonweal/mode/2up.

Welch, Roger L. *Sod Walls.* Lincoln, NE: J & L Lee, 1991.

Werner, Charles Hain. Letter to his father, Henry B. Werner, November 3, 1897.

Werner, Henry Beckley. Diaries, Special Archives Collections, Albright College, Reading, PA.

Werner, Isaac Beckley. Journal. Lucille M. Hall Museum, St. John, KS.

Werth, Barry. *Banquet at Delmonico's, Great Minds, the Gilded Age, and the Triumph of Evolution in America.* New York: Random House, 2009.

Western Outlaw Lawman History Association, "William 'Red' Angus." https://www.legendsofamerica.com/lawmen-list-a/.

White, Richard. *Railroaded: The Transcontinentals and the Making of Modern America.* New York: W. W. Norton, 2011.

White, William Allen. "What's the Matter with Kansas?" *Emporia Gazette,* August 15, 1896. http://www.kancoll.org/articles.what's_the_matter_with_kansas.html.

Whitehead, Fred, and Verle Muhrer, eds. *Free-Thought on the American Frontier.* Buffalo, New York: Prometheus Books, 1992.

Wiebe, Robert H. *The Search for Order, 1877–1920.* New York: Hill and Wang, 1967.

Winkler, Adam. "Corporations Are People is Built on an Incredible 19th-Century Lie." *The Atlantic,* March 5, 2018.

Zygmond, Jack, ed. *Panorama of Progress: A Century of Living, Pawnee County, 1872–1974*, Larned, KS: Tiller and Toiler, 1972.

Index